What Others Are Saying about
Let Your Path Find You

"This book is a fantastic collection of stories, life lessons, quotes and most importantly, takeaways and things you can do to improve your own personal situation."

KERRI STRUG
Olympic Gymnastics Gold Medal Winner,
1996 Atlanta Summer Olympics, Atlanta, Georgia

"The many teachings and values from *Let Your Path Find You* have helped me in my personal life and business leadership role. Bob Logan's formula is simple, but hard to implement—hard work, meticulous study of details, passion, strength, enthusiasm, sacrifice, resilience, and intellectual honesty. Follow Logan's formula and this book will take you on the path to success."

ANDREA PANZANI
CEO and General Manager, Valsoia Spa Food Group, Bologna, Italy

"An inspiring personal narrative of self-discovery and endurance. No matter where you find yourself in life, you will learn and gain insight from Bob's story. Good work."

JONATHAN ROTHSCHILD
Mayor of Tucson 2011-2019, Attorney & Partner,
Mesch, Clark and Rothschild, Tucson, Arizona

"As a coach, I usually dislike sports cliches, but *Let Your Path Find You* includes a few we all may benefit from in our own lives. Work hard, get up when you get knocked down, treat people right, never give up. None of these should ever go out of style. Buy the book, and you will be better off in the end."

CHUCK CECIL
Asst Football Coach, University of Arizona, Consensus All-American, 1987,
College Football Hall of Fame, 2009, NFL Pro Bowl 1992, Tucson, Arizona

"Bob Logan's life experiences have been so challenging, so varied and so upbeat that I was always hoping he would write a book about his discoveries and how he made the best of a fascinating career path. *Let Your Path Find You* is that book. It's an incredible journey and he made it all work. A great read."

GREG HANSEN
Sports Columnist, Arizona Daily Star, Author of *Hansen's 100,* Tucson, Arizona

"There seem to be no coincidences in life so it's no surprise that Bob would become a mentor and friend to me. We found each other through our shared history of sports, military life, and our love for community. But you don't need to walk the same path as Bob to enjoy his storytelling and thoughts. You will feel like Bob is your friend, too, after enjoying this book."

CRISSY AHMANN (PERHAM)
Olympic Gold Medalist & World Record Holder (Swimming),
1992 Barcelona Olympics, Rociada, New Mexico

"I would never write an endorsement without getting to know the author and why they wrote the book. Bob's book, *Let Your Path Find You* tells stories, shares experiences and provides strength and hope. I am always looking for other teachers that I can learn from to help me help those I am coaching and mentoring. Buy the book! You'll be glad you did."

CLINT HURDLE
Major League Baseball Manager, Colorado Rockies and Pittsburgh Pirates

"There are a million books on leadership and success, but not very many on how to navigate a life. *Let Your Path Find You* is that book. It is not perfect, but life is not perfect."

JIM CLICK
Founder and President, The Jim Click Automotive Group

"Looking for a book that will challenge your thinking and set you on a direct path to success? Read Bob Logan's *Let Your Path Find You*...now!"

DR. KEVIN LEMAN
Founder of the Leman Academy of Excellence, and *New York Times* Best-Selling Author of
The Way of the Shepherd and *The Birth Order Book*

"As a two-time cancer survivor and one of the first women in the country to work directly with a Division 1/FBS football team, I relate strongly to every chapter of Bob's book. His insight and inspiring life experiences from *Let Your Path Find You* provide life lessons we all can use to find our own personal path to a life of meaning."

KATHLEEN "ROCKY" LAROSE
Retired Acting Director of Athletics and Deputy AD/C.O.O.,
University of Arizona, Award-Winning Photographer

"This book really hit home for me. I have always preached about living in the moment, and clearly the message from *Let Your Path Find You* is exactly that. If you are looking for direction or facing challenges, this is a book you must read."

MIKE CANDREA
University of Arizona Softball Head Coach (36 years), 2004 Athens Olympics Gold Medal winner, USA Softball National Hall of Fame, Tucson, Arizona

"Life…it certainly is a complex and challenging journey. Bob's book is filled with great stories, important life lessons and key takeaways that will open your mind to your personal journey in life! Do yourself a favor and read this book!"

DAVE HEEKE
Vice President and Director of Athletics, University of Arizona, Tucson, Arizona

"It's not the path you take in life that determines your life's outcome. It's the road that you didn't take that determines your fate. Bob's collection of stories and anecdotes is a must read on how we learn to adapt and embrace our own winding path called Life. A great book. Trust me."

CHRIS DEL CONTE
Vice President and Director of Athletics, University of Texas,
Texas Christian University, Rice University

"Bob Logan is one of the best persons I've ever known. So, it doesn't surprise me that he would write such an insightful book that shows us how to continue pushing forward through life's challenges, while appreciating every step of the journey."

BRENT DERAAD
President & CEO, Arlington Convention & Visitor's Bureau, Arlington, Texas

"Life is full of challenges. Bob Logan has been transparent in sharing his path to overcoming the challenges we face in life. His stories are easy to find inspiring for your own personal journey."

ANDY LOPEZ
University of Arizona Baseball coach (2001-2015), two NCAA National Championships, American Baseball Coaches Association Hall of Fame, Tucson, Arizona

"Inspirational, funny, sad, and at the same time, very personal. His stories resonated with me. It made me think about what is really important in life."

LEA MARQUEZ PETERSON
MBA, President, Márquez Peterson Group, LLC, Chairwoman, Arizona Corporation Commission, Phoenix, Arizona

"This is a great true story of grit, determination, and sheer belief in yourself. I was so inspired by the message to never be afraid to make a change, accept new challenges, and take risks. Trust me, you will feel inspired, and it will give you the courage to take a chance!"

MATT MUEHLBACH
Senior Vice President & General Counsel, 5Lights Group, LLC, UA Basketball Player, 1987-1991; PAC 12 Tournament MVP, 1990

"It doesn't matter what country or what language this is in; Bob Logan's message works anywhere. This is a must read, no matter where you live. Being a good human works anywhere."

ENRICO MAMBELLI
M&A Senior Advisor Fashion and Sport, Milan, Italy

"Have you ever wondered what you are missing in your life? Finding one's path is the true key to finding happiness. This book will set you on that journey. Thought-provoking and moving. A must read."

DIANA MADARAS
Nine-Time Winner of Tucson's Best Artist Award, Tucson, Arizona

"Bob Logan discusses the human factor one moment as gently as a butterfly with sore feet landing on a flower, then brutally as a middle linebacker demolishing a ball carrier with violent intent. *Let Your Path Find You* shows us in vivid detail how life often requires the gentle touch and sometimes the brutal in us to find success."

JAY DOBYNS
Federal Agent (ret.) *New York Times* Bestselling Author of *No Angel: My Harrowing Undercover Journey to the Inner Circle of the Hells Angels*, and *Catching Hell: A True Story of Abandonment and Betrayal*

"When celebrities write about life and loss, overcoming obstacles, and reaching their goals, it can be hard to relate. Bob Logan is no celebrity. He's an ordinary guy who has achieved extraordinary success. In this lovely book, Bob offers honest real-life lessons and inspiration to us all."

KATE MAGUIRE JENSEN, MPH
President & CEO, Ronald McDonald House Charities of Southern Arizona

Let Your Path Find You is both captivating and empowering. If you deserve a higher-quality of confidence, pride, recognition, relationships, and joy,… this book offers you that opportunity!

DR. JOHN C. "BJ" BJELLAND, MD (RET)
Co-Founder Arizona State Radiology PC (1989), University of Arizona Medical Center (UAMC) Department of Radiology Associate Professor, Tucson, Arizona

"What a great collection of personal lifetime experiences, woven into an easy to relate to and follow book. Bob showcases how it's often the smallest things that derail people, organizations and ideas. If you've been knocked off your horse, this read will help get you back in the saddle."

MARK IRVIN
President, Mark Irvin Commercial Real Estate,
Tucson Man of the Year, 2019, Tucson, Arizona

"We read a memoir to experience a life different from our own and to learn vicariously from the adventures of others. Bob Logan's *Let Your Path Find You* compellingly fulfills that desire to learn from another. It is well written and very engaging as you learn of a life well lived. His reflections on lessons learned are especially inspiring."

DR. THOMAS GROGAN
Founder, Ventana Medical Systems-Roche, Author of *Chasing the Invisible*, Tucson, Arizona

"Bob Logan has had a positive impact on many people. His message is extraordinary! This book is a must addition to your library!"

SCOTT THOMPSON
Former NCAA Head Basketball Coach (Wichita State, Rice University, Cornell College)

"Bob Logan has spent his entire life working with people. And it is clear through this story that he understands people. Read this. What it told me is your life is YOUR life, not what others do or what happens to you. Truly, if you want to live, let your path find you. You will be happier for it."

LARRY FINUF
Executive Vice President, Wells Fargo Bank Corporate Office, Charlotte, N.C.

"Bob Logan has been building strong relationships over his many years. This story highlights his understanding of people and what motivates them. The insight in this book provides a great foundation in learning how to deal with people in your life who cause you stress."

JOHN WOODS
Assistant Vice President, The Ohio State University, Columbus, Ohio

"Sometimes the random book you read is the look in the mirror you desperately need. Take the time to enjoy the journey of Bob's book. It will definitely be entertaining, and it will challenge you to learn, grow, and be better."

KURTIS DAWSON
President & CEO, YMCA of Southern Arizona, Tucson, Arizona

"Life can be a wonderful journey. The life lessons Bob Logan frames through *Let Your Path Find You* helps us navigate that journey."

MICHAEL FRANKS
Founder and President, Seaver-Franks Architects, Tucson, Arizona

"One thing that impressed me about Bob Logan was his ability to take risks and find solutions to obstacles in his path. He lived and coached abroad, and now I have coached in nine countries. If there is one thing I know, those lucky enough to hear his messages and listen to his stories in this fantastic book will be better off. He will inspire you, just like he inspired me. This is a must read."

JOHN SAINTIGNON
Head Basketball Coach and Consultant,
Japanese Professional League, Yamaguchi Patriots, Yamaguchi, Japan

"Read this book. There is no better storyteller, or teacher, than Bob Logan. He has reinvented himself and lived a life filled with incredible experiences. The stories in *Let Your Path Find You* will humor you and make you think at the same time. He will inspire you to achieve more in your life. Buy this book; you will not go wrong."

JIM NICHOLS NCCM(SW), USN (RET)
Vice President of Franchise Development, Threshold Brands, Boston, Massachusetts

"A book that tells it like it is. Life is challenging, life is difficult, and life can be a never-ending string of disappointments and failures. Once you understand that life is not what is done to you but rather, life is what you make it out to be, you will be better off. Bob Logan's life and his stories put all of this in perspective."

JACQUELINE BUCHER
Head of the Office of Communication,
Fermi National Accelerator Laboratory, Batavia, Illinois

"Bob Logan has woven many important lessons into the fabric of *Let Your Path Find You*: Integrity matters. Gratitude is important. Life is hard and perspective helps us grow from difficult experiences. Kindness and compassion in all areas of life are critical. The lessons are imparted with humor, humility, and vulnerability—a wonderful gift to readers!"

MARCY EULER, MED, CFRE
President, Pima Community College Foundation, Tucson, Arizona

"Like a fullback, Bob has blocked and dodged his way through the adversity that life offers to us all. Yet he has accumulated a set of lessons of great value that have helped him find joy in uncomfortable situations. His passionate support for friends and respect for life as a team sport shine through this book as a beacon for those who could use a helping hand."

DR. PETER SMITH
Principal Investigator, Mars Phoenix Mission (2008), Planetary Sciences,
University of Arizona, Tucson, Arizona

"Finally, a book that speaks to your heart, your soul and challenges you to take action. I could not put it down. Read this today and you will never be the same!"

DAVE SILVER
ABC News, KGUN9 TV Sports Director, 1983-2011, Tucson, Arizona

"If there is someone, I would ever take advice from, it is Bob Logan. When he speaks, it is from the heart. Always. His stories in this book are powerful. Buy this book; you will not go wrong."

JAMES "JR" LYDA
Command Chief Master Sergeant (Ret), Davis-Monthan Air Force Base, Tucson, Arizona

Bob Logan's recipe for life - honesty, humility, thoughtfulness, and a dose of humor is something we could all follow. I hear his confident and compassionate voice flowing from the pages of this book. This book helped me focus on what's important in my life, and it certainly helped me find my path."

QUAN NGUYEN
Founding Partner, Nguyen, Tarbet (NTIP) Patent Attorneys, LLC, Irvine, California

"Bob Logan's *Let Your Path Find You* is an intensely intimate sharing of a life well-lived. Relying on his own experiences "in the arena," Bob guides you on your own "random walk" to embrace a meaningful and purpose-filled life. Don't miss this gem!"

KAY SULLIVAN
President, Salpointe Catholic High School, Tucson, Arizona

LET YOUR PATH FIND YOU

EMBRACE YOUR OWN WINDING ROAD TO A MORE FULFILLING LIFE

BOB LOGAN

SABINO PRESS
SINCE 1937
TUCSON, ARIZONA

LET YOUR PATH FIND YOU
Embrace Your Own Winding Road to a More Fulfilling Life
Copyright © 2023 by Bob Logan. All rights reserved.

This publication is designed to provide accurate and authoritative information in regard to the subject matter covered. It is sold with the understanding that the publisher and/or author is not engaged in rendering legal or any other professional service. If legal advice or other expert personal assistance is required, the services of a competent professional person should be sought.

Published by:

Sabino Press
Tucson, Arizona
info@sabinopress.com

All Rights Reserved. No part of this book may be used or reproduced in any manner whatsoever without the expressed written permission of the author. The scanning, uploading, or distribution of this book via the internet or any other means without the expressed permission of the author and publisher is illegal and punishable by law. Your support of the author's rights is appreciated.

Address all inquiries to:
Bob Logan
bob@boblogan.net
info@boblogan.net
www.boblogan.net

ISBNs: 978-1-7377508-0-2 (paperback)
         978-1-7377508-1-9 (Kindle)
         978-1-7377508-2-6 (ePub)

Library of Congress Control Number: xxxxxxxxxxx

Editors: Tyler Tichelaar, Superior Book Productions
         Marni McCrae
         Tracey Maxwell
Cover Design: Kendra Cagle, 5LakesDesign.com
Cover Copywriting: Dennis Welch, BeArticulate.com
Interior Book Layout: Yvonne Parks, PearCreative.ca
Index: Russell Santana, E4Editorial.com
Author Photo: Courtesy of Jeff Smith, Fotosmith

Every attempt has been made to properly source all quotes.
Permission to reprint the poem "The Man in the Glass" by Dale Wimbrow provided by family members Heather Matthews and David Evans.
Cover Photo: Provided by Bob Logan, on the Camino de Santiago just outside Ciruñea on October 9, 2015

First Edition

DEDICATION

To my Dad, Major Edward Logan
A Great Man
A Great Father
A Great Military Leader
I hope you are proud of me.
I Miss You

CONTENTS

Introduction ... 1

PART I | LOSS ... 7

Chapter 1 | Failure ... 9
Chapter 2 | Fear ... 27
Chapter 3 | Criticism ... 41
Chapter 4 | Adversity ... 55
Chapter 5 | Grief ... 73

PART II | RECOVERY ... 89

Chapter 6 | Life Is Messy ... 91
Chapter 7 | Challenge ... 107
Chapter 8 | Change ... 125
Chapter 9 | The Seven Most Important Words ... 145
Chapter 10 | Laughter ... 157

PART III | REDISCOVERY ... 173

Chapter 11 | Happiness ... 175
Chapter 12 | Vision and Visualization ... 195
Chapter 13 | Leadership ... 213
Chapter 14 | Simplicity and Balance ... 229
Chapter 15 | A Random Walk Through Life ... 239

Acknowledgments ... 261
Endnotes ... 263
Reading List ... 273
Index ... 277
About the Author ... 291
How to Connect with Bob Logan ... 293

INTRODUCTION

We have just endured one of the most difficult periods in our human history, the coronavirus pandemic. Tragically, more than 1,000,000 people have died in the United States from this dreaded virus. Worldwide, the number is almost unbelievable—more than 6.3 million. The United States and countries all over the world went into lockdown, businesses were shuttered, travel came to a standstill, people lost their jobs and livelihoods, and the elderly were locked in isolation in their homes and assisted living facilities.

During the spring of 2020, George Floyd was murdered by a Minnesota police officer, and the Black Lives Matter movement stirred across the world as protestors rioted and burned down police stations and filled city streets throughout the summer months. Only a few years ago, we witnessed the MeToo movement as well, where women were finally able to stand up and speak out against sexual abuse from bosses, politicians, and men in positions of power.

And now, in our world of 2022, we see the ongoing destruction of the democratic nation of Ukraine at the hands of Vladimir Putin and the Russian regime. For the first time since the Cuban Missile Crisis and the Cold War of the 1950s and 1960s, there is real concern about the use of nuclear weapons and the possibility of a World War III. It is a scary time, indeed.

Our politics have become so divisive, we risk being subjected to verbal assault if we mention our political position during casual conversations. We as Americans, and as a human race across the globe, don't seem to be able to get along anymore. Our society seems to be totally polarized right now. Life is difficult, and if you watch the news every day, it seems like our world is falling apart.

Have the current events of the recent years got you in a funk? You're not alone. Maybe you have marital or financial issues. Or you might have unrelenting issues with your family members. Possibly a toxic work environment has pushed you to the edge. Or maybe you're trying to find your own path, just as I have found my very crooked path to a sometimes sad, but at the same time wonderful, life.

Believe me, you are not alone. I have dealt with premature loss of family members (Mom at age fifty-four, Dad at age fifty-eight, and my only brother at thirty-seven); I have dealt with financial issues and toiled for many years in low paying jobs; I have been a dishwasher and a door-to-door salesperson in the summer heat to make ends meet. I have had friends and family die of cancer and suicide. Does any of this sound familiar? For most people, it likely hits close to home.

The point is, as bad as your problems are, the people to the right and left of you also have similar, or, often, problems significantly worse than yours. What exactly is one supposed to do? To me, it is pretty simple—grind yourself through life and ask for support when you need it.

I have seen it all and experienced gut-wrenching issues that I never could have imagined over my lifetime. And the back story is this—I have still had an amazing, wonderful life. I have had a list of careers that would make most people's heads spin. From a high school, college, and international football coach, teaching high school history, selling multi-million-dollar computer systems for AT&T, athletic director in one of the largest universities in the country, to associate dean in a college of science, and now as a motivational speaker and consultant. My wife Judy and I have been together since 1980 and we have two very successful sons who make us proud. It has been an amazing ride.

We have all heard the term, "Past events are not indicative of future results." I feel this applies to life as well. We are all walking on "the long path of life," and too many of us tend to live in the past instead of living in the moment. Just like when you drive your car, you need to spend most of your driving time looking out the front windshield and glance in the rear-view mirror from time to time. If you spend too much time looking in the rear-view mirror, and studying what's behind you, you will ultimately crash—guaranteed. So, our walk together in these next few pages I hope will encourage you to always be moving (and looking) forward and not be stuck living in the past (and worrying about what "could have been").

Which brings me to why you have decided to pick up this specific book. This book is part memoir and part self-help book. It covers topics in myriad areas from our lives that are issues and problems for all of us. Chapters include fear, failure, change, and adversity. Conversely, other chapters include happiness, laughter, and having a balance in our lives. Based on a lifetime of family, work, and personal experiences, I can honestly say I have quite a bit of familiarity in all these areas. I hope to share some nuggets you might find helpful in your life challenges, so please, read on. This is not meant to be a novel, so it is not necessary to read it from beginning to end, feel free to jump around here and there.

Another note regarding this book: it is meant to be an immersive experience. There are numerous references to websites, videos, interesting stories, etc. To facilitate this, QR codes have been liberally placed throughout the book. I am a believer that people learn through all the senses, not just the eyes. So when you sit down with this book, have your smartphone by your side. Just hover your smartphone camera over the code, click on the yellow boblogan.net that pops up, and it will take you immediately to that link. Watch the videos, listen to their stories and be inspired. I hope you will enjoy the journey with me.

The Camino de Santiago Experience – One we will never forget

In the pages ahead are many references to the Camino de Santiago, a 1,500-year-old pilgrimage in Northern Spain. I have walked the Camino on three occasions, and for me, each was a humbling and life-changing experience. If you have not heard of the Camino before, do yourself a favor and Google it. You will be amazed, and maybe it will end up on your bucket list. You may frequently come across the words "path" and "Camino" during this reading. You should know that these two words are synonyms and interchangeable. The only difference is one is in Spanish, the other English. Path can either mean the "Camino" or it could mean one's personal Camino, i.e., your "Life's Path." Life is meant to be a journey and to improve the path you are on, let its lessons be meaningful to you. Every now and then we should stop…and cautiously listen to the lessons your Path teaches you.

To become more Camino proficient, you may want to spend time on my blog on the Camino (see QR code below). Better yet, rent the movie *The Way*, starring Martin Sheen on Netflix. The entire movie was filmed on the trail, in the *albergues*, and in the churches as part of the Camino de Santiago. Whether or not you ever decide to walk the Camino yourself, I think you will find *The Way* a wonderful movie.

The Camino trail in the middle of Spain

Logan Camino 2018
https://BobLogan.net//LoganCamino2018

I welcome you to allow "Your Path to Find You" with me over these next few pages. Hopefully, you will discover some answers and some inspiration to help you deal with this crazy thing we call life. Enjoy, and feel free to reach out if you like.

Bob Logan

www.boblogan.net
bob@boblogan.net

The Man in the Arena

"It is not the critic who counts; not the man who points out how the strong man stumbles or where the doer of deeds could have done them better. The credit belongs to the man who is actually in the arena, whose face is marred by dust and sweat and blood; who strives valiantly; who errs, who comes short again and again, because there is no effort without error and shortcoming; but who does actually strive to do the deeds; who knows great enthusiasms, the great devotions; who spends himself in a worthy cause; who at the best knows in the end the triumph of high achievement, and who at the worst, if he fails, at least fails while daring greatly, so that his place shall never be with those cold and timid souls who neither know victory nor defeat." [1]

BY PRESIDENT THEODORE ROOSEVELT

PART I
LOSS

CHAPTER 1

FAILURE

"Remember your dreams and fight for them. You must know what you want from life. There is just one thing that makes your dream become impossible: the fear of failure."

— PAULO COELHO

I started out my adult life as a massive failure.

It was such a disaster that my very own father didn't speak to me for six months, even though we lived under the same roof. To understand why this failure was such a blow to my family, you probably need some background about my early life leading up to 1975, when I went away to college at the United States Air Force Academy.

My dad was a twenty-eight-year veteran of the Air Force, retiring at the rank of major. He flew in three wars, B-17s at the end of World War II, F-86s in the Korean Conflict, and F-4s and F-101s during Vietnam. As a result of his Air Force career, my family lived all over the United States, stationed at a new base every 2-3 years. It was a nomadic life for a young boy, but you learn how to adjust and adapt, something essential since I attended six different schools in my first twelve years of education.

Major Edward Patrick Logan, a decorated veteran.

My dad visiting me at the U.S. Air Force Academy during Parents Weekend, Sept. 1975

I was a chubby kid most of my youth, and I grew into my body by playing football. I loved the camaraderie football brought to me, and it became my ambition to play college football. It was also clear that football needed to be a way for me to attend college since we were not a wealthy family.

Fortunately, the sport became my college ticket when I received a scholarship to play at the U.S. Air Force Academy. My dad was incredibly proud of my landing a coveted appointment at this esteemed institution. He told all his Air Force buddies with great pride that I was going to the Academy. After the intensive mental, physical, and emotional pre-Academy testing results, I was approved as a pilot-qualified cadet candidate. This meant upon graduation I would be flying jet airplanes just like him! He knew I was following in his footsteps, and he was probably more excited and prouder than I was at this achievement. My entire life was set, according to him.

You can also imagine his anger, frustration, and disappointment when I quit less than a year after I started. I was homesick, had a first-time girlfriend I missed terribly, and after basic training and all of the traditions of a first-year Academy cadet, I certainly wasn't sure I wanted this Air Force lifestyle. All typical excuses to quit for a disillusioned eighteen-year-old young man. It was too much to handle. That was my mindset at the time.

Almost everyone tried to talk me out of my decision to quit the Air Force Academy. Probably more so because of my dad's extensive Air Force connections. I endured several different lectures about my fatal decision—from my dad, from the Academy squadron leadership, from my football coaches, and from one of the highest-ranking officials at the Air Force Academy. It was all fruitless because I was stubborn and had made up my mind. I would not listen to anyone.

Let me give you some background on what happens when you announce you are quitting the U.S. Air Force Academy. It's a long and very complicated process.

The U.S. Government has identified you as one of their future leaders and made a significant investment in you. They drag the 'outplacement' process out for 30-45 days. It was excruciating. Once a cadet announces they're washing out, for whatever reason, the Academy wants to brand you as 'different. To make you stand out in the crowd, they require all the 'outplacement cadets' to wear olive green fatigues instead of the standard dress blue uniforms all cadets wear every day at the Academy. When you're leaving the Academy, you must wear these fatigue greens until the final day when you leave the premises.

Every day, the entire cadet nation lines up in uniform and marches to Mitchell Hall for breakfast, lunch, and dinner. The 4,000+ cadet wing is divided into forty squadrons of about 100 cadets each. I was a member of the 39th squadron, so we were one of the last squadrons in this three times a day meal parade/march. The squadrons all line up in formation on the terrazzo tile walkways and they all walk in perfect unison to Mitchell Hall. It is quite the spectacle. To see this spectacle for yourself, feel free to watch the videos below:

Academy Noon Meal Formation (1 minute)
https://BobLogan.net/AcademyMealMarch1

No Ordinary Walk to Lunch (1:35 mins)
https://BobLogan.net/AcademyMealMarch2

One can also imagine how easy it is to spot the 'quitter in green fatigues' in a sea of blue uniforms during these daily marches. It wasn't enjoyable, but looking back on it, I understood what they were doing.

When I announced I was leaving, I was determined to prove to *everyone* that this decision had been my choice. I didn't want people to think I was a loser and couldn't handle it. The Academy has a never-ending string of metrics a cadet must follow. How clean is your room? How tight are the 45 degree corners of your bed? How perfect is your uniform? How shiny are your shoes and your belt buckle? How do you perform in P.T. (physical training)? And on and on. Again, for your entertainment, here are a couple of videos to show you how to make your bed and set up your drawers.

How to Organize Your Cadet Dresser Drawer (:35 secs)
https://BobLogan.net/CadetDresserDrawer

How to Make a Cadet Bed (1:35 mins)
https://BobLogan.net/MakingCadetBed

They grade everything you do, and everyone is ranked, from best to worst. Then they give out various awards to the best of the best—Cadet of the Month, Cadet of the Week, Squadron Leader, etc. Even though I had been pegged as a washout and had to endure wearing the green khakis every day, I was determined to win one of these coveted cadet awards before I left. I wanted to show them something about myself.

I am proud to say I dominated in meeting all these Cadet-of-the-Week metrics, and I won the award during one of my final weeks on campus when I was in the outplacement process. As one can imagine, my success did not bode well for the rest of my squadron cadet's compatriots. After all, how could a quitter like me be considered one of the best of all the cadets? With pride, I walked out of the Academy with my head held high in green fatigues, knowing full well that I would have been one of their best cadets had I decided to stay.

Standing by your convictions and defending your choices is a lesson everyone should follow in their personal and professional lives. A lesson learned.

When I entered the Academy, I had very low self-esteem. At the time, it was hard for me to believe I was good enough or could compare to the other outstanding cadets in the wing. Each year, nearly 11,000 high school students apply to the Academy and only 10 percent are accepted. A US senator or congressman has nominated all these cadets. For myself, this included former US presidential candidate, Senator Barry Goldwater. These cadets were the smartest in the country, the best athletes, active in their communities back home, and involved in their student governments at school. How could I possibly measure up to them?

But there I was, a star football player myself, an outstanding student, active in the community, but when I entered the Academy doors, for some reason, I still thought everyone else must be better than me. I was my own worst enemy.

Paradoxically, I was also aware of some of the politics involved in how some lesser qualified cadets were admitted, and I knew immediately many of these cadets were not going to make it. They just were not good enough, but because they had influential parents or had highly ranked military parents, they got in. But many of these 'privileged' cadets stuck out like a sore thumb. They did poorly in the physical training and whimpered emotionally when the going got tough. Truth be told, historically, approximately 20 percent of all cadets ultimately end up dropping out of the academy.

Even though my father was a twenty-eight-year Air Force veteran, I was not one of these "privileged" cadets. I was recruited to play football, I was an early leader during basic training, and was a leader when I was assigned to my squadron. The academics of the Academy were also stressful. On top of the football practice, the military training, and learning how to be a "doolie" (a first-year cadet), I had a twenty-one-credit hour workload of classes. That translates to seven hard classes, and most freshmen at other schools take twelve or fifteen hours, max. And trust me, there was no break being a football player either. None of these classes were easy, and I honestly struggled to keep up academically.

The bottom-line reason I left was because I was incredibly homesick. Although I moved many times as an Air Force brat, it was always with my family, making it more comfortable and an easier transition, moving from base to base. Now, being so far away from them in such a demanding atmosphere took a considerable toll on me. As I mentioned before, I had a girlfriend back home and just thought I was not cut out for military service long term; I ached to be back home.

As much as I missed home, when I returned to Tucson, living in my own home and being there as a "quitter" in my father's eyes was no picnic. My mom was an invalid and spent much of her life in bed. Can you imagine how my dad treated me when I returned home? He ignored me entirely and didn't speak to me for nearly six months. He was incredibly disappointed and bitter toward me and my decision to leave the academy. I dealt with a lot of shame and uncertainty about what I was going to do in the next chapter in my life. I knew if I wanted to finish college, that burden would largely fall on my shoulders. I would have to earn money myself because, the situation being what it was, I could not face asking my father for financial support for college. The best I could do for work was as a dishwasher and a lunch cook at a local restaurant with plans to attend Northern Arizona University as soon as I had saved enough money for tuition.

When I was not at the restaurant, I was working in a door-to-door salesperson/delivery role with the Fuller Brush Company. What is Fuller Brush you ask? It was-and still is-a different version of Avon Cosmetics where salespeople visit homes one-by-one selling cleaning supplies. Some of you may even ask what is Avon? Back in the 1960s and 1970s, door-to-door sales were quite commonplace. There was no internet, no Amazon; it was a different time. Obviously, this is hard to imagine today. Today, somebody showing up at your door unannounced is something most people dread. Most people don't even answer their door when the doorbell rings. We run to our spouse, "Oh my, someone is at the door! Were you expecting someone?" We check our video doorbell to see who is there before we respond. Crazy how times have changed.

About door-to-door sales—trust me, you better get used to rejection-because about 98 percent of the people you visit say no. Talk about being at the low of all lows.

A few months earlier I was preparing to become a jet fighter pilot at the U.S. Air Force Academy and now I was doing one of the most menial jobs possible, going door-to-door selling cleaning products. While it was depressing at the time, I knew what I had to do, and I was in no position to complain to my dad. I'd brought all of this on myself, and it was up to me to figure out my new path in life. It took me nearly a year to save enough money for the first year of college, and this entire process taught me self-reliance. It taught me how to work hard, no matter the circumstances. I had to learn how to apply for school, investigate scholarship opportunities, research various academic areas of study, where to live on campus, etc. all by myself. It was time-consuming.

Looking back on it today, arguably the biggest failure of my life, I do regret not finishing my time at the Air Force Academy. I realize now that I wasted a lifetime opportunity. It was a mistake in many ways, but I also learned so much from the experience that it has led me to be the person I am today. I learned that I was better than I thought I was and began to develop a healthy level of self-esteem. I learned how important it is to follow my heart and not worry about what other people think. In hindsight, I can see now how much courage it took to walk away when there was so much pressure to stay. I know now that many people live their entire life trying to live up to other's expectations, and I'm grateful that I rebelled against that at such a young age, even though it damaged my relationship with my father for quite some time.

I also recognized the critical role that athletics played in my life and began to see it as my path to success and a future career. My high school best friend and college roommate, Jay John and I were both walk-ons to the NAU football team. We had a great time playing, but Jay went on to be a basketball coach, and I stopped playing intercollegiate football for NAU during my sophomore year. However, I still loved the game of football, and I began to volunteer as a football coach at various schools around Flagstaff, all while I was still an undergrad. After college, I went back to teach at my old high school, Salpointe Catholic, but after 3-4 years of teaching and coaching, I had bigger ambitions.

I wanted to be a Division I football coach. However, I also knew the following fact: to become a Division I coach, I needed to return to college and obtain my master's degree. Most football graduate assistant coaches take the easy route and enroll in the easiest master's program possible. Preferably one that did not require a thesis. However, that was not the route I was going to take. I felt it was essential to attain a degree that would provide the greatest benefit long-term since I could always return to education if this college coaching dream did not work out. For me, that best option was to get a business degree, an MBA. I knew an MBA would open many doors for me in the future, even though it was a rigorous program of study and would take me many years to complete.

Like most worthwhile things in life, getting admitted into the University of Arizona Eller College MBA program is not easy. It was one of the top public school MBA programs in the country and highly competitive. My internal stigma about being a "dumb jock" began to rear its ugly head. It did not help that my NAU degree was in history, not quite the necessary academic background to enter an MBA program. Admittedly, I had zero business background and had never taken a marketing, accounting, or finance class in college. When I took the standard business school admission test, the GMAT (Graduate Management Admissions Test), I failed miserably. Disappointed but not deterred, I studied and prepared for a second try. I bought all the guidebooks and spent hours poring over practice problems. I was ready. I took the GMAT a second time, and again, I produced a low score. Better, but not by much. Due to these GMAT scores, the University of Arizona business school denied me admission into the MBA program twice. I still have the rejection letters as a reminder. I didn't know what I was going to do. I had failed again, how could I possibly achieve this dream?

However, my persistence paid off as I went to meet with my faculty advisor, Dr. David Tansik, and asked him what I could do to gain admission into the program. Knowing the system, Dr. Tansik opened a small side door for me to slip through, enrolling me on a probationary status as a 'non-degree' seeking student. He allowed me to take the first twelve credits (four classes) of the MBA program. The deal I had with Dr. Tansik was the following: if I successfully completed these twelve credits with a 3.5 GPA or better, my GMAT scores would be removed from the admissions criteria, and the business school administration would admit me as a full-time, regular MBA student! Now I had a chance, and all I had to do was prove myself. I was excited—no-ecstatic—about this possibility.

What was the takeaway? First of all, I will never forget Dr. Tansik for taking a chance on me. It proved to me that there are ways around "the system" especially if you find the right people who are willing to help. You must find this kind of person. Would this situation have occurred if I had not been persistent in my mission and explained my passion for getting an MBA to anyone in the business school who would listen? Don't ever accept no for an answer—keep navigating the system until you find the yes.

Looking back, I can see now that my short time at the Air Force Academy and my grind to achieve an MBA degree have paid huge dividends, serving as cornerstones of my success throughout my career. The U.S. Air Force Academy still appears on my resume, even though I was a cadet for less than a year. Many times, I was asked about the academy experience in job interviews. Clearly, people are often impressed that I was even accepted into the Academy, even though I never graduated. It has that type of reputation. In a way it signified to others that I was not a "football player" and I brought real value to organizations. I began to realize that I was "good enough" and through sheer determination, I could be a success.

During the spring of my final semester for my Eller MBA, several major companies recruited me, including IBM, Proctor & Gamble, and AT&T. Ultimately, I was hired by AT&T Computer Systems, a Fortune 500 company at the time. My career since then has been filled with incredible successes and life-changing experiences. Still, that first big Academy failure was vital in overcoming my fears and inadequacies and learning persistence. Failures are a necessary part of life, and wins wouldn't be as sweet without the contrast of our defeats.

Failure is surprisingly connected to happiness and leadership in the sense that everybody can learn from failure. As I have learned, the field of science is often a compilation of multiple failures until suddenly something works, or discovery occurs. I have learned this during my more than twenty years in the College of Science at the University of Arizona. Experiments are just that. If your results are disappointing, you just keep track of what you learned and try again.

FAILURE ON A MASSIVE SCALE

To illustrate this point, the UA College of Science is one of the premier institutions in the world as it relates to space and astronomy. Our astronomy program builds the largest mirrors in the world for telescopes that will see as far back as the big bang. UA Astronomy professor Dr. Marcia Rieke developed the camera on the recently launched James Webb Space Telescope. This UA-developed camera will be 100 times more powerful than the Hubble Space Telescope! The images due later in 2022 are sure to be stunning.

Another one of the esteemed departments is the Lunar and Planetary Laboratory (LPL). LPL has been involved in every NASA mission since its inception. In fact, in the 1950s and 1960s, scientists from LPL mapped the entire surface of the moon to identify the landing sites for the Apollo moon missions. To have worked closely with these UA professors and experience their innovations and discoveries firsthand for so many years is one of the highlights of my professional career.

LPL has been involved with numerous missions to Mars in recent years, and one of the things I learned early on is that space and Mars missions are dangerous, and failures are commonplace. However, these failures are the fuel to identify what to fix, change and alter to improve the next mission. As catastrophic and disappointing as they are, failed experiments are a part of life in the scientific community.

MARS CLIMATE ORBITER (MCO) – SEPTEMBER 1999

The MCO was a $127,000,000 mission designed to orbit the planet Mars, and with our UA high-resolution cameras, map the surface of the planet for future landing missions on Mars. It was also to study the atmosphere and climate of Mars. NASA and Lockheed Martin were some of the MCO mission partners that joined together with the UA effort.

The critical part of the MCO mission was the precision needed to execute final orbital insertion into the Mars atmosphere. In layman's terms, the best way to explain it is for the orbiter to successfully enter Mars's gravitational field and orbit the planet, it needs to enter the atmosphere at the *precise* proper angle. It's like hitting the side of a piece of paper from 140 million miles away. If the orbiter came in too deep, it would plunge to the surface of Mars and burn up. If it came in too shallow it would bounce off the Mars gravitational field and fly forever into the solar system, never to be heard from again. MCO's orbital insertion position had to be *exact* for the mission to succeed.[2]

At the critical time of orbital insertion, the thrusters on the MCO needed to receive a rapid communication stream of very small, minute, and precise course correction adjustments. And these adjustments had to be precise. NASA and Lockheed Martin partners were responsible for different thruster communications, individually sending what they thought were the correct adjustments for their individual MCO tasks. And in this tragic case, they were not perfect, they were not precise, they were not even close. When the MCO began the critical orbit insertion sequence, everyone waited anxiously for the MCO to communicate back to Earth. But after a long couple of minutes, there was nothing but silence. Mission control was dead quiet when they realized the mission had failed.

During the post-mission investigation, an amazing fact was discovered. As it turned out, Lockheed Martin was sending their necessary communications and thruster adjustment signals in English Standard, or foot pound measurements. NASA was sending its thruster adjustment signals to MCO in Metric, or Newtonian measurements![3] Talk about a lack of communication. MCO missed the perfect orbital insertion point by more than sixty miles! This was a 127-million-dollar mission failure. Two huge space agencies were responsible for a huge mission failure by arguably a stupid mistake that could have been avoided by simple communication. Incredible.[4]

MARS POLAR LANDER (MPL)—DECEMBER 1999

But the story gets better. Just a few months after the MCO disaster, the Mars Polar Lander (MPL) launched its own mission to Mars. The MPL was a 327-million-dollar probe that was to land on the surface of Mars and conduct experiments to help in future missions. The mission was going as planned, all the way to entry into Mars's atmosphere and the ultimate touchdown. Communication was steady, all systems were in order, and the science team was poised for celebration. Suddenly, literally seconds before touchdown on the surface of Mars, everything went silent again. Just like the MCO, after several minutes of silence, everyone knew this mission had failed and that the lander had crashed on the surface of Mars.

What possibly could have happened? Again, the post-mission investigation identified the culprit. It was two $20 sensor devices affixed on the legs of the lander. The sole purpose of the sensors was to detect direct contact with the surface of Mars. Once they felt the jolt of hitting the surface, the sensors were to shut down the engine thrusters to complete the landing.

Unfortunately, these specific sensors had not gone through full and complete pre-mission testing, with a comprehensive review of all possible scenarios. What ultimately occurred was disappointing to everyone involved when they realized this simple mistake caused a catastrophic failure.

As the MPL was descending, at an altitude of only 150 feet above the surface of Mars, the legs of the lander deployed at the proper time and locked into place for landing. But this leg deployment step was a violent process incorporating small explosive charges to propel the legs into position and lock them in place. The landing sensors (which were on two of the legs of the lander) felt this sudden jerk and they thought the lander had just touched down on the surface of Mars. Therefore, the sensors released the parachute and shut down the thrusters like they were supposed to do.[5]

But the MPL had not landed yet, it was still 150 feet above the planet's surface. With the thrusters now shut off, the Mars Polar Lander plunged rapidly at fifty miles per hour to its doomed crash landing. A $40 mistake resulted in a $327,000,000 mission failure.

After these two massive failures in the span of four months, the NASA professionals went back to work. They made huge changes, several upcoming Mars missions were scrapped, and NASA scientists and engineers went back to the basics, rebuilding the entire Mars program from top to bottom. And what NASA learned from these mission failures was stunning. Future missions like the Mars Exploration Rovers, Spirit and Opportunity, scheduled for short ninety-day missions ended up running for fifteen years! And in 2008, the University of Arizona and LPL managed the highly successful Mars Phoenix Mission, which landed on the surface of Mars and discovered sub-surface ice, which could mean that life exists beyond Earth.

Living in Tucson, many people have asked me over the years, why did we name this Mars mission the "Phoenix"? If you didn't know, there is a heated rivalry between Phoenix and Tucson, the two largest cities in Arizona. Arizona State University (ASU) is located 120 miles north of Tucson in Tempe/Phoenix. The UA, located in Tucson, is often considered Phoenix's little brother. Aside from the sports rivalry, well, we just don't like each other very much.

But scientists are not sports fans. They named the Mars lander the "Phoenix" after the mythological bird the Phoenix that continuously rose from the ashes. The Phoenix mission had many components reused from previous failed Mars missions in the past. In essence, the Mars Polar Lander "rose from the ashes" and became the Phoenix. It took me a lot of explaining to the UA donor community the thought process on naming the Mars Phoenix Mission. These scientists come up with crazy ideas from time to time.

SPACE SHUTTLE MISSION STS-80 AND A FAILED SPACEWALK[6]

Astronaut Tom Jones was a graduate of the UA Department of Planetary Sciences and one of our most distinguished alumni. He had an outstanding career at NASA and served as an astronaut on four shuttle missions. Like all astronauts, Tom's lifelong goal was to exit the spacecraft and perform an EVA (Extra-Vehicular Activity), otherwise known as a spacewalk mission. How exhilarating it must be to be floating in space, tethered to your spacecraft with a small line.

UA graduate and space shuttle astronaut Tom Jones waves during his spacewalk on mission STS-98 (Feb 12, 2001)

In 1996, when Tom Jones was selected for Shuttle Columbia mission STS-80, he and his female astronaut partner, Tamara Jernigan would be performing an EVA to repair a few items outside the Shuttle. The EVA Day of the mission had arrived. Astronaut Jones and Astronaut Jernigan donned their EVA space suits and entered the small cabin to exit the spacecraft. However, when they tried to turn the handle to open the outer airlock hatch, it would not move. It was stuck. After several hours and many more attempts to open the hatch, NASA decided to scrub the EVA. What a disappointment!

Again, just as the two Mars missions described above, an infinitesimal detail caused the failure of this spacewalk. In a post-mission analysis of the Columbia, it was determined that a small forty-nine-cent bolt had the incorrect threads and had worked its way loose during liftoff and lodged in the gear actuator that operated the airlock hatch handle.[7] Can you believe that? A tiny bolt any one of us can buy from Ace Hardware stopped two astronauts from their lifelong goal of a spacewalk. Unbelievable.

The good news is Tom Jones was finally able to accomplish his long-awaited goal of a spacewalk many years later on Shuttle mission STS-98 in 2001 (photo above).

THE FIRST LIGHT BULB

An old story about Thomas Edison said his first 1,000 attempts to make the light bulb were considered failures. But when the 1,001-attempt worked, he was suddenly considered a genius! If you're not failing, you're probably not trying hard enough. Ambition naturally brings failure. To use an analogy, whether water skiing or kayaking, if you don't find yourself from time-to-time face down in the water, you probably will never enjoy the thrill of barreling into the waves, catching air, or pushing yourself to the limit. Not taking chances is safer, for sure, but certainly not as much fun.

Having something to seek out and embrace is equally important. Ambition is the engine that keeps us moving forward. Otherwise, we may find ourselves in a rut, doing the same old thing year after year with little to show for it.

To make up for my Air Force Academy failure, I had a brand-new start a year later in Flagstaff at Northern Arizona University (NAU). When I entered as a freshman, I set a personal goal to graduate with high academic honors upon graduation four or five years later. I thought that would finally make my dad proud of me. I researched all the NAU graduation award honors requirements:

1. **Summa cum laude 4.0 GPA**
2. **Magna cum laude 3.8 to 3.99 GPA**
3. **Cum laude—3.5 to 3.79 GPA**

I decided I could realistically try to graduate Cum laude (3.5 to 3.7 GPA) and that was the goal I set for myself.

I missed many a college party to stay home and work on papers or go to the school library to work on research. I took this GPA goal seriously and was well on track to graduate with a minimum 3.5 cumulative GPA. I was driven to succeed and was excited to achieve this high academic standard. How did I do you ask?

Again, I failed.

I barely missed it, and can you guess by how much? My final cumulative NAU GPA was 3.496! I missed this amazing academic achievement by .004 points! Sadly, there was no rounding up; this type of honor was black and white—3.5 and you achieve it, anything less, you fail. All this hard work over many years was for nothing.

Was I angry? Absolutely! Was I disappointed? Of course!

Looking back, I realize all the hard work was so worth it. There is a lesson to be learned in there somewhere. Do you think my grades would have been as high as they were if I hadn't set that goal for myself? Doubtful. I likely would have gone to many more parties and chased more fun. The reality is because I set that aggressive academic goal, it made me a better student and a better person. I learned more and became popular with my professors because they saw I wasn't a "football guy" and was taking my academics seriously. Even though I missed the mark, setting the goal prompted me to study when I could have instead been wasting time, drinking beer, or hanging out with friends. It kept my eyes on the prize.

Some Thoughts and Takeaways on Failure

1. When you get knocked down, dust yourself off and put yourself back in the game.
2. Be persistent. No one is a more prominent advocate for you than you.
3. Have confidence in yourself, and it will inspire the faith of others too.
4. Always set lofty goals in your personal and professional life. You may not always achieve them, but you will always be better off in the pursuit.
5. Understand that failure can occur through no fault of yourself. Control what you can control, and don't worry about the rest.
6. Know that rules, standards and testing requirements are all made up by people. If you do not get the answer you want, be persistent and find out who is in charge. From time to time, they may give you a break because of your passion.
7. Sometimes working menial jobs can make you a better person. After all, there is nowhere to go but up. These situations also provide perspective for the future.
8. Always strive to be your best. No matter the situation. No matter what others may think of you.
9. Try to be an "overnight success." In reality, people who have achieved "overnight success" have overcome many mistakes, missteps and failures in their past.
10. Life is 10 percent what happens to you and 90 percent how you respond to it.

CHAPTER 2

FEAR

"I learned that courage was not the absence of fear, but the triumph over it. The brave man is not he who does not feel afraid, but he who conquers that fear."

— NELSON MANDELA

I believe most failures in life occur because of the individuals' reaction to fear going into the situation. Fear is the great equalizer, and it causes one to hesitate, to hold back, or to totally fail to act in a reasonable manner. While the field of psychology has identified many types of fear, the two types of fear that effect most people are the following:

1. **Physical:** You fear bodily harm, like riding in a car with a reckless driver or being pursued by a barking dog. This fear is when bodily harm is very real and quite possible.
2. **Emotional/Social:** You fear emotional harm, and the fear of being rejected. like when dealing with a difficult person, or the stress from asking someone out on a date. Family issues, job difficulties are all examples of emotional and social fear..

We all experience these various types of fear from time to time in our lives, and we are bound to fail many times. But you *cannot* be afraid to do something solely because you might fail. If there is one thing that will hold you back in life, it is fear and fear of failure. To take a different view of fear, believe it or not, it isn't even real. You may have heard of the acronym FEAR—False Evidence Appearing Real. Think about that for a second. Much of the fear we deal with in our day-to-day lives is all in our mind. If we can overcome our false worries and just go for it, it is clear we will fail from time to time, but it is also clear that as long as we continue to get up again, dust ourselves off, and keep moving forward, we will eventually come out ahead in the end. You must have trust in this concept. Fear makes us stronger if we use it correctly.

The study of brain science has clearly shown that the avoidance of fear and danger is hard-wired into our brains. The brain stem or the "reptilian brain" was the first part of man's brain to develop hundreds of thousands of years ago. Going back to when man was living in a cave, he was terrified of the many things that could bring him harm. Animals, enemies, and geographical dangers all would trigger his "flight or fight" mechanisms in his brain. And those very same "flight or fight" triggers still exist in our brains today. When someone runs a stop sign and nearly hits you, your body tenses up and you take that deep breath as the adrenaline rushes through your veins. This is your "reptilian" brain taking over all aspects of your body. In today's society, there may be times when we experience "caveman" physical fears. Things like wild animals, criminals, or extreme weather, but let's be honest, these reptilian-type fears are extremely rare today.

The fears we face on a day-to-day basis are normally internally generated. We fear calling someone we want to ask out on a date; we fear the big presentation to our boss and senior staff; we fear the difficult conversation with our spouse or partner, but the reality is these fears are all in our mind. We can overcome these fears if we choose to do so.

Sure, external factors can impact us negatively, but our fear of internal scenarios is far more potent than any actual outcome. There are many books about worst-case scenarios, with the premise being preparedness, but putting those negative thoughts into our minds is damaging. Our mental state would be much better in the long run if we concentrated on imagining best-case scenarios. We know our ideas strongly influence what happens to us, so why not think of the best scenario rather than the worst?

In his book *Stumbling on Happiness*, Harvard Psychology Professor Dan Gilbert introduces a concept called impact bias.[8] Impact bias deals with our imperfect ability to predict our emotional states. We naturally think that when "good" things happen to us, we will continue to feel good, and when "bad" things happen to us, we'll always feel bad. In reality, it doesn't work that way—at least not for very long.

Research shows that the initial highs and lows based on external events are extremely short-lived.

Dr. Gilbert says part of the reason this phenomenon occurs is that we tend to imagine both positive and negative outcomes in a vacuum. We think about a singular event without considering how that event will impact us for the rest of our lives. When something difficult occurs in our lives, our friends and family rally around us, our passions give us purpose, and our appreciation of simple things gets us through the day. Conversely, when something great happens to us, there are still bills to pay, life dramas to navigate, traffic, and other daily annoyances we all contend with day-to-day. Think about how excited you are when you're buying a new car. Suddenly, all over town, you see the same model driving on the roads over and over. They seem to be everywhere you look. Then you buy the car, and you show it to your friends in excitement. Many months later, the high has worn off, the new car smell has diminished, and suddenly, your fabulous new car is just that, a car. It becomes just your mode of transportation. In both cases above, the impact of significant positive and negative life events evens out over time, and we return to a state where we are neither excited nor depressed.

THE CAMINO DE SANTIAGO—A BACKGROUND

A continuing theme throughout this book will be various references to the Camino de Santiago. I have walked the Camino on three different occasions, in 2012, 2015, and 2018. Let me give you a brief history of the Camino so you might have a better reference. The Camino is a 500-mile pilgrimage across Northern Spain, and it has been in existence for nearly 1,500 years. Each year, more than 300,000 pilgrims (on the Camino "people" are referred to as pilgrims) walk this spiritual trail, many starting in the traditional starting point of St. Jean Pied de Port, a small town in southern France high in the Pyrenees Mountains. One must cross the Pyrenees on the first two days (a terribly difficult ordeal) and then walk due west to Santiago de Compostela, Spain. Most pilgrims walk between 15-20 miles a day, and the entire journey takes five to six weeks. Along the way, pilgrims stay in small towns where there are albergues, little inns or hostels to stay the night. The albergues provide a communal living environment, with rows of bunk beds and many people sleeping in the same room, sometimes twenty or thirty in a room. What is the goal? The goal is to reach the massive Cathedral in the center of Santiago where the remains of the apostle St. James are buried. Catholics and other Christians walk this trail in honor of St. James because he preached the gospel throughout Spain in Roman times. While the Camino was established by Christians, pilgrims from every faith, color, and creed come together and walk hand in hand.

For the readers who are uninitiated to the Camino de Santiago, take a few minutes to watch this wonderful short video by PBS travel expert Rick Steves:

Rick Steves PBS video – The Camino de Santiago (3:06 mins)
https://BobLogan.net/RickStevesCamino

WHY WOULD ONE DO THIS?

The spiritual dimension of the Camino is a central feature of most peoples' journey. Many are devoutly religious or affiliated to a church, others are secular, and some are atheists. It would be hard to find a person who has dedicated a month of their lives to walk 500 miles across Northern Spain who does not engage in some soul searching. There are multiple Camino routes to choose from all over Spain, as well as from many parts of Europe. However, the most traditional route to Santiago is called the Camino Francés, or the French Way. The Camino Francés has grown rapidly in popularity since the turn of the century as a place for people to reconnect with something outside of themselves. That connection might be with their fellow pilgrims, the natural world, a simple lifestyle unencumbered by unnecessary material wants, or their own perception of God. What each pilgrim discovers along the way is a product of their own intentions and openness, and the random factors that chance, fate, or God puts in their way. No one who walks the Camino in full or in part will be unchanged by the experience. The Camino Francés is a Camino of seeking, be it atonement, peace, or redemption. The emptiness that often lies at the heart of contemporary Western culture is one factor that accounts for why so many people are willing to forego lives of comfort and put their bodies and minds through a comparatively grueling ordeal, even if it is only for a few weeks.

The Camino is all about the basics of existence. Your entire life is cradled in a backpack. You walk until you are tired, and you eat when you are hungry. You do the exact same thing every day. Get up, walk for much of the day, stop for rest and for food, find a place to stay and then exhausted, sleep. Then you do it again. And again. For days on end. You meet people from all over the world, and everyone is walking in the same direction. The stories you hear from others are truly inspirational and humbling. Everyone is carrying some type of burden on the Camino, maybe it is dealing with cancer, the loss of a loved one, a messy divorce, losing a job, or starting a new retirement, there are many reasons. It is an incredibly spiritual experience, and it was a life-changing one for me. My experience walking the Camino brought me back two more times, and I fully expect to go again many more times during my lifetime. It is that powerful of an experience. While I would love to go into greater detail, just Google the Camino de Santiago and you will spend hours being enthralled. Better yet, go on Netflix and watch the movie *The Way*,[9] starring Martin Sheen and directed by his son, Emilio Estevez.

When I decided to walk the Camino de Santiago in 2012, I was terribly afraid. Not so much from pushing myself to make the commitment, but most of my fear came from my physical condition. Once a successful athlete, I was not exactly in the best shape of my life after so many years as a fundraiser, sitting at a desk and eating many extravagant donor lunches and dinners. I had become sedentary and gained some weight, like many of us do as we get older.

The 2012 timeframe from my deciding to walk the Camino and then starting the walk was very short (about two months), and I had very little time to put in any significant training. Luckily, I was adequately prepared for what to pack and how to navigate the albergues (basically hostels) along the way. But I was seriously concerned with whether I had the physical stamina to complete this challenging journey.

My fear of this adventure even had an impact on determining the appropriate starting point for my first Camino in 2012. Since I only had three-and-a-half weeks available to walk the Camino, I knew I did not have enough time to complete the entire 500-mile pilgrimage on this visit (Typically, walking the entire 500-miles of the Camino takes 5-6 weeks). My choices were to walk the first-half of the Camino, finishing in Leon, or the second-half and finish in Santiago de Compostela. As I mentioned, the traditional starting point for the Camino is in St. Jean Pied de Port, a small French town nestled into the base of the Pyrenees Mountain range.

In 2012, I could have started in St. Jean Pied de Port, and walked the first half of the Camino, but that decision would entail a strenuous climb over the top of the Pyrenees Mountain range, which divides France and Spain geographically. The Pyrenees Mountains stretch 270 miles across the entire French-Spanish border with a high point of Aneto Peak at 11,169. This trek would happen all on the first two days of the Camino.

This climb is, without a doubt, the most challenging part of the Camino. The Napoleon Route, as it is called, begins just outside of St. Jean Pied de Port and has 5,249 feet of elevation gain with another 1,650 of extreme steep descent more than 27 kilometers concluding in the Spanish town of Roncesvalles. I was unsure if I was physically ready to take on that mountain climb, and honestly, I was scared. I could not imagine committing to do the Camino, telling all my friends about the adventure, train for months and then failing in the first day or two because of the Pyrenees Mountain stage. The fear of failure enveloped me from the start and felt utterly unprepared for what lay ahead.

These fears of the Pyrenees cemented my decision to walk the second half of the Camino, starting in Leon and finishing at the cathedral in Santiago de Compostela. I would cover just over 200 miles and experience some of the best parts of the Camino. If I had time, I hoped to continue on after Santiago for a few days and walk to Finesterre, a small town on the Atlantic Ocean on the western coast of Spain considered the "end of the world."

My reason for undertaking the Camino challenge was to figure things out, mentally, physically, and emotionally. As it turned out, most of my fears centered on the physical demands of the Camino and whether I could handle them. When I departed for Spain, my wife Judy was not pleased about my Camino decision and was not very supportive. She was rightly concerned about me and my physical condition, but in the end, she understood this was something I just had to do for myself.

FEAR OF THE UNKNOWN – COACHING IN BOLOGNA, ITALY

There was a time in my coaching career when fear almost brought me to my knees, but only momentarily. It was also quite complicated because, like the Camino, it involved foreign travel. From 1984-1986, I was a full-time graduate assistant football coach at the University of Arizona, working for a great man, Head Coach Larry Smith. At the conclusion of the 1986 season, he left for an amazing opportunity, to become the head coach at the University of Southern California (USC). As much as I would have loved to continue working for Coach Smith at USC, it was clear I could not afford to be a graduate assistant on his staff. The cost of living in Los Angeles was prohibitive, and there were no spots for me to take a full-time paid coaching slot. So, what do I do?

As they say, timing is everything. When all these coaching changes were occurring, a local headhunter friend of Coach Smith contacted me about becoming the head coach of a professional football team—where, of all places? Bologna, Italy! And the team name? The Bologna Doves no less.

I could bring two American players and another assistant coach from the United States with me. As it turned out, a coaching friend of mine connected me with a junior college head coach in Phoenix, Glendale Community College (GCC). GCC is a school with a great football tradition, and they were often national championship contenders. I was fortunate to be able to recruit a coach of his caliber. Fred Haeger was unmarried, had no kids in the picture to worry about, and he was a little bit of a free spirit kind of guy, and I thought he would love this new coaching adventure. When I offered the job to him, he was all in.

All this took place immediately after our University of Arizona football season concluded in November. The Italian football league plays opposite their American counterparts, and their season runs with preseason camp during the early winter months, and the regular season from early spring through May. The playoffs begin in June and July. Knowing this, it was necessary for me to move immediately to Italy to begin training with the team. I traveled to Italy in early December to begin pre-season training while Fred resigned his Glendale head coaching position and prepared for his own move to Italy. He had to rent his house and put the rest of his affairs in order. I told him to wait a few weeks, and I would send him a plane ticket to join me in Italy in early January.

Soon after I arrived in Italy, the Bologna Dove ownership group of ten to twelve prominent Italian businessmen hosted an extravagant dinner to welcome me to Bologna. However, I was soon to find out that the dinner was a ruse to deliver some unexpected news. After a couple of hours of drinking, laughing, and eating Italian food, as only the Italians can do, we got down to some business regarding the team. As it turned out, they had recently determined that the budget wouldn't allow me to hire an assistant coach after all, so I would need to tell my coach that he could not come. Are you kidding me? I was shocked, but I kept calm at dinner. I did say that this could be a problem, and asked if we could meet tomorrow night and reconvene? I told the ownership group this was a big change and I needed twenty-four hours to think about this new development and I requested we meet again for dinner the following night. I told them I needed to call the coach I had offered the assistant position to and break the news.

As I left the dinner, I was sweating bullets thinking about what I was going to do. I pulled out my contract, which was written in Italian, and thought about Fred Haeger, whom I had hired and promised a job. Fred had already resigned his position as head coach of GCC, again one of the best junior college programs in the country. And I knew he was sitting at home preparing for the coaching adventure of a lifetime. He was willing to pack up his life and move to another country based solely on my word that he had a guaranteed job as my assistant coach. How would he take this news? How would I explain this to Fred? Would I ever be able to make it right by him? I doubted it.

I knew what a disruption this big move had been in my own life, and I could only imagine what news like this would mean for Fred. Here I was, sitting in a foreign country, not able to speak the native language, and not knowing what the culture was and how things worked in Italy. I was unsure what politics might be in play. I didn't understand the financial aspects of the situation, and I couldn't even read my contract written in Italian! I was uncertain of my next steps. I was in a panic and total fear on the inside, but tried to remain calm on the outside.

Making that phone call to Fred was one of the hardest things I have ever done. I thought long and hard about what to say and how to communicate this disastrous news. I must've picked up the phone and hung it up again half a dozen times. When I finally got him on the line, I said, "Fred, I have some good news and some bad news for you. The bad news is that the Italians have just told me they only have money for one coach. And I just found this out last night for the first time. I am so sorry." Fred was devastated. He couldn't believe what he was hearing. I continued, "Fred, the good news is the following—I am meeting with them again tonight at another dinner to discuss this, and if they stick to their guns on not hiring you, I'm going to tell the owners that if there is only enough budget for a head coach, then your new head coach is Fred Haeger. I will return to the States and Fred will be the new coach of the Doves. Fred was dumbfounded that I was taking this stance. He said he would be honored to come over to Italy in either capacity, as my assistant or as the new head coach of the team.

I went to dinner the next night and after some antipasti and a few glasses of wine, it was time for me to deliver my message to the ownership group. I identified whom I felt was the best English-speaking owner in the group, Giacomo, the team President, to translate for me. I slowly stood up in front of the group and said, "Giacomo, I need you to translate what I am going to say word-for-word. I will try and talk slow, but I want the owners to hear exactly what I am saying."

"If there is one thing you will all learn by working with Bob Logan, it is that I am a man of my word. I understand you have financial issues with the team, and you need to do what you need to do. That is your problem, not mine. I was hired to coach an outstanding football team, and I am excited about the prospects for this season. However, just like each of you need resources to successfully run your various businesses, I need resources to run a football team. I promised a coaching job to an outstanding coach in the United States, Fred Haeger. And he is every bit as good a coach as I am. I promised him this job based on your original offer and your original agreement with me. So here is the bottom line; if you can only afford one coach, then that coach is not me. I will resign right now, and we will bring Fred Haeger over here to be the new head coach of the Bologna Doves. I promised him a coaching job in Italy, and I will not go back on my word. My word is my bond. I am sorry it has come to this, and I want to thank all of you for the opportunity." I then sat back down in my chair.

I didn't know the culture, and I had no idea what was really going on here. As soon as I told the owners my position, the table exploded into boisterous Italian conversation. It was interesting to sit back and watch all of them discuss, posture, and yell with one another while I sat there patiently for what seemed like ten minutes, having no idea what they were saying to each other. Finally, one of the English speakers let me know that they had worked it out financially, and Fred could come after all as my assistant coach. In essence, I had called their bluff, but I was also fully prepared to fly back home and let Fred have the job if they maintained their stance. Looking back now, if I had to do it all over again, I would not have changed a thing. I felt that strongly about my position. Challenging, absolutely, but I needed to be able to look myself in the mirror and say I did the right thing.

Looking back on this many years later, it did teach me one thing. Do the right thing, always.

I stayed a year and coached the team, with Fred, to the Italian national championship semi-finals. Our team dominated nearly all our opponents throughout the season, and, in the end, we just ran into some bad luck. We had a fantastic team and led the league in nearly every offensive and defensive category. Our final record was 12-1-1 and we nearly played in the Italian Super Bowl for the national championship. We lost in the semi-finals by a score of 20-12 to a team from Milan. So close.

I was proud of the season we had and how far we progressed in the playoffs. Just a couple of bounces our way and we would have played for the Italian National Championship in the Super Bowl. Not bad for a first-year American coach, in my mind.

The Italian owners had a different perspective on football success. When I arrived, I replaced a beloved coach, Jim Emery, who had led the Doves as head coach for the first three years of their existence as a team. In 1985, Emery led them to a victory in the Super Bowl in the Italian National Championship. This same team went on to win the European National Championship (the Eurobowl) in Amsterdam.

This was clearly the high-water mark for the Bologna Doves and Italian football for this group. Not having a long history of football, the Italian owners saw this instant success and felt it should be an automatic to win the championship every single year. They invested in the best coaches and the best players, so if we had a championship team this year, then we should win it again next year. As we all know in sports, it just does not work out that way in reality.

And my reality was the ownership group felt our final 12-1-1 record was not a good year, and simply earning a spot to play in the national championship semi-finals was a failure. They thought we had failed because we didn't win the title as the team had done two years earlier. While our semi-final loss was tough, through my eyes I saw our total season as a huge success, building a solid foundation for the future. We had built a team and a program while learning a new language and culture at the same time. I felt good about our prospects. We had great players and I knew we would contend for the Italian Super Bowl title next year.

But the Italian ownership group saw that semi-final loss as a failure. In reviewing the season with the ownership, I had thoughts on what we needed to do to improve going forward, but many of them disagreed with my analysis and feedback. They could only remember the final loss of the season in Milan and while they may not have said it, it was clear many of the owners just thought we should change the head coach. In the end, we decided to go our separate ways, very amicably. I wished I could have stayed a few more years, but it is interesting how perception is everything.

> ## NOT ENOUGH
>
> *"My philosophy is: It's none of my business what people say of me and think of me. I am what I am, and I do what I do. I expect nothing, and I accept everything. And it makes life so much easier."*
>
> — ANTHONY HOPKINS

One of the biggest fears I faced and the most destructive internally is the feeling of just not being "enough." I certainly faced it as I prepared to walk the Camino, when I decided to quit the Academy, when I picked up the phone to call Fred, and when I met with the Italian Bologna Dove ownership group. In every case, I wondered; would this play out the same way if I had been "more"—more qualified, more prepared, more responsible, more curious, better, different? How often did I step back and ask these kinds of questions about myself? How often did I question my abilities? How much do I hold myself back, not taking on any risk, not standing up for myself simply because I don't feel good enough? This fear is entirely premised on what we think about ourselves, and it can be one of the biggest things that hold us back in life. We all have that "voice" in our head, and we must strive to make it stop talking to us.

I spent ten years working in the Athletic Department at the University of Arizona as a coach and as a fundraiser. I felt comfortable there. It was my life and represented my entire make-up as a person. I had been an athlete my whole life, and I knew how to navigate that environment. I was defined by what I did, and it felt good.

In 2002, I was offered the opportunity to transition to a leadership development position with the University of Arizona College of Science. Even though it was a nice promotion with a hefty salary increase, I said to myself, "Are you out of your mind?" While it was a great opportunity and an exciting new adventure, I was hesitant, and I was scared to death. I didn't see how I could ever measure up in the eyes of the scientists and academics. I saw them as so much smarter than me. After all, my college degree was in history!

While it was true I didn't know anything about science, I also realized I was an expert in fundraising and development. This was just like any other scary situation; I knew if I could tackle my fears head-on, I would ultimately be successful. It took some time to convince these academics that I was a renowned expert in my field of fundraising and development, just as they were experts in their individual scientific disciplines. Over time, we found great success in working together, and they realized I had specific knowledge and a skillset they did not have and slowly came around to respect me. Sometimes skillsets can be complementary, and this was a perfect example.

Even when we are out of our comfort zone, as I was when moving to Italy where I didn't speak the language or being hired as a "dumb jock" to raise money for the highly esteemed College of Science where I felt totally out of my element, there is one continuing theme and message. If one can overcome internal fears and stand up for ourselves, we can tackle anything. The outside stuff is not as big a deal as we think it is. Our internal voice is the one we must overcome to take the risk to be successful, and even happy.

Recap of Lessons About Fear

1. You are better than you think you are. Fake it till you make it.
2. Everything you ever wanted in life is on the other side of fear. You cannot enjoy any level of success unless you face your challenges, accept the risk and stifle your fear.
3. Don't worry about what other people think of you. You can't please everyone anyway, so you may as well please yourself.
4. Follow your heart no matter what. Sometimes that means doing the right thing when it is the hardest. Sometimes it means walking away. Have the courage to march to the beat of your own drum.
5. You are not what you have become, you are what you have overcome. Always remember this.
6. Discover what will make you happy or successful, and don't be afraid to ask for it.
7. At worst, you might get no for an answer.
8. If others doubt your ability (prove them wrong). If you doubt yourself (prove yourself wrong).
9. What you think about yourself and say to yourself can be more potent than anything else. Give yourself positive messages and reinforcement always.
10. Don't let fear stop you. Fear kills more dreams than failure ever will. Courage is the ability to be afraid and take action anyway.

CHAPTER 3

CRITICISM

"If you're not open to constructive criticism, you're not open to truly growing as a person."
— STEPHAN LABOSSIERE

DEALING WITH VARIOUS TYPES OF CRITICISM

There are myriad ways to look at criticism, too many to review here. I thought it would be helpful to focus on three forms and perspectives on criticism. First, the most common and most accepted is constructive criticism. When delivered sincerely and gently, and received openly and gratefully, constructive criticism is worth our time to listen and learn from others. One must consider that someone important in our life cared enough to share something with us to provide an opportunity for improvement, as hard as it may be to hear at the beginning.

Second, criticizing others is a necessary part of life, either in the workplace or in our personal lives. From my many years of work in coaching and the business world, I will share a bit about effectively using the skill of criticism. This is an acquired skill and often times criticism is delivered in a form of diplomacy.

Finally, there are times when it is essential to realize when you are in a situation where the criticism isn't about you but more about the other person's fears and perspective. In that specific case, it is best to ignore it altogether.

Outside of a formal workplace performance evaluation (often a mandatory exercise, if not an endearing part of nearly every job), offering constructive criticism is genuinely courageous. We have all been on both sides of this valuable conversation, either receiving criticism from a friend or doling it out to someone else. At first, receiving or giving criticism is not smooth or enjoyable. Think about it for a minute. If one of your closest friends or a close associate at work had bad breath or body odor, what would you do? If it is offensive to you, then it surely will be offensive to others. A true friend or colleague would step up here. You engage in this difficult conversation for one of two reasons:

A. You genuinely care about the person, and
B. You see them as a valuable contributor worthy of your time and attention.

Now, taking this to the extreme, if a person never receives criticism of any kind in the workplace, this may be a strong signal that they are not very important to the organization. There is an old adage in coaching that goes something like this— *"If I am never yelling at you or your performance on the field, then I would be a little worried about your status on the team. My riding you constantly means I genuinely care about you as a player, and I want you to improve."*

Now think about your own workplace. Are there co-workers who just seem to "exist" at work, never being recognized? You know who they are, employees just punching the time clock and getting by from day to day. Marginalized members of an organization or team are rarely singled out for personal or professional development. Most people aren't going to take on the difficult task of having this uncomfortable conversation if they don't see a payoff for themselves or the organization. When someone is seen as unwilling or unable to change, perceived as unproductive, is a poor listener, or is defensive to any feedback, they are less likely to receive and accept feedback from anyone. They are just not worth the effort. However, when someone takes the time and effort to provide criticism in a practical and caring way, it may still sting a bit, but they wouldn't do it if they didn't care and see the potential.

There is a saying about criticism, which goes something like this: *the uninitiated hear criticism and get defensive, the novice hears it and thinks there may be something to it, but when the wise are criticized, their response is, "but of course."* To clarify, which one are you? How do you take criticism: as the uninitiated, a novice, or as a wise person?

Being able to hear, graciously receive, and even be grateful for feedback, when delivered with care, is the mark of a wise individual and a strong leader. Welcome criticism and learn from it, and at the same time, don't take it too personally or allow criticism to wound you. Afterall, it is just someone else's opinion.

Early in my career, when I was a high school history teacher, I recall handing out the end-of-the-year teacher evaluations to my students. I told the students I certainly appreciated hearing about all the positive aspects of my teaching. But I also told them for me to improve, I sincerely wanted to know what they disliked about my class. I told them that hearing the bad was the only way I could grow as a successful teacher. Was I fair to everyone? Too demanding? Did I play favorites? These were the things I needed to hear. And those were some of the negative comments I received from a handful of students. It was enough for me to step back and truly evaluate what I did well and identify areas where I needed to improve.

I once heard a great story that illustrates the power of embracing negative feedback. It was told by Mort Utley, a salesman extraordinaire, in a keynote address to college students working for Southwestern Books. Southwestern Books, back in the 1980s, gave college students summer jobs selling books door-to-door all over the country, not an easy task, as you can imagine. These college students were taught the best sales techniques and could make a ton of money if they worked hard. I had many friends from Salpointe and the UA who worked for Southwestern Books each summer during college, and they raved about the experience and came home with gobs of cash.

Mort Utley's speech included conventional wisdom about the importance of memorizing the boilerplate sales call presentations and staying on script during each sales call in order to be more successful. Utley's speech also included sage advice about accepting and appreciating the many rejections you were bound to receive from customers as much as the occasional "Yes" for a completed sale. Utley related the specific story of a student salesperson being happy, excited, and vociferous in his appreciation when a specific customer delivered his strong objection and firm "No" to buying the books from this student.

The customer was clearly confused with the student's enthusiasm for being told "No." The student responded, "We know from our Southwestern Book sales training that more than 66% of customers will tell me, 'No.' Honestly, sir, I welcome the 'Nos,' because they get me one step closer to my next 'Yes' and my next sale. So, congratulations to you, Mr. Customer, because my last customer told me 'No,' and now you are telling me 'No.' This means my next customer will likely be a 'Yes!'" Mort told the audience the student's explanation about 'Yesses' and 'Nos' created a visceral reaction with the customer. So much so, that the customer changed his mind because he did not want to be perceived as a 'No,' and he dragged the student back inside to complete the sale!

A CAMINO STORY—WALKING MY OWN PATH

In 2010, a movie that has been highly rated by Rotten Tomatoes (over 80 percent by both the critics and the fans) was released that had a significant impact on my life. As mentioned earlier, it is called *The Way*,[10] directed by Emilio Estevez, and starred his real-life father (and movie father in this role), Martin Sheen. It was the story of an estranged father going to Spain to recover his son's remains, who had died in a hiking accident crossing the Pyrenees Mountains that divide France and Spain. His son was walking the Camino de Santiago, the 500-mile pilgrimage across Northern Spain. Before this film, I had never heard of the Camino de Santiago, but after watching it, I was inspired. I felt I was being pulled to accept the challenge of this 500-mile path of discovery in Northern Spain. The very film that helped me discover it has helped others as well, and as more people walk the Camino and talk about it, the Camino legend continues to grow.

There were many similarities to my own life. I saw myself in the main character (slightly older and slightly out of shape). He was totally consumed by his work, at the expense of his family. It wasn't until I faced some professional challenges that I decided the Camino would be a great place to seek answers. The difficult situation at work stemmed from the constant criticism I was receiving from one of my supervisors.

Let me be clear; I was very good at my job, and as a university development professional. I was one of the leading development professionals on campus for almost thirty years and was highly respected by my peers. With this experience, one could imagine that I was comfortable with how I did my job. I always exceeded my fundraising goals, so the total annual dollars brought in were still impressive, often in the tens of millions of dollars.

However, I will be the first to admit that I can be stubborn, and I like to do things my own way. While I was doing all the necessary tasks I needed to do to get the job done and achieve great results, I was not too fond of the menial and tedious task of paperwork and the computer metrics that needed to be entered and tracked in the computer system. As a result, I was not too diligent about documenting my contacts, meetings, follow-up calls, and other essential development metrics, theorizing that total dollars raised would be the only metric management should really be worried about anyway.

However, at the time the UA had a new management team overseeing the entire campus development operation, and my direct supervisor came down on me regularly for all the things she knew I wasn't doing. However, I also knew the College of Science was consistently one of the top two or three fundraising units on the entire University of Arizona campus, so I felt it would all work out in the end.

Our College of Science development office was severely under-resourced and under-staffed, and I felt the limited time I had should be spent dealing with donors and securing gifts, rather than inputting information into the computer. However, she was right, for sure, and she had a job to do and needed these metrics to manage her development officers. But I just couldn't force myself to take time away from the tasks I felt were truly important to do what I saw as meaningless and trivial, and the constant criticism about it was wearing me down.

The tension between us deteriorated to the point I was willing to leave my job over it. As they say, "life is too short," and I was ready to do something completely different at this stage of my career. I contacted headhunters and started to investigate other positions around the country.

It was during this challenging time of extreme criticism at work when I discovered the Camino de Santiago. It was a revelation, and it was then that I decided to walk the Camino. While the decision was the right one for me, once I began to share my plans, I immediately began facing some strong critics from nearly every aspect of my life.

The first person to weigh in was my wife. Telling her my idea of walking the Camino de Santiago was not fun. Even though she knew how much stress I was facing at work, she was generally not a risk-taker and could not understand how I thought this trip could possibly be so cathartic. How could walking hundreds of miles alone carrying a heavy backpack be a positive experience she wondered? Besides, she was worried about my physical condition and my ability to complete the journey, but more importantly, she hated the thought of my being away for so long. My Camino pilgrimage in Spain would last about three-and-a-half weeks, and I was combining this Camino experience with a two-week work trip to Italy for some prominent donors from the College of Science. All-in-all, I would be gone for about a month and a half—the longest we had ever been apart since getting married nearly thirty years before.

Next, I faced criticism from almost everyone I talked to about my plans to walk the Camino. At the time, the Camino was nowhere near as well-known as it is today. You can imagine the reaction when I told people about my plans. When I disclosed I was taking a month off from work to walk some religious pilgrimage that most people had never heard of, they all thought I was nuts. I received comments such as, "Clearly, your job must not be that important if you can take that much time off," or, "Your work must not be that valuable if they can do without you for that long." Those who had heard of the Camino got it, but because so many others didn't, I decided to stop sharing my plans with most people. I didn't need the criticism and I didn't need everyone judging my decision to do something decisive. There is a lesson here—stop listening to your critics and follow your heart and gut. More times than not, you will be correct and pleased with the ultimate outcome of your decisions.

Finally, I learned something very important during my Camino preparations. I discovered many Camino *experts* held strong opinions and judgments about the "right" way to walk the Camino. Purists believe there is only one way, and if you don't do it the "proper" way, you are not a true pilgrim. They feel anyone who deviates hasn't indeed had the real experience of the Camino.

From their perspective,

1. First, you must walk the full 500 miles. (No partial Caminos)
2. Second, you must walk from beginning to end and all at once
3. Third, you cannot skip any sections.

For me, in 2012, I did not have the requisite time to do the entire 500 miles in one continuous hike, so I did it in two stages. As I mentioned, for my first Camino in 2012, I started in the middle of the Camino in a city called Leon. Leon was about 200 miles from Santiago de Compostela. My second Camino began in 2015, I started in St. Jean Pied de Port and walked 300 miles to Leon. In essence, I did the full 500-mile Camino de Santiago in two trips. This was not unusual for many pilgrims. Not many people have the time or money to spend 5-6 weeks in Spain.

The Camino purists also believe that pilgrims should spend all their time eating and sleeping only in albergues (basic hostels just for the Camino, where they sleep in bunk beds and mingle with other pilgrims). I stayed in albergues 75-80 percent of the time, mainly to enjoy the camaraderie and relationships with pilgrims on the trail. I will admit, however, from time to time, I needed to sleep in a comfortable hotel bed with a hot shower and room service to keep my sanity. It was a way to refresh myself and regain my purpose for the Camino, and I did not feel I was any less of a pilgrim for doing so. I was not worried about being judged by other pilgrims.

Camino purists also feel it is cheating not to carry your fully loaded backpack every day. Many pilgrims arrive in Spain to walk the Camino and they suddenly realize they have brought too much stuff (I was one of these). It only takes a day or two of carrying 5-10 pounds of extra weight that you realize you have a problem. To capitalize on this common occurrence with pilgrims, many backpack transport services have popped up on the Camino to help the tired pilgrim.

Essentially, these services will take some of your extra weight and transport it ahead to your next town 10-15 miles away. In this scenario, a pilgrim will have their regular pack and a small day pack to hold just what they need on the trail for that day (water, change of socks, and some snacks). While I initially felt guilty on some days when I shipped my bags ahead, I realized the Camino is about the journey, not about punishing yourself. The purists believe that carrying everything on your back is the authentic way to do it. I now tell people considering walking the Camino—this is *your* Camino, so don't be afraid to do it *your* way.

I believe that walking the Camino in whatever way you can is always preferable to not doing it at all. My misgivings about climbing the Pyrenees and inability to take off even more time from work might have stopped me from going had I not figured out a way to do it within the limitations of my fitness level and schedule. Once I had completed the first half in 2012, there was no question I would return someday to complete the full 500 miles. I did return in 2015, and I am so glad I didn't listen to the criticism of others to keep me from my goal.

CRITICISM—DISHING IT OUT

> *"Criticism, like rain, should be gentle enough to nourish a man's growth without destroying his roots."*
>
> — FRANK A. CLARK

Brené Brown, in her book *Rising Strong*,[11] says this: "Not paying attention because you're not the one getting harassed or fired or pulled over or underpaid [or gossiped about—Bob] is the definition of privilege." Just because you're not the one who started the gossip, if you spread it or even allow it to continue in your presence, you are part of the problem. In this same book, Brown shares an acronym relating to trust, which is crucial for effectively sharing feedback—BRAVING. It covers the seven elements of trust that emerged from her research.

1. **Boundaries:** You respect mine, and when you're not clear what they are, ask. Be willing to say no yourself.
2. **Reliability:** Do what you say you'll do. Don't overpromise and communicate when you are having problems or will be late with a commitment.
3. **Accountability:** Own your mistakes and clean up your messes with an apology.
4. **Vault:** Don't share confidences that you aren't authorized to share, including gossip.
5. **Integrity:** Choose courage over comfort. Practice your values and do what is right.
6. **Nonjudgmental:** We can both ask for what we need and talk about how we feel without judging each other.
7. **Generosity:** Choosing the best possible interpretation related to others' intentions, words, and actions.

Early on in my football-coaching career, like most young coaches I screamed and yelled at my players all the time. After many years of experience, one realizes the authoritarian approach (i.e., yelling) is standard with most new coaches and mirrors advice given to new schoolteachers as well. The thought is you should rule with an iron fist from the start, and classroom management will be much easier and allow for softening down the road. Otherwise known as "let the rope out slowly."

It certainly didn't take me long to realize that players (and your students or your employees) begin to tune you out when you are always yelling at them. If you make everything a big deal all the time, then ultimately, nothing is a big deal. Your fire and brimstone tactics eventually fall on deaf ears.

Experience taught me that I could be a far more effective coach, teacher, or manager if I put my arm around the shoulder of one of my players, students, or employees and pull him/her aside to offer some guidance in a caring manner. I also appreciated being seen as a one-on-one teacher rather than an authoritarian blowhard. Masculine stereotypes can harm sports in general, not just with coaches, but also with players and even with fans. The passion with which some fans approach their teams can have both positive and negative consequences.

Everyone is a critic when it comes to his or her team. Coaching decisions are made on the fly without the benefit of instant replay, and it is easy to play Monday morning quarterback from the comfort of your living room. Athletics is one area where everyone involved is second-guessed all the time—Hiring the right coach. Firing the coach. Recruiting the right players. Making the right plays. Starting the right players. Executing the plays correctly. Officials making the right calls. The world of sports can be brutal as it relates to criticism, and this is a nice segue to the next section on criticism—ignoring it.

CRITICISM—IGNORING IT

"The artist doesn't have time to listen to the critics. The ones who want to be writers read the reviews. The ones who want to write don't have the time to read reviews."

— WILLIAM FAULKNER

In the end, you are the one who must live with yourself. If you can sleep at night and feel good about the way you show up in the world, that is all that matters. When you are comfortable with yourself, it doesn't matter what other people think or say. One of my favorite football coaches is former Notre Dame head coach Lou Holtz, truly a legendary coach and one of the wisest people I know. He said, "Never tell your problems to anyone else...90 percent of the people don't care at all about your problems, and the other 10 percent are glad you have them!" It's funny and said with tongue in cheek, but also very accurate. Most people really don't care about your problems. They are worried about their own problems!

The same sentiment can be applied to the subject of criticism as well. We spend so much time worrying about what other people think about us, and most of them aren't thinking about us at all! Another great coach, John Wooden, said, "You can't let praise or criticism get to you. It's a weakness to get caught up in either one." When we can genuinely maintain confidence in ourselves, and live according to our values, then the winds of change and controversy can blow all around us, but they won't blow us off our course.

We all remember Michael Jackson's hit song "Man in the Mirror." The lyrics of that song remind me of a famous poem with a similar name that delivers a very similar and powerful message. It was originally written in 1934 by Peter Dale Wimbrow, Sr., and it has been reprised many times since the original, but the words today are still as relevant as they were back then.

The Man in the Glass
by Dale Wimbrow (1934)[12]

When you get what you want in your struggle for self
and the world makes you king for a day
Just go to the mirror and look at yourself
and see what that man has to say

For it isn't your father or mother or wife
whose judgment upon you must pass
The fellow whose verdict counts the most in your life
is the one staring back from the glass

He's the fellow to please never mind all the rest
for he's with you clear up to the end
And you've passed your most dangerous difficult test
if the man in the glass is your friend

Some people may think you a straight-shooting chum
and call you a wonderful guy
But the guy in the glass says you're only a bum
if you can't look him straight in the eye

You may fool the whole world down the pathway
of life and get many pats on the back as you pass
But your final reward will be heartaches and
tears if you've cheated the man in the glass.

A CAMINO STORY—A SPIRITUAL AND LIFE-CHANGING EXPERIENCE

Not six months after I returned from my first Camino in 2012, the local United Way organization began to recruit me for an executive level position. This came with significant responsibility and the salary to match. It was amazing this opportunity came my way at precisely the time when I was looking for a possible career change. I have no doubt my soul-searching on the journey played no small part in this miraculous job offer coming my way at just the right time.

I went to my boss, Joaquin Ruiz, the Dean of the College of Science, to tell him about the offer, and I let him know I planned on accepting it and moving on from the university. Joaquin and I were very close and had been together as a team for nearly fifteen years. He did not want me to leave, and he asked if I would wait a few days before responding. I was happy to do so, and I did a lot of soul searching over the weekend. When I returned on Monday, he provided me with an even more lucrative salary and a significant promotion to stay on as Assistant Dean for External and Corporate Relations. I was stunned, surprised, and elated.

In my mind, the offer was unexpected and welcome. I realized my entire life had changed in dramatic ways because of the Camino de Santiago pilgrimage. What

I learned while walking is there is more to life than work and being defined by your job, a fancy title, or an attractive salary. Those definitions are traps that too many people fall into. Gaining an understanding of what "life purpose" means started for me after I had stripped away all the trappings and distractions I was carrying with me every day, in all I was doing.

Everyone loves to have a witness. When my wife told me that she was seeing the incredible benefits that were coming into my life after taking this Camino journey, I was grateful for her perspective. Over the few years since I'd returned from my first and second pilgrimages in 2012 and 2015, she heard my many Camino stories told time and again to friends, family, and anyone else who would listen. While she was growing tired of hearing them, she began to notice the impact they had when I told them to other people. Her formal view of my "crazy" endeavor of mine shifted in a positive direction. She now understood and accepted the importance of the Camino and seeing my goal through to the end.

It is crucial to use our discernment about when to listen to criticism and when to ignore it. I am glad I didn't let the Camino purists or other detractors deter me from doing it and doing it my way.

In the chapter on fear, I told the story of my transition from the comfortable world of intercollegiate athletics to the unknown world of the College of Science. And trust me, I had to deal with a tremendous amount of criticism when I made this decision. People in my athletic circle were critical in my decision and adamant that this was a poor career choice for me. And faculty in the College of Science were critical about my being hired without any demonstrable science background. I was definitely out on an island with no boat in sight. No pun intended, but it was a sink or swim situation.

What transpired was the exact opposite. I realized the constant second-guessing commonplace in athletics wasn't the case in this new world of science. I may not have understood science initially, but I certainly knew the world of fundraising. And I certainly knew and understood people. People were my skillset. And that was what I was hired to do—manage relationships. Connecting to people with the means and interest in areas and programs within the College of Science was my task. I knew what we did in the College of Science made it possible to fulfill the potential donor's passions, wishes, and desires. Connecting with this resulted in philanthropic gifts of support. This was what I was good at, even if I could not describe the science or understand what a Gamma Ray Spectrometer does. However, after many years in the College of Science, I can honestly tell you what it does now. (Hint: it has something to do with Mars). It also means this newfound knowledge and access to complicated terms allows me to be very impressive and I can now hold my own pretty well at a cocktail party!

With the full value of perspective and hindsight, now I can see that perhaps there is a correlation between the subjective, emotional, seemingly never good enough world of sports, and the objective, fact-based, data-driven world of science. Both areas—sports and sciences—needed the ability to view my work through their particular lens. Moving to the College of Science made me appreciate that maybe it was not *that* important to beat Arizona State University in a football game. In the whole scheme of things, I now realize the tremendous impact I can make on the world by facilitating (through fundraising) some of the fantastic science discoveries that came out of the University of Arizona.

When the economic crash of 2008-2009 occurred, there was tangible fear throughout the financial world, and even more so in fundraising. Our dean was suddenly worried that donations to the College of Science would plummet, and significant projects would have to be put on hold. However, this is where the power of experience was useful. I had lived through other recessions in the past, and I wasn't worried. I knew and understood that donors at the upper levels of the economic spectrum would still be able to give, and they would give at the levels comfortable to them, but they would not *stop* giving. People with high net-worth assets *still* have high net worth after a crash, just not as much. It is all relative.

I also had data from the last seventy years showing philanthropy in the United States over the past seven major recessionary periods. What it showed were these recessions have traditionally caused only a minor blip in total giving levels. Trusting the data, trusting myself, and not letting the critics get me down has always served me well. It will serve you well too.

A Brief Recap of Lessons About Criticism

1. People only give you constructive criticism when they care about you and see you as a productive and contributing member of the team.
2. Criticism should only be about performance and never personal. If it's personal, then it's a problem. Name-calling, gossip, and passive-aggressiveness are not useful.
3. Delivering constructive criticism should only be made in a deliberate, planned, gentle, and supportive manner.
4. Sandwich criticism between authentic praise.
   - "I appreciate that you…"
   - "One area for improvement I can see is…"
   - "Thank you for…"
5. Criticize in private, praise in public.
6. Don't take either criticism or praise too much to heart.
7. Use discernment to determine what to take in, change, and ignore.
8. What other people think of you is none of your business.
9. Don't worry so much about what other people think. Be true to yourself and realize most people aren't even thinking about you at all.
10. You are always building a foundation. There will be difficult days along the way. You are always working on your foundation; watch for flawed situations, keep calm and be prepared with remedies.

CHAPTER 4
ADVERSITY

"All the adversity I've had in my life, all my troubles and obstacles, have strengthened me... You may not realize it when it happens, but a kick in the teeth may be the best thing in the world for you."

— WALT DISNEY

A CAMINO STORY—DEALING WITH CAMINO ADVERSITY: ONE SMALL MISTAKE

It was day two of my Camino adventure, and I was ninety minutes into my day's walk. I had walked about five miles, it was a beautiful day, and I looked forward to getting into the "Camino rhythm" of walking for many hours to come. When you walk the Camino, you find yourself reliving events—last night's albergue, who you had dinner with, how your bed was, and how well you slept. On this particular day, which seemed like a typical Camino day, I stopped in my tracks when I suddenly remembered I had left behind my only gym shorts and a light fleece top I sleep in back in last night's albergue.

In my mind's eye, I could see them hanging on the wooden hook by the shower where I'd left them that morning. At first glance, and to most everyone who hears this story, it might not seem like such a huge problem. But one must understand the plight of the Camino "pilgrim" and what they experience day after day. As a pilgrim, you walk for hundreds of miles carrying everything you absolutely must have every day neatly stuffed into a backpack. You have a very strict schedule to keep to each day, so any alteration can be a significant issue. Many items you carry have multiple purposes. For example, the gym shorts were my *only* pair, and I wore them at night around the albergue for casual wear, and I also used them as my sleeping shorts. I needed to have them.

Your backpack's total weight is a significant issue. That's why the fleece top was the *only* medium-weight coverup I had, and if it was frigid in the albergue, I could wear it in my sleeping bag at night. It wasn't as if I had an extra set of sleeping togs to sleep in. I had meticulously packed my clothing items for the Camino, and I had only one of each essential item except for my socks and underwear.

There I was, standing in the middle of the trail at a total standstill. I was deep in thought, dealing with what to do as pilgrims continued to walk past me as they looked at me quizzically. Suddenly, questions flooded my mind: Should I turn around and backtrack the five miles to retrieve them? That would easily add three plus hours to my day to get to where I am standing right now! This one incredibly dumb mistake meant I likely would not make the next town before dark. I would now be an entire day behind on my Camino. And I had only just begun my Camino the day before!

You might ask, couldn't I just replace them in the next town? (Truth be told, I am a big guy, and it's not as if there are many department stores along this pilgrimage. Since I had lived in Italy earlier, I knew the sizes in Europe were generally much smaller. Finding anything in an American size XXL anywhere along the Camino and the many small towns would be problematic, I was sure.)

Then there were the other questions. If I did go back, would the albergue even be open? (They are typically closed during the day for cleaning.) What if I walked back all those miles and then discovered my stuff wasn't even there? How would I make up the miles and all the lost time? For a long moment, I was paralyzed with no idea what to do next.

Finally, I knew I had to go back. It was the best option. I would figure the rest out. It was depressing to walk backward on the trail and see all the pilgrims going in the opposite direction. They would give me strange stares and wonder what was up with me. I felt stupid, and it was genuinely depressing.

Dealing with adversity can sometimes feel overwhelming, and sometimes it may feel small and somewhat insignificant, as this story appears at first glance. My Camino problem was complicated by several other factors, including not having anyone to reach out to for advice. It didn't help that I didn't speak Spanish, I didn't have a model for dealing with something like this, and there wasn't anyone I could call on for help in this situation. I was on my own. Totally alone.

When I finally arrived back at the albergue, a sign on the door said it would be closed until 2 p.m. I looked at my watch: 11:30. Now I would have to sit in front of the albergue for two-and-a-half hours before I could even get my things! Doing the math in my head, at this point, I knew I had just blown an entire day on the trail because it was clear I was not going to be able to complete today's route. What a stupid mistake; and to stay on schedule, I would likely have to catch a bus to the next town. While technically it was okay, taking a bus violated the fundamental tenet of the Camino in the eyes of many Pilgrims. And oh, by the way, I had no idea how the bus system worked or where to catch the correct one.

There I sat, for two-and-a-half hours until the albergue opened, mulling over my dumb mistake. Finally, the front door opened, and I raced in to retrieve my clothes. Luckily, they were still hanging right where I had left them. I headed into town for the next part of my excellent adventure—how to catch a bus in a tiny town in Spain.

I poked my head in the local butcher's shop to ask how to catch a bus in Spain. The butcher was a very nice man, but he spoke *zero* English. In my broken Spanish, I tried to explain my dilemma, and I was surprised to find out from him there was a bus stop/bench right outside his shop where I could wait for the bus. I sat down with no idea how long I'd be waiting for the next bus.

Two hours later, I was still waiting for the bus to arrive, and this was quickly turning into the Camino day from hell—what a comedy of errors I had brought unto myself. I began to worry, and along came a German guy (who spoke good English *and* Spanish), also looking for the bus to Astorga, the same town where I was headed. I was thrilled to find someone who could possibly help me.

He went inside to ask the butcher about the bus times, and at the exact moment when he opened the front door to come back outside, a bus rapidly approached from our left. I stood up. This bus whizzed around the corner just in front of where I was standing on the curb and continued on down the road. There was only a split second to read the sign on the front before it went barreling past. I missed what the sign said but it didn't stop—it just rolled right on by, and I was standing there like a deer in headlights. What just happened? The German guy freaked out, wondering if that was the bus we wanted and started yelling at *me*, asking why I didn't stop it.

The German guy said it is customary in Spain to stand up and wave the bus down to stop it. Otherwise, they just keep on going. How could I possibly know this? In America, you sit on a bus bench and the bus stops in front of you. You calmly stand and get on the bus. Simple, correct? I clearly had no idea how this Spanish bus system worked. The German guy said, "I sure hope that was not the bus to Astorga, because if it was, we will be sitting here a long time." So there I was, sitting on the bus bench with someone I thought could help me, and now he was angry with me. Not much fun for me on this day!

Luckily, within 15-20 minutes, along came the correct bus to take us to Astorga. I was tired, embarrassed, and discouraged. I felt guilty for taking the bus on only my second day on the Camino, and I felt like a burden to everyone who had tried to understand my terrible Spanish. At the same time, I was also relieved that I wasn't sitting alone and feeling clueless anymore.

In looking back on that day now, I realize I was not alone. The butcher had been super kind to me, despite our difficulty to communicate, and he did try to explain the bus system in his broken English. Finally, for all his bluster, the German guy was also good company, and he made me feel more comfortable since he knew what he was doing.

What was eye-opening about this bus ride was the amount of time it took. It put the entire experience of the Camino in perspective. Here I was, on the second day of my Camino, and I had wasted nearly 5-6 hours because of an incredibly dumb mistake. Now, I was riding on a bus to my next town—Astorga. How long was the bus ride to get there? About twenty minutes! A twenty-minute bus ride to cover ten miles would take a typical pilgrim 4-5 hours to travel the same distance by walking. Clearly, time has a totally different meaning on the Camino.

The good news was I met a very nice woman on the Astorga bus. She was from Toronto and would become a close walking companion for the next three to four days. She was beginning the Camino, just like myself, but she had a different approach to the Camino than I did. In advance, she had built complex spreadsheets and a structured plan for each day—how far she would walk and where she would stay each night—all figured out for the entire trip. The details were unbelievable! I was incredulous. For me, on the other hand, I just planned to let the Camino decide my day. When I got tired, I would stop. When I became hungry, I would eat. My new friend and I laughed at each other, and we agreed we could be confused together on our differing Camino strategies for the short term. We walked together for several days and had a great time along the way.

As I look back on that entire situation now, I realize I didn't do much to make it better. I was reasonably anxious the entire time, and my internal self-doubt didn't help. I was more inclined to beat myself up than calm myself down. I internalized the problem and made myself the victim for most of the day. I was frustrated at my poor Spanish, angry that I was so forgetful about leaving my essential clothes behind, etc. For five hours, I made myself miserable, alone, and helpless. Even though it was only a small-scale crisis, it indeed was the low point of the entire Camino for me. It just shows how important the little things are in one's life.

DEALING WITH ADVERSITY IN A HIGH-PRESSURE SITUATION—UA VS. ASU FOOTBALL RIVALRY, 1986

On November 22, 1986, the UA played arch-rival ASU in one of the more significant games in this long-storied history. ASU came into Tucson undefeated (9-0-1), ranked #4 in the country, and had already clinched a berth in their first-ever Rose Bowl. They were legitimate contenders for a national championship. UA, on the other hand, was 7-2 and ranked #14 in the country. The UA had a strong team and was ready for the challenge. The game had such a high profile nationally that it was selected as a national broadcast on CBS Sports and was to follow the famed Ohio State vs. Michigan rivalry game. Unbelievable. More than 58,000 fans crammed into Arizona Stadium, and they wanted to see the UA end ASU's undefeated season. The pressure and the tension surrounding this game were palpable.

Chuck Cecil's 106 interception return vs. ASU in 1986. The greatest play in University of Arizona history! (And that is me holding the clipboard on the sidelines-35 years and 40 pounds ago!) Courtesy Arizona Daily Star

This game produced two of the greatest plays in UA football history (one being Chuck Cecil's 106 yd TD interception return), and sad to say, I was instrumental in the second play you are soon to learn about. I was in my third year as a coach on the UA staff and I worked with special teams and on the defensive side of the ball. My game day responsibilities were to handle all defensive substitutions. Basically, it was my job to always have the correct players on the field that matched the defense that had been called. There was no margin for error. Our defensive coordinator, Moe Ankney, was high up in the press box and he would call down each play's defense to linebacker coach Tom Roggeman on the sideline. I stood next to "Rogge," and if the defense included a change in personnel, I had to check my chart, send the correct players on the field for that defense, and at the same time, pull the replaced players currently on the field "off" the field, all before the offense broke their huddle for the next play.

For example, on a 3rd and long situation, we might want to play a nickel or dime defense, meaning an additional defensive back goes into the game and we take out a lineman or a linebacker. These substitutions happened in a span of seconds. There was no time for conversation. As soon as I saw "Rogge" signal the next defense, I immediately had players coming on and off the field. Most of the time, the substitutions were simple, but from time to time, it can be incredibly stressful. Usually this occurs during key situations when we were unsure what was the best defense to call at that time. When this happens, there are only seconds available to implement these quick player substitutions. It was these rare, crucial situations that made this job much more difficult than it had to be.

And in this case, it happened to be one of the biggest plays in one of the biggest games in UA history. To set the stage, we were playing a flawless game and the crowd could sense the possibility of an upset. We led ASU at halftime, 14-10. However, ASU was a powerful team (and in total transparency, was likely a better team than us). ASU racked up more than 500 yards of total offense and our defense was constantly on our heels just trying to keep them out of the end zone.

Fast forward to the third quarter. We are leading ASU 21-10 at the time, but again, ASU is driving deep in our territory. A touchdown will make it a one-score game. Here is the sequence of events that took place:

Play #1 – ASU 3rd Down – 6 yards to go from the Arizona 10-yard line
- ASU completes pass down to the 3-yard line
- Officials need to measure for first down and ASU gets first down by one inch!

Play #2 – ASU First Down from 3-yard line
- ASU inside run for gain of one yard

Play #3 – ASU 2nd Down from 2-yard line
- ASU inside run off tackle for gain of one yard

Play #4 – ASU 3rd Down from 1-yard line
- ASU inside run off tackle for no gain

Play #5 – ASU 4th Down from 1-yard line
- ASU kicks an 18-yard Field Goal

PENALTY – TOO MANY PLAYERS ON THE FIELD!
- ASU ACCEPTS PENALTY AND TAKES FG POINTS OFF THE SCOREBOARD
- ASU DECIDES TO GO FOR IT AND ATTEMPT TO SCORE A TOUCHDOWN INSTEAD!

Play #6 – ASU 4th Down and inches
- UA stops ASU for NO GAIN!

Let's go back and review this entire sequence. We have stopped ASU four consecutive plays inside the 10-yard line and three of the plays from inside the three-yard line. Between play #4, when ASU has 3rd and goal from the one, we are ecstatic with the amazing stop. However, there is pandemonium on the sideline because we're not sure if ASU is going to kick a field goal, run a fake, or have the offense go for a touchdown to make the score 21-17.

The fans are screaming, the players are jumping around with the goal-line stand, and I'm trying to stay composed to watch "Rogge" and the defense he signals to me and the team. An important point here—inside the one-yard line, we have three different defenses we can call, all with different personnel. I see "Rogge" call "90" and I send a lineman onto the field and call for Chuck Cecil, our All-American safety to come out of the game. The "90" defense is an all-out, fill every gap of the offensive line and sell out to stop a quarterback sneak one normally sees at the goal-line. We need big bodies on the field to prevent the inside run. It's a great call for this situation. Chuck sees my call and begins to jog off the field.

Now, just as "Rogge" makes the call and I send in the right player, here comes our Head Football Coach, Larry Smith, racing down the sidelines, screaming to change the defense. He wants us to be in "Trojan" defense, which is an entirely different group of players with an entirely different philosophy. ASU is in the huddle, and we don't know if they're kicking a field goal or going for a touchdown. "Rogge" and Coach Smith start arguing with Moe Ankney on the headset on what defense we should be in. I'm standing there in shock because I know the implications. I look on the field and scream at Chuck Cecil to "Stop!" He does and is standing at about the 10-yard line, not knowing what to do. I yell at him to "hold on." I look at Coach Smith and "Rogge," still arguing over the call, and now ASU is breaking the huddle. Who do I listen to, "Rogge," who is technically my boss in this situation, or the head coach of the entire football team? I still don't have an answer and ASU is about to line up for their play. As it turns out, they are going to kick a field goal. But by now, there is no time left. I wave to Chuck— "Go back, get back in the game!" He races back to the line of scrimmage to try and block the field goal.

Chuck Cecil goes onto the field, ASU kicks the field goal to make the score 21-13, which is a huge victory for our defense and a relief for the team. It was a great goal-line stand. But hold on, Chuck now became the 12th player on the field, and the flag was prominently thrown on the turf for everyone to see. Penalty. Twelve players on the field. This type of penalty is inexcusable and should never happen with a well-coached team. You could hear the fans saying to themselves, "How can you possibly have 12 players on the field for a field goal? That is the stupidest thing I have ever seen!" I had Coach Smith and Coach Rogge asking what happened and I had nothing to say. Bottom line, it was *my* fault.

Here is the rest of that story. ASU decides to accept the penalty, take the three points off the scoreboard, and go for a touchdown with the ball only inches from the goal line. I'm thinking to myself, if ASU scores here and ends up winning this game, I will never live this down for the rest of my life. I'm devastated.

I go to the other end of the bench with my head down. At this point, there's nothing I can do. ASU breaks the huddle, lines up, and hands the ball off to their 220-pound fullback, Channing Williams. He rumbles toward the goal line, and, initially, it looks like an easy score. However, just shy of the goal line, literally at the 6-inch line, Williams is stood up by James DeBow, our 180-pound defensive back. Williams is stopped cold for a moment, and they start to work their way down the line of scrimmage, almost like a dance. DeBow is underneath Williams' shoulder pads, driving his legs hard to keep him out of the end zone. Seconds later, a host of UA defensive players join the scrum and stop Williams in his tracks. *No gain* and *no touchdown*! The 58,000 fans erupt, and the UA sidelines explode in jubilation. We have stopped the #4 team in the country for six plays inside the 10-yard line. Incredible. We go on to win the game 34-17 and this play was the catalyst for this victory. I will never forget it.

I had lunch with Chuck Cecil recently, and this is what he remembered about that sequence,

> *"I wasn't sure what was happening, but when I was told to go back on the field I did. After the DeBow stop all I remember is how the stadium was rocking. It was pandemonium! I thought the stadium might actually buckle it was so loud. I had to stand on a bench and try and quiet the crowd when our offense had the ball. The fans were totally out of their minds."*

That one call, made under the most incredible stress and adverse conditions, changed the way I think about pressure forever. In that moment, what do you do? You have a job to do, you've gone through every substitution possible in your head and you're ready for any situation. But what happens when the situation changes. Who is your chain of command in this situation? Do I answer to "Rogge," or do I answer to our Head Coach, Larry Smith? This is a tough question. In reality, it comes down to the following—you are hired to make a decision. You are trained, you are confident, and you cannot back down from adversity. In this case, in my opinion, my boss was "Rogge," not Coach Smith. I made a decision, I stood by it, and I took the consequences.

The final story, the ending of this one play, is quite gratifying. After the game, I was in the coaches' locker room showering and getting dressed. Coach Roggeman came up to me, put his hands on my shoulders and said, "Coach Logan, you didn't make a mistake out there today. Never, never think what happened out there was your fault. I will take care of this to ensure it never happens again."

About fifteen minutes later, Coach Smith entered the locker room after his post-game press conference and Coach Roggeman stopped him in his tracks. Roggeman, a former Marine drill sergeant, got right in Coach Smith's face and said, "Coach Smith, I was hired to do a job. And I will always do my job the best I possibly can. If you don't like the way I do my job, just tell me now and I will leave. But you need to hear this loud and clear. Never, never step in front of me doing what I am paid to do. If I make a mistake, we can talk about it later. But never in the heat of the moment. Do you understand me?" You could hear a pin drop in the locker room, and the coaches all turned away, not knowing what to do. Coach Smith was aghast. However, he also knew he was wrong for what transpired, and he apologized right there to Coach Roggeman.

The message here is clear. When dealing with adversity, own the situation and make a decision. It may not be the correct decision but facing adversity head-on is always the answer. Secondly, if you do make a mistake, you also need to own that mistake. Two very important lessons in life.

Note: Here is the video link of this entire goal-line stand sequence of plays. Enjoy!

ADVERSITY | 65

James DeBow Goal Line Stand vs. ASU 1986 (5:47 mins)
https://BobLogan.net/DebowASUGoalLineStop1986

James DeBow Goal Line Stand (short) (18 seconds)
https://BobLogan.net//JamesDebowASUStop1986

AN EPIC STORY OF ADVERSITY—MIKE CANDREA

One of my friends from my ten years working in the University of Arizona Athletics Department has demonstrated incredible resilience in his life, amid unfathomable challenges and adversity. His name is Mike Candrea, and he recently retired as the head coach of the Arizona women's softball team after thirty-six incredible years. Candrea is arguably the best softball coach in US history, winning eight NCAA national championships. He is a five-time National Coach of the Year and a three-time U.S. Olympic softball coach. Candrea was the head coach of the women's national softball team in 2004, when Team USA won a gold medal, and in 2008, when they won the silver. For many years, Candrea lived in Casa Grande, a town halfway between Tucson and Phoenix, and he achieved all this while commuting seventy-five miles each way from Casa Grande to Tucson every day for twenty years.

**Mike Candrea, University of Arizona women's softball coach
36 years, 8 NCAA Championships, 3 Olympics**

In 1997, Candrea experienced the tragedy of losing one of his softball players. As a coach, the worst thing you can ever deal with is the loss of a player. Julie Reitan, a local Tucsonan, was a GTE Academic All-American and one of the team's more popular players. Reitan, an extremely religious person, had gone to the wedding of one of her high school classmates and returned late that evening to her townhome. Unfortunately, Reitan had diabetes, and while sleeping that night, died from complications from that disease. More than 1,200 people attended her funeral services, and Candrea said at the time, "She was more than just a player, she was the spiritual leader." Candrea still says it was one of the most challenging times in his entire coaching career.

A few years later, in the summer of 2004, Candrea was preparing for the Athens Olympic Games as the head coach of the U.S. Olympic team. Candrea had to deal with another tragic loss in his tight-knit world—the sudden death of his spouse. Over that past year, his Olympic softball team had played exhibition games all over the United States, and they were winding down their exhibition schedule and in a few short weeks would be in Athens, Greece competing for the Olympic gold medal. One of their final games was in Stevens Point, Wisconsin, just prior to the Athens Olympic Games. Upon their arrival, Sue Candrea, his wife of twenty-eight years, collapsed in the airport and ultimately died of a brain aneurysm. The team and the Tucson community were in shock. How did Candrea handle this? After much soul searching and discussion with his family, friends, and players, they all said Sue would want him to complete the task.[13] And complete the task he did. The U.S. Olympic team totally dominated, winning all nine of their games, outscoring their competition 51-1 and won the 2004 Gold Medal. Sue Candrea would have been proud.

Think for a second about the adversity Mike Candrea had to deal with in the span of a few years at the heyday of his outstanding coaching career. Unbelievable. How does one deal with adversity at the scale that he did? One can learn a lot from Mike Candrea.

To be successful in life, you must learn how to ask for help and be comfortable doing so. The challenge is almost entirely internal. We seem to play out all the various scenarios in our minds and develop multiple worst-case scenario outcomes. In the end, the outside "noise" we need help with is often never as complicated as the stories we make up or the feelings we have inside. When we can let go of that and just ask for help and receive it without getting defensive, we will be much better off.

This is one reason why the Camino was so important to me. It was quite literally my first exposure to mindfulness practice and a socially acceptable way to work things out. It gave me an outlet for my vulnerability when I was feeling over-stressed, overworked, and over-burdened. Besides providing a great way to build resilience and strength, it also offered an ego boost and some validation that I could complete this challenging trek—both physically and emotionally.[14] Other people who knew that I did it saw me somehow as a "good person."

The second time I returned to the Camino in 2015, I was very conscious of not being perceived as an ugly American. I worked on my Spanish, and I made a concerted effort to always greet people in Spanish before asking if they spoke English. While it was clear that I was not fluent, I was determined to communicate with Spaniards my questions and/or issues in their native language. I noticed how much the Spaniards always appreciated my attempts to speak their language. We all tend to take the "easy way out." And the easy way out is to ask everyone you meet on the Camino if they speak English. I found that the genuineness and politeness of that effort to speak their language were vital. People were more inclined to help if I were willing to show my vulnerability and weakness in Spanish communication. They all wanted to help when I tried. There is a message in there someplace.

When I finished the pilgrimage, I took a couple of extra nights relaxing in Santiago. The day before my departing flight, I had no idea how to get to the airport, and it was on my mind all day. I discovered a local travel office in the town's central square. I entered, sat down, and explained what I needed in my broken Spanish and asked for help. The woman looked at me and smiled. She said, "First of all, I speak English, and second of all, you look like you're a little stressed." We had a big laugh at that, and what a relief to know I could talk easily with someone about my travel issues.

When I explained my needs, she took charge of the situation and handled every detail, including arranging a taxi to pick me up at my hotel at 5 a.m. to take me to the train station. Next, she pre-printed my train ticket to the airport. This small act meant I did not have to deal with the ticket booth at the train station, which is always a challenge. She then took care of the required Madrid train transfer to ensure I made the correct train to the Madrid Airport. What a relief to know that my next day of travel stress was totally taken care of—all because I took the time to ask for some help from a stranger. I'm so glad that I had become much better at seeking out and accepting help by the end of the Camino. It made things so much easier. Don't be afraid to ask, and you will learn most people are willing to help.

SOMEONE TO BE VULNERABLE WITH

I am very fortunate to have three confidants in my life. One is my best friend from high school and college, Jay John. We played football together at Salpointe HS, and Jay was also a fantastic basketball player. Although he was a year younger than me in high school, because of my Air Force Academy year-long detour, we started college together as freshmen at Northern Arizona University in 1976. We both competed on the NAU football team; we were roommates, and many years later, we served as the best man in each other's weddings. We have been friends for more than fifty years and we have stayed in touch all that time, even though he lives in California, while I'm in Arizona.

We also walked very similar paths in our university careers. I was a football coach and athletic administrator, and Jay was a basketball coach and an athletic administrator. After we were both done coaching, we both spent time as major gift fund-raisers and senior administrators, Jay at UC Berkeley, and me at the University of Arizona. Even though we don't talk on the phone as regularly as in the past, with kids, work, etc., when we do, it's like we just spoke yesterday. I can talk to him about anything.

I was also lucky to have a great career mentor in a man named Tom Sanders. In 1992, under the leadership of Athletic Director, Cedric Dempsey, Sanders hired me to be part of his development team at the UA athletic department, and we worked together for ten years. Many years later, after we moved on to different university positions, we would still get together once a month to check-in and talk about our respective work and family issues. It was great to have that touchstone and know that I could bring up items to run past him during our get-togethers. I could tell him work-related things I couldn't discuss with anyone else. He was a safe harbor. I knew my issues and problems were safe with him, and it was always great to have a different perspective to help me decide how to react. Sadly, a few years ago, he went in for surgery to repair some chronic back issues. What sounded like a simple surgery, if that is possible, became very complicated. Amazingly, he developed an infection, developed sepsis, and died within a week. It was truly tragic. I miss him terribly, and our time together. Having a mentor, or even a peer, to talk things through with can be so helpful.

Finally, my wife is my confidant and my best friend. We met when I was a junior at NAU and we had a long-distance relationship for a while (it was 250 miles from Tucson to Flagstaff/NAU). During our time in Flagstaff, we had been dating long enough to know our relationship was serious, and during my senior year, we became engaged. Sadly, at the same time, my dad was diagnosed with lung cancer and given a short time to live, the doctors said less than a year. On top of this, my mom had passed away the previous year, and my only brother, Jim lived across the country in Pittsburgh, Pennsylvania. He had a big job and five young children, so he would not be able to provide much help. There was no one else, and it was evident this crisis with my father was all going to fall on my shoulders. There was no one but me to look after my dad. I was also in my final senior semester of college, and I didn't know how to handle my dad's healthcare and finish my college education at the same time. It was an impossible situation. After much thought, it was apparent I would have to drop out of college and return to finish my degree at some later date. As disappointing as this was, I had little choice. I had to deal with this. Family comes first.

Judy, my then-fiancée, understood not only our relationship but also the terrible predicament I was facing. In one of the most selfless acts I have ever witnessed, she volunteered to help. And when I say help, I mean helping in a way few people would be willing to do. She unflinchingly said she would move into my house while I was away at school and take care of my dad. What exactly did this entail? It meant feeding him each day, changing his dressings after his surgery, taking him to the VA for doctor's appointments, etc. It meant taking care of his every need, twenty-four hours a day! And she committed to this level of support for more than six months while I finished my degree at Northern Arizona University. And while Judy is not a trained nurse, she is an unbelievable person of compassion and support.

Who does this? Talk about an incredible source of support during a life crisis I was going through. Without her help, I have no idea how I would have done it. Needless to say, I can talk about anything with her with no risk. She is an incredible listener and partner to me, and I am happy to say we have now been married for more than thirty-seven-plus years.

Recap of Lessons About Overcoming Adversity

1. Use tools to calm yourself when needed (and forgive yourself too).
2. Don't dwell on the negative; focus on solutions. As hard as it is, be positive.
3. Take stock of your skills and separate them from experiences (especially the painful ones)—draw on your skills to apply them to the situation at hand.
4. Call on a friend or mentor for advice or help. You can even call upon a stranger with some expertise in the area you are struggling with.
5. Tell the people you love how you feel—often. You just don't know when they won't be there anymore.
6. Guidance can sometimes come from a paid professional who can help.
7. Go back and read the ten ways to build resilience and start working on them so you will have some tools to call upon when you need them.
8. Ask for help. We are not put on this earth to deal with problems by ourselves.
9. Invest in yourself. There is no greater investment than in your own well-being. Look for ways to improve through personal development.
10. Embrace adversity as an opportunity. There is no greater tool for preparing for the future than learning from the past. Use this adversity as a springboard to success. Don't give up.

CHAPTER 5

GRIEF

"Halfway along our journey to life's end I found myself astray in a dark wood, since the right way was nowhere to be found."
— OPENING LINE OF DANTE'S INFERNO

For all intents and purposes, my wife and children have been my only real family for most of my adult life. I lost my entire immediate family when I was just out of college. It was challenging to experience my parents' deaths and my only brother just a few years apart in the 1980s. I was in my twenties, and suddenly, I had no immediate family to depend on and help me through life. I had no father to guide me through the very basics of becoming a man, acquiring my first job, learning how to navigate getting a mortgage, or buying my first car.

Regarding family, I have six cousins from my father's side, all originally from the Irish Catholic south side of Chicago, and I subsequently lost touch with all of them. It has been awkward and sometimes strange to be untethered to any real family relationships. There are times I get jealous when I see photos on Facebook of large gatherings of families celebrating Thanksgiving and Christmas holidays. I realize I will never have that in my life. Oddly enough, there have also been some silver linings from losing my parents so young in life that provided tangible benefits to my long-term success, as strange as that may sound.

First, let me provide some background on my family. You must be wondering what happened to them? Neither one of my parents were the picture of health. As mentioned earlier, my mom, Jean Logan was a sick woman throughout my childhood. She suffered from diabetes, high blood pressure, and many other ailments for as long as I could remember. She was an alcoholic, a three-pack a day smoker, and by most doctors' evaluations, she would be considered morbidly obese. When I was seven or eight years old, she had a massive stroke at the young age of thirty-nine and lost the functionality of her entire left side. This was especially difficult for her since she was also left-handed.

It was not uncommon for me to come home from school and have my dad tell me "Bobby, we need to go to the hospital; Mom is sick again." She was principally a functional invalid who spent most of her life in a bed, and to be honest, I was never able to develop a strong mother-son relationship with her. It always bothered me that she never once saw me play in one of my high school football games. Football was the most important thing in my life at the time, and my mom was not healthy enough to navigate getting in a car and walking the hundred yards or so to the stadium to watch me play. Her health situation and her life were so unfortunate and terribly sad. When she died from a massive stroke on Thanksgiving Day, 1980 at the young age of fifty-four, it was undoubtedly a wake-up call for my dad. Every Thanksgiving, I think of my mom and the difficult life she lived.

The Air Force lifestyle of the 1950s and 1960s was one of drinking and smoking. It was just what you did back then. You can see it in advertisements of the day; celebrities always had a drink and a cigarette in their hand. I'm sure you have seen the famous pictures of the "Rat Pack"—Frank Sinatra, Sammy Davis, Jr., Dean Martin, Joey Bishop, and Peter Lawford. All of them holding a Scotch in one hand and a cigarette in the other. It was an accepted practice back then and not frowned on at all like it is today. My parents were always heavy drinkers and smokers, my father's preferred drink was Scotch and water, and my mother's was red wine. It was not unusual for my father to consume a quart of scotch and my mother a large jug of wine over just a few short days.

Cigarettes were another thing altogether. Incredibly, they both smoked three packs of cigarettes a day. When my mother died on Thanksgiving night in 1980, it was the end of a ten-to-fifteen-year labor of love for my dad. Her long, slow death at such a young age was a real tragedy. But it was an ordeal and, ultimately, a shock to him; in that moment, he decided to make a drastic change in his life. On January 1, 1981, literally weeks after Mom had died, my father decided to quit smoking cold turkey. Can you imagine how difficult this must have been? Smoking three packs a day to zero? To his credit, he never smoked another Terryton cigarette again.

I admired him for how tough he was to do this. It is a shame he did not think of doing it earlier.

Looking back many years later, it showed me how strong a man he really was. There were no nicotine patches back then or Nicorette gum to contain the urges. He just decided it was the right thing to do, and he just stopped—totally. Who does that anymore? Unfortunately, it was too late. Ironically, later that spring he went in for a standard annual physical, and he came out with terrible news. He was diagnosed with lung cancer when doctors discovered a grapefruit-size tumor, and he was given about five months to live. He again bucked the odds, lived for more than a year and a half. However, just like my mom, he died at the young age of fifty-eight.

As I was having some early success in college at Northern Arizona University, Dad and I had become very close. I think he finally forgave me for quitting the Air Force Academy, but it took a few years to get to this place. And it was a wonderful place. Now, he was not so much my dad, but more of a friend, so it was strange to switch roles with me suddenly becoming his caretaker. Judy was there during the early days of helping dad, but I helped every weekend and after I graduated in May. During this long battle with lung cancer, I bathed him and changed his dressings. There is nothing more humbling than helping your own father sit on a stool in the shower and bath him because he is so weak. I will never forget those moments. If you have ever experienced cancer with someone close to you, you will understand there is a distinctive and recognizable odor involved with the disease, and I can still smell that "cancer odor" when I think about those last months of his life.

Not only were their deaths emotionally devastating for me, especially being just a couple of years apart, but they occurred just when I was beginning to build a life of my own. Their deaths also put a strain on the relationship with my brother, Jim. Jim was five years older than me, and he had moved to Pittsburgh, where he married, and worked in the newspaper business. Like most siblings, because of the gap in our ages, we didn't have much in common as kids. When he was in high school, I was in grade school. When he was in college, I was in high school. We cared about one another, and we loved each other, but our lives were different.

As young adults, we occasionally visited each other, but Jim now had five young kids, a busy life, and travel for either one of us was difficult. All the difficult and emotional duties of taking care of my dad's final year and taking care of the various estate issues fell entirely on me—pretty heady stuff for a twenty-five-year-old young man.

After Dad's death, Jim's wife Sue began pressuring him to make sure he got his share of the "estate," even though there wasn't much to it—very little money to speak of, and most of the rest of the assets had little sentimental or monetary value. I didn't want disagreements over this "stuff" to infect our brotherly relationship, and I could tell his wife was pushing Jim hard to get what he was deserved from the estate. Remember, I was living in the house where we grew up, so all the furniture was in its original place—even though half of it legally belonged to Jim.

I told Jim to bring a truck and take whatever he wanted, and it was a strange scene seeing the two of us walking through the house together, dividing up the accumulations of our parents' lives and our childhoods. In addition to the various furniture pieces, Jim took all my father's Air Force medals and ribbons. I still regret that to this day.

It was only a few years later when Jim died at age thirty-seven from an asthma attack. It was a shock, and I had never heard of someone dying from asthma. I went back to Pittsburgh for the funeral, my third funeral for a family member in just a few years. Also, I had only met Jim's wife on two occasions—at their wedding and at Jim's funeral, so it was hard to develop a relationship with her and my five young nieces and nephews. Today, I don't even know where she lives, I don't know if she has remarried or what her name is now. And I have not seen my nieces and nephews since the funeral so many years ago. Really sad.

My dad grew up in an Irish Catholic family on the south side of Chicago. When his family descended into Tucson for his funeral, they took over all the funeral arrangements. Looking back, I know they were doing the right thing, but at the time I felt marginalized, from my perspective. I'm sure they thought they were doing me a favor, being a young adult who was grieving, but they made some decisions that I didn't agree with, and I didn't think Dad would have either. The final straw came in the basement of the funeral home. My aunt Eileen and I were selecting caskets, and she wanted to choose one that was ridiculously expensive in my opinion. I knew my dad would flip out spending that amount of money on a coffin.

Exasperated, I stood up to my aunt and said, "Aunt Eileen, I have been taking care of my Dad for the past eighteen months, and I think I know him pretty well. I know what he would have wanted. I am making this decision, not you." Aunt Eileen only knew me as "little Bobby," and I think it shocked her that I had challenged her. It obviously put a strain on our relationship. This became evident to me since she chose not to attend our wedding. Then the Christmas cards stopped coming, and eventually, a few years later, we stopped communicating altogether. For the better part of thirty years, I completely lost touch with that side of the family. Again, really sad and probably a lot of it is my fault.

My internal grief was profound because I felt like I had lost my whole family in one day. All of it happened so fast. It's a burden I have been carrying for years, and I think about it all the time. For me, my entire family history exists in just a couple of boxes of photos. One day, I was sorting through my parents' old family photos from Chicago and realized I had no idea who any of these people were! Wedding photos, graduation photos, picnics in the countryside, portraits in front of homes, and photo after photo were people from my own family I did not recognize! These were photos of my mom and dad's life in early Chicago, and without them around, I would never be able to tell if any of these people were my relatives.

So many years had passed, and I thought it was time to reconnect to the only family I had left. I wrote a heartfelt letter outlining my life, marriage, kids and told them I think about them all the time. I boxed everything up and sent it via FedEx to the last known address I had for my aunt and uncle in Chicago. It took a few weeks to get a response, but one of my six cousins wrote back, and I discovered both my aunt and uncle had passed away. None of them had bothered to tell me. While hurt, I still try to keep in touch with them now and occasionally visit them. It's just not the same, however.

Only a few of the things I inherited from my parents have any real significance for me. Most of everything was material possessions, like furniture, etc. However, two items have an enormous emotional attachment for me. They are two separate silver chains holding Catholic medals that I wear around my neck every single day. One chain holds a Saint Christopher medal my dad gave me when I was a young Catholic schoolboy. The other chain was my dad's. It holds two medals that my dad wore during his life along with his Air Force dog tag. One medal was an Air Force St. Christopher medal, and the other was a Saint Jude Thaddeus medal he purchased when he was diagnosed with cancer. St. Jude Thaddeus is the patron saint for "hopeless causes," and Catholics appeal to St. Jude for strength, especially during trying times.

On the day he passed away in the hospital, I said goodbye, wiped the tears from my eyes and kissed him on the forehead. I slowly and gently, removed this chain with these two religious medals from his head. I said a prayer and let him know he would always be with me, always.

To remember him, I have proudly worn them every day since, for more than forty years. He is still with me.

My father's Air Force dog tag (top), St. Jude Thaddeus medal (left) and military-issued WWII St. Christopher medal (right)

For all the tremendous grief, sadness, and despair their premature deaths brought into my life, looking back now, I can now see some unexpected blessings. First, in the early years of our marriage, my young family lived in my boyhood home, something that was pretty special. Since my father had nearly paid off our mortgage, it lifted a huge financial burden from our shoulders. I recall our monthly mortgage payment was only $150/month, allowing me to take a low-paying teaching job at

Salpointe HS, a Catholic school. Additionally, as I look back now, I can see how I took several risks early in my life that I ultimately may not have taken if other family members had weighed in on my choices. The burden was all on me, and I would have to live with the choices I made. Kind of liberating if you want to know the truth.

HEALING FROM GRIEF

There is no doubt that time is the biggest factor in dealing with significant grief in one's life. Trusting that you will ultimately heal and giving yourself adequate time to mourn are essential principles. Sometimes distraction can be helpful. During these early years, I became immersed in reading and learning about "the ways of life" from leaders. Devouring self-help and motivational books saved me after my parents died, and they provided me with an outlet and a great deal of inspiration for moving forward. Even today, I have books all over the house. They are next to my reading chair in the living room, and there are multiple bookshelves filled to the gills. Books are one of my greatest vices; I still buy books regularly, and I probably am working on 5-7 books at any one time. Books allow you to "step away from life" for a short time, and they will enable you to imagine how your life can be in the future. There is a message here—books (and learning) are good for a person's soul.

Some of my Catholic lessons from childhood have served me well through the various stages of the grief process. I believe when you lose everything, the best response is to give back to others. A few years back, there was a wonderful segment on CBS News, "On the Road" with Steve Hartman.[15] It was about a young six-year-old boy named Jaden who tragically had lost both of his parents within a period of a couple of months. As you can imagine, *everyone* Jaden ran into was sad for him. They all felt so sorry for the genuinely terrible situation this beautiful little boy had been placed. After a while, Jaden was tired of how everyone treated him, so he had a plan to change things. First, he asked his caretaker aunt to do him a favor. He wanted her to go to the dollar store and buy a large bag of toys. Not for him, however, but for others. Small things like dinosaurs, rubber duckies, army men, etc. Jaden wanted a bag of these small toys so he could turn around and give them away to people on the street. He said he was tired of everyone feeling sorry for him, and instead, he wanted to bring a smile to other people's faces.

Needless to say, every person Jaden touched on the street smiled and laughed when they learned what Jaden was doing. This little boy was only trying to do one thing—make people smile! What a fantastic act of kindness! We all find our own ways to get through the trials and tribulations of our lives, and nobody in our society is spared from dealing with tough times. Even today, when I give one of my motivational talks, I show this clip and then give out rubber duckies and toy soldiers to the audience. It always brings a smile to their faces. It is not uncommon to run into people who have attended one of my talks and have them tell me they still have that little rubber duckie! Cool stuff.

Steve Hartman CBS News On The Road – "Smiles" (2:55 mins)
https://BobLogan.net/SteveHartmanSmiles

Though I have mostly healed, there have been some long-term effects from my losses. Those significant losses haven't been the only ones I've faced over the years. I have had friends die in car accidents, take their own lives, and suffer from cancer. However, attending the multiple funerals of my family members during that early time in my life was so hard that I now have an aversion to funerals. I realize one should "pay their respects" when a close friend passes, but I cannot bring myself to attend funerals very often. At most, I have summoned the courage to attend just one or two funerals in the past thirty-five years.

Along these lines, I also wait a long time to send a sympathy card. I know from experience that the first few weeks following a tragic loss are so stressful and busy, and the number of communications (phone calls, visits, cards, etc.) is just overwhelming. When I send my card, I want to be sure my message is received fully and heard loud and clear, so I send it many weeks later when things have quieted down. I believe this has a much more significant impact on the grieving family.

A CAMINO STORY—REMEMBERING OUR LOVED ONES - 2012

A couple of years later in 2012, I was preparing for my first walk on the Camino de Santiago. We had close family friends, Jeannie and Manuel Gadea, from our son Sean's elementary and high school days. We had known each other for nearly ten years and spent time playing golf and having dinners. The Gadeas were wonderful people and the perfect family. They had two sons, Mario and Diego and the Gadeas were fixtures at all the St. Cyril school and church events. Diego was close friends with Sean, all the way back to 3rd grade at St. Cyril Catholic School and they played football together at Salpointe H.S. Diego was a state champion level wrestler (38-7 record), a great student and National Honor Society member, and very popular at school. As always happens in cases like this, you would love your own son to be like Diego Gadea.

But the secret many did not know was Diego suffered from depression for most of his adolescent life. Sadly, in the summer before his senior year, the depression took over and Diego took his own life. Sean was devastated, as was the entire student body at Salpointe Catholic High School. Since Sean was incredibly talented in photography and videography, the Gadeas asked Sean to create the memorial video that played at Diego's service. Not a dry eye in the church and a sad memory I will never forget.

The night before I left for this first Camino in 2012, I was incredibly excited. To celebrate, Jeannie and Manuel invited us to join them for dinner. Manuel had Hispanic roots (Peru), and they were both familiar with the many traditions of the Camino de Santiago, including the Cruz de Ferro. Late in the dinner, they pulled out a rosary cross and scapula that belonged to Diego from the Vatican on a previous family trip they had taken to Rome. They also handed me a polished stone and a rubber wrist band, both with Diego's name that was passed out at his funeral.

My eyes were like saucers when I saw these important parts of their family being handed over to me. It was only a few months since Diego's passing, and the memories were so close and so raw. Manuel and Jeannie asked if I would be willing to take these precious items and leave them at the base of the Cruz de Ferro. It was a powerful and very tearful scene at that dinner table. To think these loving parents, who had suffered so much, were entrusting me to take these special remembrances of their son on the Camino is a memory I will never forget.

Diego Gadea (1993–2011)

Tragic memories and burdens left behind to honor Diego Gadea at the Cruz de Ferro (left by Bob Logan in 2012)

Camino Magic in Action
Ten Years Later - 2022

When one walks the Camino, it is very common to come across coincidences that make you scratch your head from time to time. We call it "Camino Magic." And the above story is one of these "Camino Magic" incidences. In late September 2022, I was in the final stages of getting this book ready to publish. My book consultant suggested I contact the Gadeas to get their permission to tell their story, since it was so personal. I agreed.

The next day, I called Manuel's cell phone, and when he picked up he said he was traveling with Jeannie, but initially did not say where. I told Manuel why I was calling, described the book I was writing and the story I wanted to include about Diego. There was a bit of silence on the other end. I thought I had overstepped my bounds and was ready to apologize. Manuel then said, "Bob, you will not believe where we are right now. Jeannie and I are walking the Camino de Santiago as we speak, and we were at the Cruz de Ferro YESTERDAY leaving stones for Diego!" Wow, wow, wow. The Camino is unbelievable. Camino Magic at its finest…

**Stones left at the Cruz de Ferro for Diego Gadea
(left by his parents, Jeannie and Manuel in Sept 2022)**

THE CRUZ DE FERRO (THE IRON CROSS)

You may be wondering what the Cruz de Ferro is on the Camino. The Cruz de Ferro is an iron cross mounted on top of a fifty-foot-high wooden pole. At the base is a HUGE mountain of stones. It is located on the Camino de Santiago between the tiny towns of Foncebadón and Manjarín on the trail. The Cruz de Ferro is approximately 90 miles from Santiago. The massive Cathedral of Santiago de Compostela was built in the early eleventh century, and legend says that pilgrims were asked to contribute by bringing a stone. Pilgrims have been leaving stones at the cross's base for centuries, symbolizing the leaving behind of burdens or sins or honoring loved ones. Some find a rock along the way to carry, and others bring stones with them from home.[16]

The Cruz de Ferro (Iron Cross) A Place to Remember Loved Ones

Personally, I brought a handful of shiny tumbled stones from home to honor my family and wrote my family's names—my parents Ed and Jean Logan, brother Jim Logan, Judy's mom MaryAnn, and stones for Judy and our sons Tommy and Sean.

Stones left for my family at the Cruz de Ferro, 2012

It didn't escape me that I was literally carrying a personal burden on the pilgrimage with the added weight of those stones in my pack and leaving them behind was more than the physical experience of removing that weight. More important was the emotional weight I was able to leave behind at the Cruz de Ferro. This entire ceremony was one of the most powerful, emotional, and spiritual experiences I had ever had in my life. It truly shook me to my core. One must stand at the base of the Cruz de Ferro and see the thousands of stones, notes, wedding rings, and family photos to understand the importance. The emotions of thousands of people are embedded in the rocks themselves, and you can feel the raw power of it all.

Seeing the Cruz de Ferro and the enormous pile of stones left behind over thousands of years was an incredible experience. As it turned out that day, I happened to be walking with a woman from Toronto. We had met on the bus the day before coming into the town of Astorga. When we arrived at the Cruz de Ferro, I told her I needed to be alone for 15-20 minutes while I honored my family and left my stones at the top. She totally understood. I happened to have a baggie with several additional stones along with a Sharpie marker, and I told her to find people who did not have a stone themselves and give one to them. I asked that she distribute all the stones I had left in the baggie. It was my gift to them.

About twenty-five minutes later, we started back on the trail, and she was in tears. I asked what had happened, and she replied that this experience had made an enormous impact on her. During this period of finding pilgrims without stones and giving them away, she met and talked with pilgrims from Korea, France, Argentina, and more. She heard their emotional stories and why they were on the Camino. She heard the intimate details about who every stone was to honor. She said I had provided stones for people from nearly *every* continent on the Earth! We were both crying by the time we left—it was a memorable and unforgettable place.

I give regular talks about the Camino now, and I buy beautifully polished stones in bulk to share with audience members. At the beginning of the lecture, I ask them to take a stone and write the name of someone important in their lives, living or dead.

At the end of the hour-long Camino lecture, everyone in the audience picks up their stones, and I ask them to think about the person whose name they wrote on their individual stone. I then play a song that embodies what the Camino is all about—Neil Diamond's "He Ain't Heavy, He's My Brother."[17] While the song plays, the video shows motivational words and phrases about the power of the Camino. In the dark meeting room, it is very moving, and many are brought to tears.

I am proud to say that many of these people have been inspired enough to walk the Camino themselves. We discuss that it is not about walking 500 miles but finding time to think about the people in their lives that are important to them. Regarding the stone they receive from the talk and what to do with it, I provide them three suggestions:

1. Leave the stone in a private, special place here where they are staying.
2. Take the stone back to their hometown and leave it in a memorable place.
3. Or, if they would like the stone to be left at the Cruz de Ferro, then leave it with me, and I will make sure it gets there someday in the future.

I currently have a baggie filled with stones waiting for my next trip to Spain and the Cruz de Ferro! Those important people will be remembered and memorialized someday in the future—I promise.

Lessons from Grief

1. Trust that you will ultimately heal.
2. Time is the most significant factor—be patient.
3. Sometimes, distraction or escape can help. Find ways to get your mind off it as often as you can while still allowing yourself to feel your feelings.
4. When you lose everything, the best response is to give back.
5. Find gratitude for all the blessings you do have in your life and focus on them as often as possible. Think about starting a daily gratitude journal.
6. It's your choice to keep carrying the burden or put it down. Wallowing never helps. Eventually, you are better off by letting go of your suffering.
7. When something bothers you, take action.
8. Don't live with regrets about all those things you didn't do.
9. Find a way to help ease someone else's burden, and you will, in turn, lessen your own.
10. Family is everything. But don't let family get in the way of living life the way you want to live it.

PART II
RECOVERY

CHAPTER 6
LIFE IS MESSY

"People take the longest possible paths, digress to numerous dead ends, and make all kinds of mistakes. Then historians come along and write summaries of this messy, nonlinear process and make it appear like a simple, straight line."

— DEAN KAMEN

Maybe you've heard this before: Life is messy.

When I was newly married, my wife, Judy, was faced with another difficult situation, one brought on by me, and she bore most of the brunt in our household. You remember Judy, this person I had barely met, who took it upon herself to move into my home for six months to care for my dying father while I was finishing college.

At the time, I was teaching and coaching football at Salpointe Catholic High School here in Tucson. My best friend, Jay John, had been the basketball coach at Salpointe and had just moved on to become a college basketball coach at Jamestown (NY) Community College. The team Jay coached at Salpointe the previous year had state championship potential, and one of its star players was an immigrant student-athlete from Mexico, Jose.

One day, Jay called me to tell me they had a big problem. The Mexican peso had recently plummeted in value. Tuition was costly, and Jose's family could no longer afford to send him to Salpointe. It looked like he would be forced to move back to Guadalajara, Mexico. Jose was a great student, a fantastic athlete, and he was entering his high school senior year, the best year of one's high school experience. It would indeed be a shame to see him leave because he had developed a strong cadre of friendships throughout the entire school and was one of the "popular" kids. To leave Salpointe at this wonderful time in his life, his senior year no less, and be forced to move back to Mexico would have devastated Jose.

Since both my parents had recently passed away, Jay knew that Judy and I were now living in my comfortable four-bedroom childhood home. We had plenty of room, so to Jay, it was a no-brainer for us to have Jose live with us while he finished his final year of high school. Well, easier said than done.

My wife agreed at the time, but neither of us understood how messy this situation would ultimately become. Think about it for a second; we had been married only three months, barely enough time to live independently as a married couple, when I asked her to add a teenager from another culture to our household. Who does that?

Jose was a great kid and very respectful despite the unusual situation we were all facing. At the same time, he did come from a strict, traditional, Mexican family with different expectations for how a family lived and how a home operated. This was not a negative statement on Jose in any way; it just meant a clash of different cultures living under the same roof. In the Hispanic household, Jose was accustomed to having his needs taken care of, and it was generally not expected of him to voluntarily contribute much to the household in terms of chores (like most teenagers). Judy and I both came from military backgrounds; we had grown up being expected to do assigned chores each week. This was an issue we had to address.

Looking back on the situation today, the difficulties were probably partially due to the cultural differences between Jose and a young, newly married couple and partially the standard nature of any seventeen-year-old teenage boy. It was just hard for everyone.

To make matters worse, I was rarely around the house because of my heavy teaching and coaching responsibilities. Judy had to navigate all the confusion around our role with this young man. She thought, *How am I supposed to act in this situation? Do I act like a traditional mother, a friend of the family, a caretaker, a landlord, or a disciplinarian?* "What exactly am I here?" she would say. "What is my role?" As you can imagine, the situation put a heavy strain on our new marriage. On top of that, I was still grieving and dealing with the emotional baggage of my parents' recent passing.

The great news is that, in the end, Jose thrived. He helped the team win a city championship in basketball, graduated from Salpointe, and graduated from the University of Arizona. Jose still lives here in Tucson, and he has become a successful businessman and prominent community leader. Jose is a self-made success story.

Judy and I are close to Jose and his family to this day, and many times he has acknowledged us for the role we played in his success and development. We appreciate that, and we are so proud of how successful he has become.

Bob Logan and Jose, July 2021. Sharing some stories and some memories. We get together often.

In Tucson, there is a wonderful organization called Tucson Values Teachers. This group supports local K-12 education and tries to call attention to the dedicated teachers serving our community. One year, our local newspaper, the *Arizona Daily Star*, published a special supplement promoting and recognizing special teachers from the Tucson Values Teachers organization. This piece included a front-page story and many letters of appreciation from grateful students to dedicated teachers and coaches.[18]

To our amazement, when leafing through the pages, we came across a letter from Jose. Jose took the time to author one of these heartfelt letters to Jay John (his coach) and Judy and me, thanking us for our extraordinary support during his senior year. Jose has gone out of his way to thank both of us many times over the years. It is a lifelong friendship.

Jose is now a successful pharmaceutical rep and a past president of the Tucson Conquistadors, a local organization that raises millions of dollars for youth sports. We often stay in touch, but unfortunately, in 2008, Jose's life itself had its own form of messiness.

One day, Jose called me out of the blue to tell me that his son, Jose, Jr., or "Guapo," who was about to start his freshman year at Salpointe Catholic High School, was hit and killed by a drunk driver while riding his bike home over the weekend. What an unbelievable message to receive from a friend; it was incomprehensible. How does one respond in that situation? It destroyed Jose and his wife emotionally for several years, and I still think about that tragedy. How does one cope with that type of loss? The loss of my parents and brother, in comparison, almost seem trivial to the loss of a son. We felt terrible for Jose and his wife, Adriana.

In addition to the tremendous grief involved in the accident, Guapo's loss resulted in lengthy civil and criminal proceedings. In addition to the long, drawn-out, criminal trial, there were civil suits against the city, the drunk driver, and the restaurant that served her. All this played out for many years in the local media, and Jose was diligent in making sure justice was done for the tragic loss of his son.

Throughout the trial, Jose would contact friends, provide updates, and make sure the courtroom was filled with his loved ones and supporters as a show of solidarity. I will never forget how hard he worked to keep his son at the forefront of the Tucson community's minds during this trying and stressful period. It was a fantastic and touching tribute to his son.

As a result, the City of Tucson had to redesign the street and intersection where this terrible accident occurred. In addition, near the home of Guapo's family off Country Club and 5th Street, the City of Tucson renamed a street in his honor. The street named for Guapo and his bronze plaque on a nearby wall serve as a daily reminder of the importance of every life.

GROWING UP NORMAL?

Surprisingly, I didn't even recognize the most significant messiness in my life at the time. As a young boy, I didn't know anything different about the state of my home life. Candidly, I thought to have parents who drank and smoked as much as mine did was normal. After all, that was the only world I knew.

Let me put this in a little perspective. As I said earlier, one of my weekly household chores was to empty all the ashtrays around the house. Now, mind you, these were *huge* glass ashtrays that would be heaping full of cigarette butts and ashes that needed to be emptied and cleaned out every couple of days. Needless to say, my parents smoked a lot. I mean, a lot.

One of my other chores was to retrieve the many bags of groceries when my dad returned from the Davis-Monthan Air Force Base commissary. Usually, the car had seven to ten paper grocery sacks, and I would place them all on the kitchen table before putting away the groceries in the appropriate cupboards.

Among these many paper grocery bags, two were always filled to the top with nothing but cartons of Terryton cigarettes! I had to stack all these cigarette cartons on top of the refrigerator for easy access for my parents. Doing the math, between my mom and dad, I estimated they smoked 120 cigarettes a day! Looking back on it now, I realize how crazy this was.

Not until I was in high school did I begin to recognize that my childhood upbringing wasn't exactly "normal." One day at Salpointe, the school called me to the dean's office. It is always a little stressful when someone walks into your classroom and hands you a note to visit the dean. What could I have done wrong to warrant this? I was a star football player and a good student who always followed instructions. I was the model student-athlete.

When I arrived at the dean's office, I was told my school locker needed to be searched. What? I never did drugs, so I knew it could not be that. Walking down the hall with the dean and other school administrators, I was terrified of what was happening. I was asked to unlock my locker and step away. They completely dismantled my locker, removing all the books, food, and trash accumulating in a typical high school student's locker.

They placed everything on the ground, and I had no idea what was happening. When they concluded the search, the dean turned around and asked me, "Bob, where are your cigarettes?" "What are you talking about?" I asked. I told them I did not have any cigarettes, and I didn't smoke. "Why would you think I would have cigarettes in my locker?"

Then they told me that teachers had complained I smelled like cigarette smoke and reported me to school officials. Because all of my clothes reeked of cigarette smoke, my teachers and coaches were convinced they would find contraband cigarettes. Clearly, after many years, my sense of smell was desensitized from so much daily cigarette smoke exposure that I wasn't even aware of it. To this day, I cannot stand the smell of cigarette smoke. If I go to a bar or restaurant filled with cigarette smoke, I need to leave immediately. The smell of cigarette smoke is that offensive to me now.

Thank God I was an athlete, and knowing what I knew from my parents' example, I would never become a smoker. I had such violent reactions to cigarettes. I tried a cigarette once as a freshman in high school and nearly choked. It was awful, and I never picked one up again.

As a high school history teacher, I taught an annual segment on the perils of smoking, sharing numerous alarming national statistics and photos of lung cancer patients. Why? Hopefully to get a message across since a unit on smoking did not fit into the normal history curriculum. In spite of this, I felt it was an important lesson for the students to hear. The students always groaned when I taught this section. They thought I was lecturing them not to smoke. "Come on, Mr. Logan; give us a break!"

But I persisted, and part of the lecture included showing the students full-size chest X-rays. The first was an X-ray of a healthy lung, and the second clearly showed a large, grapefruit-sized tumor in the middle of the lung. The students would always snicker and joke around as the X-rays were passed around the classroom. But I hoped for, and wanted, that specific reaction from my students.

In the end, I would stand in front of the class and hold up both X-rays in my left and right hands. I would say the normal X-ray was from someone I never met. The hospital was kind enough to provide it for this lecture. However, when they asked where the X-ray with the tumor came from, they were shocked to hear they were looking at my own father's X-ray and that he had died from lung cancer. More importantly, I told them he had died just last year. I would then pass around a large photo of my dad. You can imagine the silence in the classroom and the shocked faces of all the students.

This class had such an impact on the students, and when they heard my personal story, we really bonded as a class. There is a message here as well—when you open up and become genuinely transparent and vulnerable with people, it allows for significant relationships to build. It's not unusual for me to run into former students around town, and they let me know they still remember that powerful lecture on smoking and the tremendous impact it had on them.

So, that was the smoking side of my "normal" household growing up. There was also a very problematic alcohol side of my upbringing. Both my mom and dad were alcoholics, and we had a small, wooden, portable bar in our den filled with bottles of wine for my mom and Scotch for my dad.

I recall an incident in 1974 during our Salpointe High School summer pre-season training. Salpointe Football Camp, as we called it, was run just like a college or professional NFL team. It was impressive for a high school football program. It really set us apart and was a key reason our program was the envy of the State of Arizona. The entire football team stayed at the high school for ten straight days and slept in cots on the gymnasium floor. We practiced during the day, had meetings and watched films, and our meals were served in the school cafeteria by the football booster club parents, including my dad.

After one practice, we were in the back of the meal line when I overheard some of the guys in front of me making fun of one of the parents up ahead. They just thought he was another booster parent and did not realize he was my dad. On that specific day, my dad's booster job was helping serve food on the meal line to the team after practice. As he held out each tray of food to the individual players, you could see the tray shaking violently from his alcohol tremors. It was so embarrassing. At the time, I didn't quite understand, but it soon became apparent to me that because of his drinking, my dad was "different" from the other dads.

Looking back, it's incredible that I avoided alcoholism myself. Especially as a young coach—we were continually going out to bars with my coaching buddies to "review" practices and games in great detail, as only coaches can do. However, we would spend several hours drinking and telling stories. It was a blast. But often, we wouldn't think twice about jumping back in our cars and driving home, most of the time intoxicated. Again, how no one was ever hurt by any of our stupid and careless actions is amazing to me and something I regret to this day.

As for my mom, at one point, she decided to become sober, so she joined Alcoholics Anonymous (AA). But throughout all those years, I never attended Al-Anon or counseling or did anything formally to deal with my own internal pain and loss. I did nothing to protect myself from addiction myself in any way. How I survived and did not become codependent is beyond me.

I don't even really talk about it much, but I know now that some form of formal counseling would have been beneficial for me. Now I know that looking for help is *not* a sign of weakness—it is a sign of strength. Recalling those days now, it is surprising to me that someone from the Air Force base didn't take my brother and me under their wing after my parents' deaths. They obviously knew the situation with my mom and dad's smoking and drinking. One would think a couple of Air Force brats who just lost their parents at ages fifty-four and fifty-eight would have elicited some support from base leadership. It was sad that I had to deal with all this trauma by myself. After my parents died, I had no idea what types of services and resources were available to someone like me. Since I didn't know where to go or whom to talk to, I just moved on with my life. As they say, I just "soldiered on" as best I could.

In hindsight, although today it may look to an outsider like I had an unhealthy childhood, I must say my dad was always a rock in raising me. I want to be sure you know and understand that my father was a wonderful man and parent, despite the powerful deficiencies he had.

As discussed earlier, my mom was a sick person for most of my childhood, and her poor health forced my dad into the double-duty role of managing the household and working a full-time job. He did all the household cleaning, the shopping, the laundry, and the cooking, and I have to say he became quite the cook. His meals were fabulous, and he took great pride in learning how to create new dishes in the kitchen.

I fondly remember my dad creating wonderfully tasty casseroles, lasagna, Sunday pot-roast, and other meals. My brother and I had the typical roles and responsibilities around the house, and we lived with military discipline, but neither of us was ever abused or neglected in any way. While it was true my father was a functional alcoholic in every sense of the word, despite his addiction, he was able to be a loving and caring parent. He was very proud of me and let me know it often. And to my chagrin sometimes, he let everyone else know it—at the bank, in the restaurant, and at the golf course. He beamed with pride when he talked about my brother Jim and me. He always tried to make us happy. I have fond memories of playing golf with him in college and hanging out with my friends and him when we had the occasional college "keg party" in the backyard. My high school and college buddies still tell me how "cool" my dad was. He instilled in me a burning ambition to achieve and contribute, and I truly loved him.

One particular "Dad" event was totally shocking and embarrassing. But now, remembering the effort he put into it, I have great admiration, pride, and affection that he would go to such trouble on my behalf. In my high school senior year at Salpointe, we had a powerhouse football team and were ranked in the top five in the State of Arizona for most of the year. After the season was over, several of my Salpointe teammates were named to various all-star teams, myself included. One of our stars, QB Frank Garcia, even had a long career in the NFL. I was named to various All-City, All-State, and All-Southwest all-star teams, which was a big deal to both my dad and me.

Unbeknownst to me, my dad had concocted the crazy idea to invite the *entire* Tucson all-city football team and their coaches to our house for a BBQ on a Sunday afternoon after the season. He didn't run this idea by me beforehand, and like any high school kid, if he had, I would have stopped him in its tracks. When it was too late, after he had already begun to contact people, I was appalled and embarrassed, like any high school kid would have been.

Look, my dad was a work-to-the-bone kind of guy and a veteran Air Force pilot whose attention to detail was legendary. But that didn't mean we lived in some fancy house in the foothills. We lived a couple of miles from the base in what I would call an extremely middle-class neighborhood. I was worried our house was kind of shabby or "not good enough." And remember, there were ashtrays all over the house, and worst of all, I was afraid my dad might get drunk and embarrass himself and me. I dreaded this Sunday BBQ.

But the day came together, and it was a day I will never forget. It was great to hang out with the players and coaches from opposing teams who had been some of my biggest rivals on the football field. This day was one where I got to know them personally. Legendary coaches like Ollie Mayfield from Tucson High hung out in my backyard!

Remember, this was the mid-1970s, many years before the advent of technology like cell phones, home computers, and email. Lacking those conveniences, I cannot imagine how much time my dad must have spent tracking down addresses and phone numbers. He had to contact all these players and coaches one by one. Again, it was extraordinary that my dad would go to such lengths to honor my football accomplishments. I hope everyone has a dad as loving as I did.

KINTSUGI—A JAPANESE TRADITION FOR BEING BROKEN[19]

As I was preparing for an upcoming lecture, I came across a fascinating tradition in Japan called "Kintsugi." The literal translation of Kintsugi is "Golden Joinery." This process of Kintsugi began in fifteenth century Japan when Japanese shogun Ashikaga Yoshimasa sent a damaged tea bowl to China to be repaired. When it came back with several ugly metal staples holding it together, he ordered Japanese tradesmen to develop a more aesthetic form of repair.

Think about what we do in America when we drop a plate or dish, and it shatters. We run to the laundry room to fetch the broom and dustpan, sweep up all the big pieces and small shards, and quickly deposit the remnants in the trash. The Japanese treat this scenario very differently. They sweep up all the pieces and then lay them out on the table for reconstruction. This seems ridiculous, doesn't it? But *how* the Japanese handle the reconstruction is amazing. After they lay out all the big pieces in the correct orientation and position, they mix gold dust powder with the glue and put the pieces back together.

Therefore, all the cracks and missing chunks are highlighted by the gold dust, and everyone is aware of the flaws of the new piece. The reconstituted new piece now becomes a work of art and a valued part of the household.[20]

Kintsugi is a metaphor for life. We will never be able to go back to the way we once were. All our individual flaws and cracks in our personalities will be there forever, for everyone to see. What Kintsugi teaches us is to embrace our wounds or our brokenness; the repaired person should become stronger and more beautiful than ever before. There is no attempt to hide the damage, and the repair is literally illuminated for all to see. But it is clear the process of repair requires some transformation. The pieces may not fit perfectly together anymore, and you may have to alter the final product. It is important to understand the cracks and flaws in our lives do not mean the end. It means it is the beginning of a stronger, better, and more fulfilling life. Never, ever waste your gold dust! Things will be better soon—trust the process.

Kintsugi Gold (2:31 mins)
https://BobLogan.net/KintsugiGold

Kintsugi Golden Seams (3:47 mins)
https://BobLogan.net/KintsugiGoldenSeams

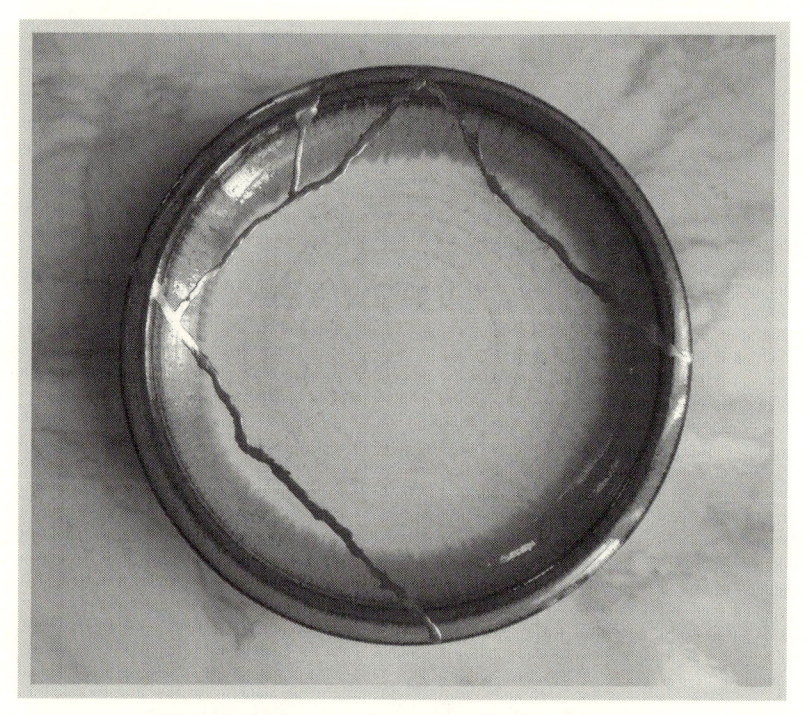

Kintsugi Plate – photo by Riho Kitagawa

DO THE RIGHT THING

I have mentioned earlier that my typical decision-making process is to leap to a decision and then figure out the details later. Let's just say I don't spend much time overanalyzing things, and often, I work from a "gut feeling. "I did that when deciding to take Jose in to live with us, walking the Camino de Santiago, moving to Italy to coach football, and taking a job in the College of Science, leaving the comfort of athletics. In reality, it is straightforward. I choose not to agonize over decisions. Obviously, a significant amount of thought and reflection goes into making hard life choices, but usually, I just know what the "right thing" is, and I run with it. Numerous details often get figured out afterward. This way of seeing things can be a blessing because I don't have to worry and stress about all the possible outcomes on the front end. It also means; however, I must navigate some "messiness" on the back end.

If there is one takeaway, it is "Always Do the Right Thing," and your life will be much easier to navigate.

A CAMINO STORY—THE CAMINO IS DEFINITELY MESSY

There are so many messy things about the Camino—the relationships, weather, planning, language barriers, and most notably, all the daily chores required to eat, sleep, and have clean clothes and water. It never goes the way you think it will, but that is the beauty of it.

The first-day hiking over the Pyrenees is by far the most challenging day physically. In 2015, I spent my first night in a lovely small albergue in Orisson, a tiny town on the French side of the Pyrenees. This albergue holds about 60-75 people, and the best part of the stay is the evening communal meal. Everyone sits at long picnic tables, and you begin to meet people from all over the world. Many of these people will become your walking partners, and you will likely see them every day for the next few weeks all along the Camino.

I immediately struck up a friendship with a woman from Salt Lake City, and we began walking together the next morning. When we walked outside the albergue and onto the trail as the sun rose, we stared into the valley below and realized we were standing above the clouds! The entire valley below was covered in clouds, and it was one of the most beautiful sights we had ever seen.

Crossing the Pyrenees Mountains—Standing Above the Clouds!

On the Camino, every task is a chore: taking your pack off to get something out; digging inside to find it; putting your pack back on; taking off a layer of clothes; putting on a layer; finding your rain jacket; finding a restroom; finding water; unpacking and repacking every night…you get the idea. After fifteen miles (and 6-8 hours) of walking, you are exhausted when you arrive at the next town and the albergue you have selected for the night. Everything in your body says you need to lay down and rest, but unfortunately, it will negatively impact your next day if you do so.

Since you typically arrive in mid to late afternoon, you have a limited amount of time to wash your clothes and hang them out to dry on the clothesline outside. You don't want to smell foul every day or put on wet clothes in the morning, so your first tasks are to immediately wash your clothes and hang them on the line so they will dry in time. After a day of hiking, your body puts you through mental calisthenics. Upon arrival, you need to do so many critical things in a short period of time. And they need to happen almost simultaneously, so it can be overwhelming. How do you prioritize tending to your painful blisters, finding something to eat, taking a nap, drinking enough liquid to rehydrate, massaging sore muscles, showering, and cleaning your clothes? What do you take care of first? There just isn't enough time in the day. Have you ever used that term before? Well, it is multiplied when you are on the Camino.

Simple things can quickly become a huge deal. I'll admit that I take having clean laundry for granted in regular life because my wife has always done it for our family. But on the Camino, it's not as simple as throwing a load in the washing machine. Most albergues do not have washers and dryers, and if they do, there is a long line of pilgrims waiting to use them. Because of this, your soiled Camino clothes are often washed by hand in a sink or in the shower and hung out to dry outside on a line. On one of my Camino stops, in the small town of Rabanal del Camino, I met a nice little Spanish lady who worked in the albergue and offered to do laundry for a small fee. I said, "Oh my God, are you kidding? How much?" She could have charged a hundred Euros and I would have happily paid it. I was ecstatic to have someone else take on this small, simple task for one night! Those clothes came back folded and fresh, and I was in heaven. It is funny how we take for granted the simple things in life.

It was surprising to me that even the act of eating could feel like a colossal chore at times. After walking for 6-7 hours, you'd think you would be starving and craving a good meal at the end of the day. Surprisingly, your appetite decreases with the amount of exercise. Many times, I was more tired than hungry when I finished a day of walking.

Each night when we arrived in these small towns, finding food, making food, and even going out to eat felt like a burden. Again, I recognize my own privilege of not thinking about food security or even what I eat most days. I have a wife who plans, shops, and cooks for us. I've been very fortunate, and the Camino helped me realize just how much.

When you're on the Camino, your whole world resides in a backpack. Things become simpler and more straightforward, and each day becomes a string of tasks necessary to get from one town or village to the next. You are totally focused on getting through each day. Combine this with the idyllic surroundings of the small Spanish towns you experience each day. These quaint ancient towns are beautiful, and they transport you back to an earlier day in our history. The townspeople live very simple lives; they still grow their own food and live off the land.

This is the way life used to be. It's a beautiful reminder of the old ways when things were much simpler and straightforward. They are not distracted by the many things that complicate our lives today. When you experience Camino life, you realize most of this "noise" from our daily lives is just that: "noise." Most of what we deal with is really not that essential or even all that important. Seriously.

I was reminded frequently on the trail that most of us don't choose to face these kinds of hardships in ordinary life. When was the last time you walked in the rain for hours on end? In our society, we don't have to deal with discomfort very often. When it is raining, we avoid it or use an umbrella. When it is hot, we crank up the air conditioning in our cars, homes, and places of work. In fact, with all the comforts we have in our lives today, we are rarely inconvenienced, and we rarely have to deal with nature's elements.

While we don't have to deal with inclement weather very often at home, I must say there is something mystical about taking on an experience like walking the Camino. It is so humbling. To think that all people lived like this at one time, and some still do—with daily hardships we can't even imagine. After walking for many hours—sometimes in the pouring rain, gale force winds, bitter cold, or stifling heat—you realize how lucky we are in our lives. We have food to eat, shelter to protect us, and friends to talk to.

At the end of the day, those are about all one really needs to be successful.

Recap of Lessons Learned about the Messy Part of Life

1. **Acceptance:** Perfection isn't possible (or even desired). Life is messy, complicated, and challenging. When you accept the way things are, you can more easily navigate through life. They say, "Live in the moment," or better yet, "Live where your feet are!"

2. **Reflection:** We can spend so much time accomplishing the small daily tasks that we neglect to see how mundane they can be. Try to step back for review and reflection every once in a while.

3. **Connection:** Getting an outside perspective can be so valuable. My wife helps me see the small things I take too seriously. Listen to those around you who look at you through a different lens.

4. **Courage:** You have to do what feels right to you. Have the courage of your convictions to make decisions that aren't always popular.

5. **Self-Knowledge:** Knowing your values and what makes you happy is critical. It is easy to spend a life following other people's dreams. Find meaning for yourself, and act from that.

6. **Release:** Letting go of the people, situations, and ideas that don't make you happy is healthy. Why spend time with people who make you unhappy?

7. **Perspective:** No matter what, don't burn bridges. Your view of the world is up to you. You've heard the saying, "Keep your friends close and your enemies closer." It's up to you.

8. **Gratitude:** Simply said, be grateful for what you have.

9. **Do the Right Thing:** When facing critical decisions, always fall back on what is the "right thing" to do. The right thing will usually present itself, even though it may not be comfortable. Follow it. The details always work their way through.

10. **Forward Thinking:** When making a decision, take a long-term view. Understand today's decisions may look very different when you have the benefit of hindsight.

CHAPTER 7

CHALLENGE

"The ultimate measure of a man is not where he stands in moments of comfort and convenience, but where he stands at times of challenge and controversy."

— MARTIN LUTHER KING, JR.

A CAMINO STORY—RESEARCHING THE UNKNOWN

When I decided to walk the Camino for the first time in 2012, there wasn't nearly as much information available as there is today. I was unable to find a single person who had walked the Camino in the past. There was no one to talk to, ask questions of, or serve as a resource for advice or counsel. In those early years, the American Pilgrims on the Camino national organization did not even exist. It was later formed in 2015, so no help there. Back in 2012, I was flying totally blind. I spoke marginal Spanish, and I had minimal experience regarding international travel. This would be an adventure of epic proportions, and clearly one of the biggest challenges in my life to date.

On top of all of this, I was dealing with some significant health issues. I had recently been diagnosed with gout and was suffering chronic sciatica pain in my back and down my right leg. I had a prominent limp from the sciatica condition, which caused problems on my long training hikes. I was very concerned that I might ultimately damage my hips or knees if I walked the mileage I was planning on the Camino.

Needless to say, my wife was none too pleased with my decision to walk the Camino, especially considering all of my recent health issues. And on top of that, I was probably 35-40 pounds overweight. She was quite concerned for my well-being. All that said, I was determined to take on the Camino challenge—when *nobody* in my circle of family or friends thought it a good idea.

Why was I going? Why was I not listening to anyone? Why had this quest become such a passion? We all have issues and problems, personally and professionally. In addition to my health issues, I had issues with my work situation. While my health issues were significant, I knew I could motor through the pain.

My primary motivation was my extreme frustration with the university development management team. I was responsible for the entire fundraising enterprise at the University of Arizona College of Science, one of the largest units on the entire campus. Each year, thanks to my twenty-five-plus years of development expertise, vision, and leadership, we were consistently one of the top fundraising units on the entire University of Arizona campus. It was not uncommon for our College of Science to raise upward of $15-20 million each year. And when I was hired in 2000, we were raising a fraction of that amount. This was a serious and highly successful operation, and I was proud to have built it to that level.

One of my proudest achievements was the occasional years when the College of Science would raise more than both Intercollegiate Athletics (something I loved to talk about, since I came from athletics) and the Cancer Center or Medical School. We were one of the best.

Yet, despite all this success, I just did not connect with some of the senior level development administrators. I wanted them to "just let me raise the dollars the way I know how and add up the results at the end." That was my ultimate form of measurement. Total dollars in the door. To me, that made the most sense, but for whatever reason, development management just could not see the value of my body of work and what metrics constituted success. So, I was considering leaving the UA or possibly retiring. Either one would not be a bad result; after all, I had spent nearly thirty years there, and I had certainly paid my dues.

Earlier in my career, I'd gone through a major organizational change when I worked for AT&T. My division was AT&T Computer Systems when word came down that NCR Corporation was "merging" with our huge computer division in a

$7.5 billion acquisition.[21] It didn't take long to realize this was more like a hostile takeover. The differences between the two organizations became abundantly clear, and it was quickly apparent who was "in" and who would soon be "out." When the new organization charts and business units were finally developed, I could see there were many more NCR employees in leadership positions compared to my AT&T counterparts. NCR was clearly making the decisions in this merger. In the end, this turned out to be true as I and 10,000 other AT&T Computer Systems employees were laid off. It was terrible.[22]

My current UA situation felt like the AT&T Computer Systems situation, so I knew it might be time to consider a change. And that was okay. Believe it or not, great value comes with experience. I had seen these situations play out many times before, and I was ready to accept a change if need be. My 2012 Camino experience would clearly include a lot of soul-searching about my future with the University of Arizona.

If there is a takeaway from this situation, it is that one must always have their antenna up in the workplace. When there is a management change, or an associate gets a valued promotion before you, or you are not included in key meetings, those are signs. Do not be so proud as not to see the signs. Once you do, buckle down and do the best job you can, but try to leverage the situation to help you find something better. Do *not* wait for the ax to fall and suddenly be on the street. Remember, the best time to find a new job is when you *have* a current job. Be smart about how you handle your work environment. There are a ton of moving parts and personalities, and you will not always win out. Be prepared, plan, and be ready to move on.

So back to the Camino…. How does one prepare for a journey so far away? Since there was so little mainstream information, I knew I was facing a ton of research. I needed to learn about everything to expect in Spain from how to pack and where to stay to how far to walk and all the journey's daily challenges. All this research took hours and hours, over many months of planning. Thank goodness for the internet! For months, I spent nearly every night in front of the computer, reading articles and stories and printing out pertinent information. I can't imagine how people managed this Camino process before the invention of the internet. It was overwhelming. Everyone had an opinion—what type of backpack was the best, how many pairs of socks to wear, whether to use hiking poles or not, and on and on.

My challenges before and during the pilgrimage were many and varied. They ranged from a lack of good sources of information for specific topics and knowing the best gear to buy, to developing and implementing a training regime and the intimate details of packing a backpack. While not an exhaustive list, so you will have some idea of what I was up against, here are a few of the things I had to consider and make decisions on before I left for Spain and the Camino.

PRE-CAMINO:

1. What will the weather be like when I am in Spain?
2. What kind and how many clothes will I need?
3. What about cold-weather gear, boots, hats, socks (do I need gloves)?
4. Should I take a poncho that goes over my pack or just a rain jacket? What about rain pants?
5. Should I use trekking poles? (I've never used them, and they looked silly to me.) If so, what kind of trekking poles should I get? How will I travel with them on a plane?
6. How heavy should the pack be? How much water does one carry?

I had never backpacked before, so I did hours of research online and spoke with many more experienced outdoor friends to answer critical questions. Trust me, the folks at the outdoor superstore REI (the Recreational Equipment, Inc.) knew me on a first-name basis. I am sure they said to themselves when they saw me, "Oh no, here comes Bob Logan again…." I asked about what kind of backpack to buy (Osprey or Deuter). I asked about how to deal with blisters. (Turns out, Vaseline all over your feet inside your socks will keep them from rubbing and prevent blisters. Who knew?) I asked what type of socks I should have and how many pairs.

TRAINING

As a former athlete, I was quite familiar with the conditioning needed to compete in a sport. I was determined to get myself into as good a shape as I could before boarding the plane to Spain. Ideally, it would be best to train for up to a year to prepare for a trek of this length and difficulty. The Camino is not technical, and it is not like climbing Mt. Everest, but you must get the body used to walking 6-8 hours a day. This type of training takes a lot of time. However, I did not have an abundance of time, just a few months. I was anxious about getting in the proper amount of mileage during my training. On the Camino, one typically walks 12-15 miles with the occasional 18-20-mile day. Finding the training time for this type of mileage in a daily routine was incredibly tricky. Not for the physical part, but for the amount of time it takes to cover this mileage. I got up daily and walked early in the morning since I live in a hot climate in Southern Arizona.

But I also had to do some miles at night after I returned home from work. And both the morning and evening walks would require me to wear a headlamp. Logging these kinds of miles takes time and fitting it into the life of someone still working a full-time job is nearly impossible. Training your body to be able to do this every day is critical. It is a mental exercise as much as a physical one, and it is so easy to find excuses to put it off until later.

I walked consistently a minimum of five miles a day 4-5 times each week. On the weekend, I would make sure to get in one or two long ten-plus mile walks. When it was all said and done, twelve miles was my longest training walk before I left for Spain. I just did not have the time nor the sunlight in the day to walk any greater distances during my training.

At a certain point in the training, I started wearing my hiking boots to break them in and finally realized I should also carry a fully loaded backpack as often as possible on my training walks. I started doing this very late in my training, and I'm so glad I did! I learned how much more tired you get when carrying a pack of twenty-five-plus pounds.

Unfortunately, what I did not do ahead of time was fill my backpack with *everything* I planned to carry to see how much my pack weighed. As you will see later, this was a critical error on my part. The night before my flight to Spain, I was frantic. I had many packing decisions to make. Should I take one or two pairs of pants? How many socks? My iPad and electronic gear? In the end, I stuffed anything I thought I needed into my pack. I never weighed my full-loaded Camino backpack before I left. This mistake turned out to be a huge albatross!

ARRIVAL IN MADRID

International travel was very intimidating. Besides my Air Force moves, I had not done much travel in my life. Not speaking Spanish and being too proud to ask for help only resulted in more frustration. Just getting from the airport to the train or bus station when you can't read the signs is a huge challenge. I discovered the Madrid International Airport is nowhere near the specific Madrid train station I needed. I also learned Madrid had multiple train stations with different names. One was for local travel (Chamartin) and the other (Atocha) for longer rides across Spain. It took a long time to learn how to buy the proper local ticket and take the correct train to connect with Leon's high-speed train. It seemed like everything was an obstacle I had to overcome. And I hadn't even started walking yet.

The backpack problem reared its ugly head when I was in transit from Madrid to Leon, my starting city. I had realized earlier that day, after getting off the airplane and carrying around my pack in the huge airport, that I would have a huge problem. I needed to take the train from Madrid to Leon, a two-and-a-half-hour ride. When I arrived at the train station in Leon, I found a map of the city. It was a short two-mile walk to the albergue where I would stay that night.

Not a big deal; two miles should be no problem, considering I was accustomed to walking 5-10 miles a day. I was in good shape. However, when I hoisted that pack on my back when I got off the train, I realized, "Boy, this thing is pretty heavy." By the time I arrived at the Benedictine Monastery albergue in the center of Leon, sweat was pouring off me. I was exhausted—after only two miles! What a great way to start this adventure. I may be done before I even begin!

Clearly, my pack was way too heavy—probably forty pounds or more. (Experts say backpacks should be *no* heavier than 10 percent of your body weight, and for me, that would be twenty-five pounds). My backpack was forty pounds *without* water, which adds another 5-6 pounds. It was now evident I had not done a very good job planning my backpack contents. For example, I was planning to blog about my Camino experience, so I had my iPad and a solar charger that probably weighed 2-3 pounds. I had too much of everything. I knew I had a problem.

When I arrived that first night, I was totally out of my element. I had yet to complete a single day on the Camino, and I knew absolutely nobody. I was so nervous I didn't talk to anyone, and I didn't eat dinner. I was overwhelmed by the 200 pilgrims in this vast, old monastery, which now served as an albergue for pilgrims. Pilgrims filled the monastery, many of whom were excited about their day on the trail. I immediately realized how small I was, how humbled I felt, and how all alone I was amid hundreds of others. I was genuinely depressed at my situation, and I had no one to blame but myself!

The next morning, I was determined to ask for help. I clearly needed help. But I would wait until the appropriate time. When 200 pilgrims are preparing for their Camino walk each morning, the activity around the albergue from 6 to 8 a.m. is incredible. Showers, retrieving laundry from the clothesline, packing your bag, breakfast, etc. No one had any time to help me. And I was not about to ask some busy pilgrim clamoring to get out onto the trail. I decided just to hang back until the albergue was entirely empty and all the pilgrims had left for their day.

I sheepishly found one of the volunteer attendants and asked if she could help me. I said in my broken Spanish, "I am so sorry, but this is my first day on the Camino, and I am afraid my backpack is too heavy. Would you mind coming over and taking a look at my pack?" She sauntered over to the long table that just an hour ago had held 50-60 backpacks. Now my backpack was sitting there upright and all alone in all its glory.

The volunteer looked at my backpack, and at first glance, it seemed relatively harmless. Then she reached across the table to pick it up. She pulled it away from the wall and, with a big sigh, lifted it about six inches off the table and quickly dropped it back on the table. She stopped, turned, and with a look of despair and a slight smile, said, "*Increíble e imposible!*" No translation needed there. Then she went and found 3-4 other volunteers to look at my ridiculous backpack. They all shared a good laugh at my expense.

Luckily, one man took pity on me and said he would help. We emptied the entire backpack's contents onto the table and went through each item (kind of like that scene in the movie *Wild* with Reese Witherspoon hiking the Pacific Crest Trail).[23] The pile on the left would stay in my backpack and continue with me on the Camino. The discard pile on the right I would send back to Arizona.

The wonderful man helping me walked me through downtown Leon to the Correos Post Office. (This was the Spanish version of the USPS here in the States). I would never have found it by myself. He helped me pack up the fifteen-plus pounds of stupid items I'd brought and mailed them back to the US. All at the cost of more than $200! Oh, the lessons one learns on the Camino! What a mistake, but as they say, what a learning experience for the next time.

DISCOMFORT

I talked about this a bit before, but there is something compelling about being uncomfortable. It was often freezing in the mornings, so it was not easy to get out of bed and get going. Then you might have to take a cold shower and have a less than satisfying roll and coffee for breakfast. You start walking, and some days (in fact, many days), you might be walking all day in the rain. Or in freezing cold. Or in windy or hot conditions. Despite all these inconveniences and daily annoyances, I was always aware that my discomfort was only temporary. At the end of my walk, in only a few short hours, I knew I would have a comfortable bed, have a glass of wine in my hand, eat a hearty meal, and meet some fascinating people. And oh, how it made me appreciate even the small comforts at the end of a long day of walking.

I recognized what might be uncomfortable to me on the Camino might be daily life for people in other parts of the world. How wonderful and blessed we all are in the United States makes this contrast of Camino life better. The Camino helps us appreciate things. The simple things. Would we value the sunshine and the light without the dark? Warmth without cold? If life were comfortable and easy all the time, we would take it for granted. Challenges and being uncomfortable touch every life experience, and I feel we desperately need to be challenged and uncomfortable from time to time to be complete humans.

CAMINO LOGISTICS

After arriving in Spain, navigating to the start of the pilgrimage, and facing some of the other challenges I detailed earlier, there were many day-to-day issues with essential communication—both language barriers and technology inefficiencies. One had to endure sleeping in a communal setting, filled with many people snoring and farting throughout the night. And, of course, various other small and seemingly minor issues can build up to make the Camino and albergue experience feel unbearable.

Over the years, as the number of pilgrims on the Camino continues to skyrocket, the Camino has developed several wonderful services. It soon became clear I was not alone in having a heavy backpack. Most albergues have a table where pilgrims strip weight from their packs and leave items behind for free to anyone who might have a need. These items range from socks and jackets to sunscreen and hats.

Capitalizing on this, many Camino entrepreneurs have created *mochila* (backpack) transport services for pilgrims. In essence, the process involved leaving your fully-loaded backpack in the albergues common area, with a small transfer fee of $2-$4 in cash attached to the strap in a small envelope. You then call the transport company with specific instructions on where your pack should be delivered on that day. I always feared my poor Spanish and the shuttle service employee's sometimes poor English would cause problems. But it always seemed to work out well.

A small van arrives each morning, picks up the pile of pilgrim backpacks in the lobby, and drives them to the next town where they are delivered to various albergues. When you walk into your predesignated albergue, there is your trusty pack, waiting for your arrival. Beautiful! Once you got used to it, the process was reasonably straightforward. The mochila transport service was a brilliant idea, very reasonably priced. A pilgrim just needs to "trust the process."

The only downside to using the transport services was the loss of flexibility in your Camino experience. Typically, a pilgrim just walks until they are tired, and they select an albergue in the town where they have decided to stop for the day. When using the transport service, a pilgrim must decide exactly how far they want to walk that day and pick a specific albergue for their pack to be delivered. So each day included the added pressure of knowing I *had* to get to the pre-selected town and albergue to meet my backpack. I couldn't quit prematurely even if I were extremely tired, sick, or injured. I *had* to make it to the next town no matter how bad I felt or how painful my blisters were. It was a constant mental battle each morning. How far do I want to walk today? Ten miles, twelve miles, fifteen miles?

The advantage to using the mochila transport service was how much more enjoyable your daily Camino walks became. Instead of carrying a heavy pack of twenty-five-plus pounds, I would carry a small day pack with a couple of pairs of clean socks, a dry shirt, some snacks, and a small water bottle. All told, my day pack probably weighed 4-6 pounds. It was heaven to walk with such a light load! It took time for me to adjust to shipping my pack ahead. There are many purist pilgrims who frown on the service; they think if you use it, you are not a true pilgrim. Baloney! One thing you learn on the Camino is that it is *your* Camino, so you can choose how you want to have the experience. Why inflict pain when it is not necessary?

Another issue I faced concerned my utter lack of knowledge of how international data worked with my cell phone plan. Many times, the Wi-Fi signal was lackluster or non-existent, so I ended up using far more data than I realized or intended while writing my blog. In 2012, after my first Camino, when I arrived back in the US, I had a more than thousand-dollar cell phone bill! On my second

Camino in 2015, I had figured it all out and learned to convert my phone to a Spanish cell phone network. Upon arrival in Spain, I immediately took a cab to a local mall to buy a Spanish sim card to make local calls with ease and not worry about huge data bills. You live and learn.

One particular day, the logistics almost sank me. I arrived late in the afternoon in Burgos, one of the largest cities on the Camino. It had been raining for many hours, and when I finally found my albergue in downtown Burgos, it was a torrential downpour. Was I glad to finally get out of that rain! It was miserable. However, my elation turned to despair when I was told the entire albergue was full. I was crestfallen. I knew from my guidebook that the nearest albergue was more than two miles away. Given my physical and mental state of mind, I knew I was much too tired and too soaked to take on another forty-five minutes (about what it takes to walk two miles) of walking in the pouring rain.

Since Burgos was a huge city, I decided to suck it up and pay for a hotel room, no matter the cost. I walked a few blocks and found a nice hotel down the street. When I stepped up to the reservation counter, I was told the hotel was full. I was shocked. I walked a few more blocks and found another hotel, and they gave me the same response. After the third hotel said it was full, I began to wonder if it was me. Was I being discriminated against as a pilgrim? As you can imagine, after walking for hours in the rain, I was dripping wet and dirty from the day's walk—I probably didn't look like the ideal guest for any hotel property.

Finally, I asked the hotel clerk at the third hotel for an explanation. As it turns out, the next day happened to be a major Spanish national holiday, and Burgos was a popular tourist destination, so all the large hotels were booked solid. Now it made sense, but you can see how your pilgrim mind races in situations like this on the Camino.

The clerk must have seen my distraught look because he told me about a small hotel/hostel off the beaten path that would likely have room for pilgrims like me. He was kind enough to make a call on my behalf and told me to use his name when I arrived. I did, and just like he promised, I lucked out and got a bed for the night. Luxury accommodations, not really—I had one of the four small twin beds in a tiny room. The beds were no more than 4-6 inches apart from wall-to-wall across the room. Each bed was individually booked, so you really got to know the fellow pilgrims sleeping on either side of you! It was crazy, but at least I had a bed. That was all that mattered.

Once I settled in, I started to wash my clothes, always the most crucial task at the end of the day, so they can be hung out to dry by the next morning. Then I realized the only available clothesline was on the balcony and exposed to the rain! I knew there was no way my clothes would be dry by morning. So, I trekked back across the street to ask the desk clerk where I could wash and dry my dirty, sopping clothes. Thank God, he took pity on me. He escorted me to a private washer and dryer the staff used for washing the hotel linens. I was ecstatic to have access to a warm dryer! However, he said it is not for public use, so not to close the door because it would lock behind me. As one always does as a pilgrim, you adapt. I lay on the ground in the laundry room for the next hour or so while my clothes dried. What one will do for the simple pleasures in life!

There is a common saying among pilgrims: "The Camino provides." It certainly did for me that day in Burgos. What started as a miserable end to my day on the Camino turned into finding a couple of kind individuals who generally cared about helping me. It would have been easy for them to let me fend for myself, but you quickly find there are good people everywhere. And the Camino provided for me many other times as well.

When you are in the middle of a challenging experience, little things can make such a huge difference. Such experiences have caused me to develop another saying I live by to this day: "The little things matter." The Camino and voluntary challenges like it are an excellent metaphor for life itself. I realize I've been talking at length about a challenge I *chose* to take. Much of what I've described so far can be categorized as "First World problems." That is absolutely true.

There are two kinds of challenges in life—those we choose and those that choose us. Both types can be precious and teach us so much if we let them. In previous chapters, I shared many of the challenges that have chosen me over the years. I thought it would be helpful to focus on challenges we choose. I believe it is essential for all of us to choose a challenge from time to time. Challenges help us grow in so many ways.

CHALLENGES CAN SPUR US ON TO GREATNESS

When I think of challenges, I often think about people like Michael Jordan, who unbelievably, was cut from his high school basketball team when he first tried out as a 5'10" fifteen-year-old.[24] "Whenever I was working out and got tired and figured I ought to stop, I would close my eyes and see that basketball cut list hanging on the locker room wall without my name on it. That usually got me going again," Jordan said in a 2015 Newsweek article about overcoming his early challenges. Did that disappointment make him work harder and develop habits that would lead him to become one of the greatest basketball players of all time? It sure seems so, looking back at his success.

What about Roger Bannister? Most people today have never heard of him. Back in the early 1900s, running a four-minute mile was thought to be impossible. It was considered the Holy Grail of athletic achievement. Scientists thought it was physically impossible for the human body to perform this feat. Roger Bannister thought otherwise. During training, Bannister would visualize himself beating that four-minute barrier, and on May 6, 1954, he finally did so with a time of 3:59.4.

What is most interesting about this achievement is what occurred *after* Bannister broke the four-minute mile barrier. Within a couple of months, another runner broke his record, and over the next five years, twenty-two other runners broke the four-minute mile barrier. And taking this to the extreme, as of 2018, 1,497 runners have broken the four-minute mile (including twelve high school runners!). The barrier has now been broken 4,518 times! Clearly, running a four-minute mile was not a physical obstacle; it was a mental barrier. It took one person, Roger Bannister, to challenge himself, train hard, and visualize the results he wanted to be the first person in history to break this record.

What challenges in your life are you willing to take on? They may seem impossible at the time, but you may surprise yourself. It is all too easy to take the easy route and avoid challenges, but being challenged regularly helps us grow, improve ourselves, and become stronger people overall.

Below are a few keys to stepping out of your comfort zone and tackling something that perhaps you don't think you can do:

1. **Quit worrying about what other people think.** As I mentioned before, the people in my life, including my wife, thought I was crazy when I told them I was taking several weeks away from work to walk the Camino.

2. **Realize you are good enough.** Believing we can't is a hard stop for most people. For others like Michael Jordan and Roger Bannister, it is

the precise challenge they needed to work tirelessly toward a seemingly unattainable goal.

3. **Be present in each moment.** While Jordan used the past basketball cut list taped on the wall to spur him on, and Bannister visualized his future triumph, both did so while living solidly in the present, doing what they could do at that moment and not giving up.

4. **Be curious.** Often, we get upset, defensive, or discouraged by our seeming failures or setbacks. What if we could get curious instead? Recognize cues better? Ask others for perspectives we don't see? Understand the situation we are in so we can create a better one?

5. **Don't fear failure.** You've heard the famous quote by Thomas Edison, "I haven't failed. I've just found 1,000 ways that won't work." Here's another from Samuel Beckett: "Never tried. Never failed. No matter. Try Again. Fail again. Fail better." And Confucius: "Our greatest glory is not in never falling, but in rising every time we fall."

> *"I've missed more than 9,000 shots in my career. I've lost almost 300 games. Twenty-six times I've been trusted to take the game-winning shot...and missed. I've failed over and over and over again in my life. That is why I succeed."*
>
> — MICHAEL JORDAN

THE CHALLENGE OF THE COLLEGE OF SCIENCE

When I made the move to the College of Science, I knew the challenge I would be facing. I went in with "eyes wide open" and embraced the attitude that it would be an incredible learning experience. Dealing with a new type of donor, high level academic faculty members, and learning about new and exciting departmental science disciplines, I knew my new life would be one of wonder and amazement.

My point I am trying to make is a challenge is just that. How you deal with and attack the challenge is the question. Are you willing to take a risk, try something totally new, and be willing to fail? To put this in perspective, Jeff Bezos, CEO of Amazon, said in his 2019 annual report to shareholders, "If our Amazon businesses are going to continue to grow, they have to have bigger failures. Because bigger failures lead to bigger successes."

Take a hard look at that quote one more time. The richest man in the world running the largest company in the world is encouraging taking on risk and encouraging failure! Let that sink in for a minute regarding your own life. Taking risks and accepting challenges will make you a better person. Just understand you are going to fail and stumble many times along the way. But said in a different way, "The road to success is littered with many failures. It will be a bumpy ride, but you will be happy when you arrive at your final destination."

To this point, when I arrived at the College of Science, I was totally out of my element and had no idea how I would make all this work. I made some mistakes along the way, but when I aligned myself with the right people who believed in what I was doing, it became a fantastic ride. One I would do again in a heartbeat if given the chance.

When I was considering this career change, I was incredibly nervous and unsure if it would be the right decision. But as they say, sometimes a seminal moment comes along and smacks you between the eyes. The College of Science had purchased a table for a charity fundraiser for juvenile diabetes. This single evening helped me put everything in perspective. After I listened to these amazing children with diabetes and learned about the groundbreaking UA research on this disease, I realized the impact I could have on our world and society by this involvement and connection to science.

In my current world of athletics, I met thousands of diehard sports fans and enthusiastic alumni (me being one of them) who lived, breathed, and died for their college team. And they gave copious amounts of money to keep those wins coming year after year.

All that is great, but sitting at that table hearing those heartfelt stories, I realized there was much more to life. When I heard these young children tell their personal stories of their fight against juvenile diabetes, I knew I could be part of something that could help find cures for diseases in our society. When they say, "What is your life's purpose?" Well, this was it for me.

I finally asked, "Why would people give money to athletics when they could be helping sick kids?" There is no comparison. Once I saw first-hand the depth and breadth of what happens in the world of science, it made me realize what a trivial thing it is to put so much emphasis on winning a football or basketball game.

THE CHALLENGE OF COACHING IN ITALY

In the late 1980s, when I was a University of Arizona graduate assistant football coach, my primary goal was to become a Division I coach and, ultimately, a head coach. Our UA coach, Larry Smith, had done a fabulous job turning around the UA program, and he was often sought after by other schools for their football jobs. I had spent three years on Coach Smith's football staff, and I was incredibly proud of what we had accomplished. Our Wildcat teams were now consistently ranked in the top ten in the AP football poll.

As discussed earlier in the chapter on fear, all this success came at a cost to me. Coach Smith was soon to be the head coach at USC, and I was soon to be out of a job. Then Italy came calling.

How this opportunity to coach football in Italy presented itself deserves repeating in greater detail. As Paul Harvey used to say on his radio broadcasts, and now, "The Rest of the Story." In the final month before Coach Smith went to USC, we were in a coach's staff meeting. Apparently, a headhunter friend had contacted Coach Smith who was looking to find a capable head coach for the Bologna Doves in the Italian-American football league. When Coach Smith asked if any of the coaches were interested, my hand shot up! I didn't even know they played American football in Europe, but it sounded like an amazing challenge and a fun adventure. (I soon learned there were one hundred-plus football teams in Italy.) When Coach Smith and I talked about the opportunity after the meeting, he thought I should go for it. He gave me the contact information, and since I had done an excellent job on his staff, he provided a fantastic recommendation to the team's owners.

The humorous part of this story is the interview process. Coach Smith handed me a paper with a phone number, and I called it. Who answered? A thoracic heart surgeon from the University of Arizona Medical Center (UMC)! Apparently, this doctor was good friends with the Italian ownership group, so my first round of interviews would be with him in the UMC cafeteria! How is that for an impressive start!

Luckily, the doctor was impressed enough with me to pass my name along. Within a week, the owners flew me to Italy to see their facilities and review the situation. A few short weeks after that, Coach Smith accepted the USC head coaching job and I was off to become a head coach in Bologna, Italy. I could not believe my good fortune. I would be jumping directly from UA graduate assistant to head coach, my lifelong goal in football. While it would be an incredible challenge, leapfrogging over multiple steps in my coaching growth meant I would secure my future path in the game.

But at the same time, picking up my life and convincing my wife to move overseas was an intimidating proposition. I did not speak Italian or know anything about the culture. I only knew that having a head coaching job on my resume would be impressive when I returned to the United States. It was a "professional" coaching job, after all!

JUDY'S PERSPECTIVE ON THIS ITALIAN ADVENTURE

We were newly married, and I had just been getting settled into Bob's parents' home and making it our own. I was not happy about suddenly having to pack everything up and put it into storage in order to rent the house while we were away. I also didn't want to be torn away from the mild Arizona winter and the pets we loved. It was a tough transition.

But I was also interested in this experience. As a frame of reference, during my college years, I had lived overseas in Paris for a year. I was only twenty-one, and my job was as a nanny to a young family's small kids. It was a life-changing experience. I also knew this was a fantastic opportunity and Bob would regret it if he turned it down. He had planned to backpack around Europe after college but couldn't because of his dad's illness and responsibilities at home.

In the end, we were both so glad we took on the challenge of living overseas in Italy. It was the perfect time in our lives to do something like that; we weren't too settled and didn't yet have kids. It was a great career move for Bob, and we both got to see a lot of Europe. We have many happy memories of those days and have been lucky enough to visit Italy on many occasions since then. In addition, we have had many of our Italian friends visit us here in the United States. We have lifelong Italian friends because of this experience.

Sage Advice from Famous People about Overcoming Big Challenges

Henry Ford—Believe in yourself. As Henry Ford said, "Whether you think you can, or you think you can't—you're right."

Mike Dooley—Visualize what you want. Mike Dooley says, "Thoughts become things. Think the good ones."

Robert Tew—Be able to walk away. Robert Tew said, "Sometimes walking away has nothing to do with weakness and everything to do with strength. We walk away not because we want others to realize our worth and value, but because we finally realize our own."

Vince Lombardi—Finish. Vince Lombardi said, "If you start it, you must finish it. The wisdom comes in knowing when to push forward and when to take a different path. You'll figure it out."

Barack Obama—Ask for help! Barack Obama said, "Asking for help isn't a sign of weakness, it's a sign of strength because it shows you have the courage to admit when you don't know something, and that then allows you to learn something new."

Ellen Johnson Sirleaf—Think BIG. Be delusional when you have to. Ellen Johnson Sirleaf said, "If your dreams don't scare you, they're not big enough."

Teddy Roosevelt—Avoid comparing yourself with others. Teddy Roosevelt said, "Comparison is the thief of joy."

Mark Twain—Do the best *you* can do. Mark Twain said: "Continuous improvement is better than delayed perfection."

Carol Burnett—Accept and embrace change (discomfort is okay too). Carol Burnett said, "Only I can change my life. No one can do it for me."

Anne Graham Lotz—Do hard things. It's how you become better. Anne Graham Lotz said, "In my experience, sometimes the richest blessings come through pain and hard things."

CHAPTER 8
CHANGE

"Everyone thinks of changing the world, but no one thinks of changing himself."

– LEO TOLSTOY

Just as with challenge, there are different types of change we experience in our lives—the change you intentionally choose and the change that ultimately chooses you. In the case of change that chooses you, there are three different types:

- **Sudden Change**
  Change that comes out of nowhere and leaves us knowing our lives will never be the same again. The sudden loss of a loved one, being fired from a job, or being the victim of an accident. This type of change is the only one we typically have absolutely no control over.
- **Gradual Change**
  Then there is the type of change we may not like, and we may even resist for a while, but eventually, we recognize it is a change we must make and embrace. Examples include coming to the realization it is time for a divorce, or to end a relationship.
- **Proactive Change**
  Finally, change that we decide to make ourselves. Still not easy (change never is), but we intuitively know it's time to shake things up and move on. You may be in a job you hate, and it is time to find something better.

I came face-to-face with the second type of change early on in my brand-new head coaching job with the Bologna Doves in Italy in 1986. It was around Christmas, and I had been on the job for just a few weeks. I flew out early in December to work with the team and get everything in order. (By the way, the Italian football league season is in the winter and spring, concluding with their playoffs in June/July). My wife would not arrive until mid-January since she was responsible for packing up the house back in Tucson. She had to put our contents in storage, get the house cleaned, and find a decent tenant to rent our home. I felt terrible about her taking on all this responsibility by herself, but she took it like a trooper, and she understood I had a job to do, and I needed to leave early.

I had begun training the team (and because of the holidays, our workouts were sparsely attended, to say the least). Before I tell the story of what happened, let me share just a little background about the team, their previous coach, and my coaching background. It is essential to get an American perspective on what football was all about in Italy.

My team was named the Bologna Doves, and their logo was a white Dove on the side of a bright red helmet. It took me a while to get used to this, coming from the United States, where our team mascots came with names like Spartans, Tigers, Wildcats, Bulldogs, etc. Most US mascots are intimidating and can either eat you or kill you! On the other hand, my team's name was the Bologna Doves, which I thought was pretty funny, compared to US football mascots. When was the last time a white dove struck fear in its opponent! To my close friends, I jokingly liked to call them the Bologna "Fighting Doves."

Doves Bologna

Bologna is a large city of well over a million people, and it lies in Northern Italy with Milan to the north and Florence to the south. It is in the region Emilia-Romagna and adjacent to the Tuscany region many people are familiar with. It is home to one of the largest universities in Europe, and it has the culinary institute for the region. Bologna's nickname is Bologna "El Grosso," which means Bologna "The Fat" because of the world-class food and restaurants there. Truly amazing food is available on every street of Bologna.

The team I inherited, the Bologna Doves, had considerable success prior to my arrival. They had recently won the Italian National Championship, and they went on to compete in the Eurobowl (basically the European Superbowl). For those who don't know, American football is played in nearly every European country, including Germany, France, England, Sweden, etc. In Italy alone, more than 115 teams were playing American football. This discovery totally blew my mind, and when I tell others about the scale of football in Italy, they cannot believe it either.

The ownership of the Bologna Doves had invested a considerable amount of time and money into their team. Over the years, they had brought many highly capable coaches and players from the United States, and the ownership had a commensurate high expectation level of success. Everyone connected to the team idolized their previous coach, Jim Emery, who was there for three years.

The star player on the team was University of Massachusetts running back Gary Pearson. It was apparent, according to the Italians, and I was told in no uncertain terms, that I was following a living legend of a coach in Jim Emery. I quickly discovered I was walking into a challenging situation, although a highly successful one. Even though I was coming from a nationally ranked NCAA Division I program at the University of Arizona, my coaching style and the potential implementation of a drastic system change would not be accepted with open arms by the players or the ownership. After all, they had just won a championship, and they thought their old system was "perfect." Who was I to shake up their successful program?

The Doves had been hugely successful in the past, and they were technically considered a "professional team." They paid salaries and all expenses for two American coaches and two players. They also recruited some of the best Italian players locally and paid them a small stipend. We had no shortage of good players and a handful of them could compete at small colleges in the US.

Still, after watching film, I knew their football level was really on par with an American junior college team at best. The Italians who were closest to the team only viewed their football experience and expertise through a European or Italian lens. They were not familiar with the level of football in the US, outside of watching the NFL on television. But while this was not major college football, for the division we were competing in, our team was quite talented, and I knew we would win many games.

Because I had been a Division I coach at a major football powerhouse, I knew what it was like to coach at the highest level. I knew how to whip players into shape, and I used a typical American style "hard-ass" approach to do so. Vince Lombardi would have been proud.

Bob Logan - Head Coach Bologna Doves (Italy) - 1987

However, after a month of training, some of the more proficient English-speaking players came to my home to discuss the team's status with me. They told me the team wasn't happy; I was way too hard on them, and many were ready to quit. To say I was in shock was an understatement. I said to myself, *I cannot believe what I am hearing*. If this is how the leading players of the Italian National Champions felt, then I must have missed something. "I'm working them too hard? Are you kidding me?"

Bob Logan—University of Arizona Assistant Coach 1984-86

I told them I wouldn't change my coaching style; I knew how to get results as a coach, and they (and everyone else) would have to toughen up. I also gave them all an ultimatum, like any typical American coach would do—if you don't like being part of this team, feel free to leave, and we will play with the players committed to winning. I would accept nothing less.

Even though I showed a lot of bravado, when they left I was genuinely shaken. These were some of my best players, and I needed them to be successful. Besides, they had been integral members of the Doves for many years, and each of them had key essential insights into the players and team ownership. I needed them. And selfishly, I really needed them since these players took care of nearly all the necessary English to Italian translation required for me to teach my skills, techniques, and schemes. I had to have them on my side.

There I was, sitting all alone in my living room, taking it all in. I had just moved my life overseas for my first-ever head coaching job. I was in a country I didn't know, living in a culture I didn't understand, and trying to do a job in a language I couldn't speak. It was overwhelming, and I hadn't even started.

I wanted to be successful, and I was worried I might have a revolt on my hands very soon. If there is one thing you need to understand about the Italians, they are incredibly proud. And this team of extremely proud Italians had just won a championship. Who was I to come in and change everything that seemed to work so well in the past? I was losing them, which led to some serious soul-searching that eventually brought me to the realization that this was *not* the NFL or even the University of Arizona. I was coaching in a completely different environment and culture from the one I'd left behind. Although these guys were technically professional football players, they all had full-time jobs. Like many Italian adults, many unmarried players still lived at home with their parents or grandparents. They were a very tight-knit group of players, and if I could capture that, it would be an incredible asset to the team's growth.

The big question was: Who changes, the team or me? It was clear I needed to adjust more to them than vice versa. I started to change how I dealt with the players by letting go of my American ideas about fraternization with players. In the United States, a coach should never become a "friend" to his players, and definitely not someone you hang out with outside of football. There are just too many bad things that can happen in that situation.

In this situation, however, I needed help. It was clear the coach-player relationship I was used to in the States would not work here. I was out of my element, learning to live in the new Italian culture, so I changed my ways. I decided to change and adjust to them. This was the best decision I could have made. Change was a quantum leap for me. I had to check my American coach ego at the door, and doing so is absolutely what made the relationship successful. I also did not realize how much the Italians *wanted* to help me. They wanted me and my wife to enjoy our time in Italy, which went far beyond the day-to-day grind of football practice.

Ironically, I did not significantly change my coaching style, but I started to change my social interactions with the players. Occasionally, I would join the guys for drinks or dinner after practice. The players and their families would often invite Judy and me into their homes, and we got to know their families over the fabulous three-hour meals typical of the Italian culture. I started listening to *them* for a change. This new level of understanding had me relate to them differently, and that made them trust me more. I needed to change to become more like them.

One of our early football successes came from my introducing the concept and importance of "special teams." Let me dive into some football specific speak so you can follow along. Special teams represent the part of a football game that is *not* the offense or the defense. The special teams represent all the special plays that take place during a football game—kickoff and kickoff return, punt and punt return, field goals and extra points, and the defensive field goal and extra point block teams.

Special teams are critical because most of these plays cover 40-50 yards and include a change of possession from one team to the other. They are high-risk, high-reward plays, and a single mistake can cause you to lose a game, or conversely, help you win a football game that you normally might not have won. They are a very important aspect of football, but many people do not notice their impact.

Many coaches say that to win a football game, you must "win" two of the three aspects of the game of football—offense, defense, or special teams. Said another way, many teams can be very successful with a mediocre offense (the part of football fans love to watch), but if you have a great defense and solid special teams, you will win 75-80 percent of your games.

Ironically, many coaches give lip service to special teams. They do the bare minimum but get the players to line up the correct way. And these coaches lose many games each year due to this lack of attention to detail. However, during my time at the University of Arizona, I was fortunate to work with one of the best special team coaches in the United States, Bobby April. Bobby went on to coach special teams in the NFL for more than twenty years. He was a master, and I was his right-hand man working, side-by-side with him for three years. I knew *all* of the best practices to create an unbelievable special teams unit.

Now, back to Italy. No one on the team had ever heard of this new emphasis on special teams. In fact, their legendary coach, Jim Emery, had the good fortune of having a dominant offense and a stifling defense, so he spent very little time on special teams and still won most of his games. Remember, you only need to win two out of three aspects of the game to be successful.

Truth be told, I could tell from watching game films from the previous year that Emery and his staff did not have the higher-level special teams' knowledge base I did. I knew my expertise in special teams could be a huge differentiator for our team. We would continue to have great offense and defense, and once we added great special teams, we would absolutely dominate in all facets of the game. The

Italians were in for a treat. They had never seen this part of the game of football run with this level of complexity.

Let me provide you a specific example to bring all of this into focus. On fourth down, when the offense is forced to punt, you have a defense on the field with 5-7 players who should not be on the field for a punt return play. Just imagine a 265-pound defensive tackle being asked to run forty-plus yards to set up a punt return. These "big" players are not built for these types of plays. Typically, what you would see in this scenario is once the ball is snapped, the big players take the play off and barely jog down the field, being a total non-factor on the play. Now think if you replace those 5-6 players with running backs, tight ends, fast wide receivers, great athletes, etc. These are skilled players who are fast, can hit, and can run up and down the field.

In the Bologna Doves case, the previous year's team just left the entire starting defense on the field and substituted one player, the punt returner, to field the punt. If he had a significant return, it was because he was a great athlete, and he did it all on his own. And could any of the "fatties" on the line ever get through to block a punt? It would never happen.

When I told our team we would now be calling our punt return team "The Raiders," and we would replace nearly the entire defense on 4th down, they were shocked. They had *never* heard of such a thing. And then I told them we would put ten players on the line of scrimmage, and our goal was to block 15-20 punts this season and score 4-5 touchdowns. Their heads were about to explode. I think they thought I was a madman!

It took some convincing for them to adjust to this new idea of special teams, but in our very first game, we blocked two punts and scored two touchdowns—one on a blocked punt and one on a punt return. The team was amazed; they had never seen anything like this before. Suddenly, I had players begging me to add them to the "Raiders" punt block/return team! They could not wait when our opponents were facing a 4th down situation. They saw new techniques and new ways to play football, and they were willing to change to be successful. I think there is a message in there somewhere…!

After that, their trust in me as a coach was complete. They began to realize while I was not Jim Emery, my style and methods could work just as well. But we never could have found ourselves here if I hadn't been willing to change. I had to listen to them, understand their culture, and change my attitude to be successful. Sometimes we need to accept that we don't always have all the answers. Building a team is like building a dependable organization. It is comprised of many people with disparate ideas and thoughts, and often, incorporating their ideas will create a better team or organization.

This experience also helped me see how fast paced and often disconnected American culture can be. We could learn a lot from the Italians about enjoying life, good food, family, connection, and a slower pace. It was a fantastic experience and one I will never forget. Ironically, one of my star players did precisely that. One of the American players I brought with me was John Knight, from my rival school of Arizona State University. He was an All-PAC10 linebacker and a great player for me, and he also integrated well with all of the Dove players.

John immediately won the Italians' respect. He was a smart man because he took this opportunity to play football in Italy and take advantage of the situation. He totally integrated himself into the Italian culture and society, learned the language, and became fast friends with the entire team. (He was an excellent sounding board for me.)

How has it worked out for John? Well, he never came back to the United States! He loved the Italian culture and people, married a local woman, and continued to play football for a few additional years. Here we are nearly forty years later, and he now runs a successful small business in a tourist area and is very happy with his life there. Amazing.

SUDDEN CHANGE

This first type of change often blindsides us. Even if we did something to help bring it about, we might not fully understand its implications. Earlier, we talked about Dan Gilbert and his book, *Stumbling on Happiness*. In it, Gilbert introduced the concept of impact bias. To review, impact bias emphasizes our innately poor ability to predict our emotional states, whether they be good or bad.[25]

Naturally, we think that when "good" things happen to us, these good feelings will go on forever. And conversely, when "bad" things happen to us, we feel terrible, and we think we will never overcome this bad situation. But as Gilbert teaches us, it doesn't work that way at all—at least not for very long. Research has shown that the highs and lows we all experience ultimately even out in the long run, and we return to a baseline of emotions.

Traumatic events tend to trigger what Gilbert calls our "psychological immune systems," which promote our brain's ability to deliver a positive outlook and even happiness from an unavoidable situation. This reaction to events, positive or negative, is the opposite of what we would expect when we imagine tragedies (or experience fear about them before they even happen). Gilbert says, "People are not aware of the fact that their defenses are more likely to be triggered by intense rather than mild suffering. Thus, they mispredict[26] their emotional reactions to misfortunes of different sizes."

In a famous study from Northwestern University (1978), results showed the happiness levels of paraplegics and lottery winners were essentially the same within a year after the event occurred.[27] That's right. Most would categorize these two events as terrible and fantastic, respectively. However, after the initial surge of emotions, participants came back to the same basic level of happiness within a relatively short period of time. This study has been replicated again and again with the same essential findings. The final takeaway is: When something terrible is happening to you, understanding the common phrase "time heals all wounds" is accurate and based on scientific research. Things will get better, I promise.

GRADUAL CHANGE

For years, I judged people by their status. I was raised to believe everyone should take care of themselves, and if they couldn't, something must be wrong with them. Either way, it wasn't my problem. My parents taught me the following: hard work = success. And I raised my kids the same way.

Often, you see a homeless man holding a sign at the stoplight or sitting outside of the grocery store with a cup for coins. Unfortunately, when I was with my young kids and came across this situation, I would tell them we weren't giving them any money and explained why—the homeless person would likely use our money to buy drugs or alcohol, and I didn't want to contribute to that lifestyle. I would also tell them there were many organizations in the community where they could go for help—places like the Salvation Army and the Gospel Rescue Mission that cater specifically to this population. Why the homeless people we see at the stoplight don't use these services is a choice. They *choose* not to go and find help. All of that may be true, and you may think or say the same things, and there is nothing wrong with that perspective; however, in recent years, I had an experience that forever changed my thinking, and now I sincerely regret what I taught my kids about the plight of homeless people.

My walk on the Camino changed how I saw lots of things, but probably none more so than the way I view people in general. Much of my career in fund-raising has been dealing with high net-worth individuals, soliciting donations from them to support noble causes like scholarships, building buildings, and other worthy academic programs.

Because I learned to talk to people on the Camino—all kinds of people from so many varied backgrounds—I also try to do that more often in my daily life here at home. You finally realize that everyone you encounter during the course of your day is a human, no more, no less. It doesn't matter what one's social status is or what type of car they drive. We are all humans in the eyes of God, and we should be treated that way.

One thing you learn early on the Camino is everyone is on the Camino for a reason. I soon found out my reasons seemed comparatively minor once I heard their incredible, and oftentimes, sad stories. Their stories put my minor work issues at the University of Arizona into perspective and changed the way I saw people forever. I will never forget some of these individuals: the woman I had dinner with who had stage IV breast cancer; the woman who had been sexually assaulted as a child; and the many pilgrims who had recently lost loved ones, etc. I soon learned everyone is carrying a cross or a burden of some type and everyone has a story to tell.

Now, back to the homeless person on the corner. I now look at that person in a very different way. I see them as a human, not just an annoyance during my daily activity. Today, our family treats the homeless much differently. My wife and I have started to build and hand out "Blessing Bags" to the homeless. "Blessing Bags" are large Ziploc bags that have 5-7 necessities like toothpaste, deodorant, soap, a granola bar, crackers and cookies, etc. In addition, we include a small amount of cash, usually a few dollar bills. We typically have 5-6 of these "blessing bags" in the backseats of our cars, and if we have an opportunity at a stoplight, we honk our horn and give them a bag. The look on their faces is incredible. Try it; you will be amazed how you feel afterward.

But the homeless are even more shocked when I encounter them at a store or on the sidewalk and am able to spend a few minutes talking to them. The homeless will tell you that just doesn't happen very often, but I take the time to ask about their stories, where are they from, how long they have been on the streets, etc. Instead of ignoring them like 99 percent of people do all day to them, I stop, listen, talk, and interact with them. I tell them God is on their side and watching over them, and I recognize they are there but for the grace of God.

I don't judge their situation anymore, and I don't care what they do with the money. If they choose to buy alcohol or drugs, which gives them some sense of relief for the condition they deal with every day, I am okay with that. I give to them freely and without any prejudice or judgment.

One day, I asked a guy how he was doing, and after a short conversation, I asked, "How often do people acknowledge you?" His response, "Never." I asked, "How often do people try and have a conversation with you?" "Never." He told me that people regularly walked right by without even making eye contact or responding to his request. Can you imagine how lonely that must make a person feel? I would imagine, though I can't know for sure, that lack of acknowledgment is more devastating in many ways than lack of a home or financial resources.

When I was training for my Camino in 2015, I had a regular routine. I typically walked a specific four-to-five-mile segment, and this trail went under a major road in Tucson, Alvernon Way. Under the concrete bridge was a ledge, and it provided shade and protection. One morning, I discovered a homeless man who had set up a camp under the cover of this bridge. He had a nice little setup. It was out of the public eye, safe from the elements, and for all intents and purposes, not a bad place. When I walked by in the morning, he was usually sleeping. In the afternoons, I would see all his stuff even if he wasn't there. Over many months of just "walking on by," I thought about him always and that maybe I should try and help him. What could I do to make his life a little more bearable? These thoughts were prior to my change in attitude toward the homeless and my "Blessing Bags" idea.

After many months, I finally decided it was time to do something to help. One day, I started looking around my home for items he might like to have. I put together a care package with some blankets, clothes, socks, food, etc. This stuff was lying around my house for a long time, and I would never need any of it. After all this time, I was finally going to act and do the right thing.

I was nervous about taking it to him from fear he might be offended, not want my stuff, or feel I was taking pity on him. In case he was not there when I arrived, I wrote a note "To the man under the Alvernon Bridge" to explain who I was and why I was giving him this stuff. I said in the letter that I had seen him nearly every day for months and just wanted to help.

The big day came. I packed all the stuff into my car and drove to the Alvernon Bridge. My heart was pounding, and I was incredibly nervous about the upcoming interaction with a man I did not know. When I got to the bridge, I was shocked. He was gone, and so was all his stuff. I have no idea what happened or why he left.

The irony is I had waited too long to act. Why? I was afraid of rejection because I was worried he would dismiss me and the help I was offering. Sadly, I imagine he feels rejected every day of his life. My takeaway was: Don't wait to do the right thing. Act, and act now!

PROACTIVE CHANGE—DON'T RESIST

Complaining, digging your heels in, and resisting change is a recipe for disaster. There is a time for sharing your concerns professionally and appropriately. My Bologna Dove team members did so when I began my coaching experience in Italy. But there is also a time for acceptance. There are times you need to step back, look around, and be able to see when resistance becomes futile and is only hurting you.

Recently, I witnessed a similar situation at work. There was considerable restructuring and lots of turnover after a change of senior administration at the University of Arizona. We had a new UA President, and the leadership all over campus was changing as well. It was an unsettling time.

If you have ever worked in large organizations, this discomfort is the norm when new leadership takes over. New people in new positions shake things up, and it is tough on everyone, but some employees seem to adjust better than others. Being able to recognize this kind of organizational change might provide a signal that it's time to be proactive and move on. As an employee, you must always remember you are just an expendable cog in the organization's machine. Staying or moving on is a conscious decision; the key is to decide the appropriate time to pull the trigger on that decision.

If you choose to stay, you must find a way to make it work. I watched as one of my colleagues, who usually does not complain about things at work, became very vocal about her disdain for the new leadership and all the changes happening. Eventually, she lost her job because of her inability to adjust, adapt, and change.

A couple of years later, after I had been promoted to assistant dean, we had a new development officer for the College of Science, and he could not adjust to the Chair of the College of Science Board of Advisors. The board chair was demanding and treated him like he was his employee. Very frustrating for him, and I tried to counsel him as much as I could. As experienced and seasoned fundraisers, it was evident to both of us that the board's chair was being unreasonable with his demands and expectations. We appealed to the dean to intercede, but unfortunately, the board chair had the dean's full support. This was clearly a no-win situation. I knew things would not end well for my colleague since he became more and more agitated and animated about his feelings of being marginalized. He would corral anyone who would listen and rant about how unreasonable his situation was.

One day, I sat him down and told him I felt he was making a huge mistake. I told him I respected his principles and his position on these issues. In fact, I told him he was right. But that was not the main issue. His issue was he was in the middle of a power struggle, and he was going to lose. He would be committing career suicide by taking on the board's chair and the dean of the college "out of principle." While the situation went on for a few more months, as I predicted, he was let go later that year in an ugly separation. If there is one skill you must master, it is how to navigate an organization's power structure.

Earlier in Chapter 7 on challenge, I relayed a similar situation when I worked for AT&T Computer Systems, when our division was being "merged" with NCR Corporation.[28] At the time, it was one of the largest corporate mergers in US history, and when I researched the NCR organization, I was not feeling good about how the merger might affect me professionally.

I knew there were many redundancies in the new merger structure so thousands of people would likely be let go, most likely from the AT&T side. Since I did not like the current situation, deep down, I was hoping for an opportunity to be "rightsized," as they say. Even though AT&T was a fantastic company, and I was proud to work for them, I knew my time with the company was coming to an end. I was lucky, though, because I could use the change we were all experiencing as an opportunity.

A few months after the merger, the company announced it was looking for AT&T Computer Systems employee volunteers to leave. If one took this option, it came with a six-month severance "Golden Parachute" package. Six months of salary, are you kidding me? I jumped at the chance to find the exit door. It was time for a change and an opportunity for a new adventure. This corporate chapter of my life was now over, thank God.

SHIFT PERSPECTIVE

One of the best things we can do when facing change is to shift our perspective. Putting it into context can help us feel like what we are facing isn't too hard. I often think of the serenity prayer when I'm facing changes that have me worried.

SERENITY PRAYER[29]

God, grant me the serenity to accept the things I cannot change,
the courage to change the things I can,
and the wisdom to know the difference.

I also think about basketball coach Jimmy Valvano. He changed people's perspective of him, and he changed the focus in his life. When Valvano was diagnosed with incurable cancer, he changed from a basketball coach to an ambassador for cancer research. He used the stage of the 1993 ESPYs when he won the Arthur Ashe Award for Courage as his platform.[30] And what a platform it was. If you have never seen it, it is one of the most inspirational talks ever given in history.

Jim Valvano Famous ESPY Speech (11:31 mins)
https:/BobLogan.net/ValvanoNeverGiveUp

Valvano announced that with ESPN's help, he would be starting the Jimmy V Foundation to raise money for cancer research. The attendees were stunned, and he ended his standing-ovation speech with this: "Cancer can take away all my physical abilities. It cannot touch my mind, it cannot touch my heart, and it cannot touch my soul. And those three things are going to carry on forever." And they have genuinely carried on through his foundation and the work it has done to support cancer research. Since it was founded in 1993, the Jimmy V Foundation has raised nearly $290 million for cancer research.

The Camino was my chance to change and to change my perspective—what I thought, how I saw the world, and what I believed—even though I had no idea going in this would be the final outcome. Change can be like that.

CHANGING ONE'S LIFE WORK—FROM FOOTBALL TOUCHDOWNS TO MARS TOUCHDOWNS

Not many people can make the claim during their career that they were involved in missions to Mars (Mars Odyssey-2001) and (Mars Phoenix – 2008) and a mission to an asteroid 200 million miles from Earth (OSIRIS-REx-2015). I am proud to say I have that distinction and to say they were memorable is an understatement.

Over the years, many people have asked me how I handled the dramatic change from working in the world of intercollegiate athletics to the methodical college of science. More specifically, they ask if I miss the excitement of athletics and attending football bowl games and Final Fours, etc. Truth be told, the world of athletics pales in comparison to the excitement one sees when a mission many years in the making fails or succeeds right before your eyes.

Let me give you a couple of examples to help you understand what I mean.

MARS ODYSSEY, 2001–TODAY, $297 MILLION[31]

The Mars Odyssey was a satellite probe that was to orbit the planet Mars and map the surface to find potential landing sites for the Mars Phoenix mission to come a few years later. To do this, it first had to successfully enter Mars' atmospheric orbit. As discussed earlier with the Mars Climate Observer mission, entering orbital insertion is like hitting the side of a piece of paper from 140 million miles away! Not an easy thing to do.

At 7:26 p.m. on October 23, 2001, Odyssey began its orbital insertion, and the burn would last twenty minutes. The spacecraft would disappear behind the planet for twenty minutes and be in total radio darkness. No radio communication. Radio silence for all to hear. The scientists would know the results of the Odyssey orbital insertion at about 8 p.m.

On this specific evening, I was in the auditorium of the Lunar and Planetary Lab on the UA campus with 200 scientists, researchers, family friends, donors, etc., all listening in to the NASA/JPL mission communications. The twenty minutes of radio silence was deafening. It was so quiet, and everyone was on the edge of their seats, hoping and praying. When the first signal came through, the entire room exploded with cheers, tears, and hugs all around. It was a moment I will never forget.

MARS PHOENIX MISSION, 2003–2008, $420 MILLION

After the Mars Odyssey mission identified water ice on the surface of Mars with its gamma ray spectrometer, the next mission was the Mars Phoenix, a probe to land on the surface and dig up and analyze the soil of the red planet. Dr. Peter Smith ran the mission, which was the first NASA mission to have its entire operations center managed and run on a university campus. It was a huge deal for the University of Arizona. NASA selected Smith's proposal in 2003 and Phoenix launched from Cape Canaveral in August 2007.

It took more than nine months for Phoenix to make it to Mars, and the key aspect of the mission was called EDL (Entry, Descent, and Landing). It is important to note that the big science of space exploration is fraught with failure. Of the thirty-plus missions to Mars to date, less than one-third have been successful. Here were Peter Smith and his team, who had worked for nearly ten years on this project, down to what is called the "Seven Minutes of Terror," the amount of time it takes for the EDL sequence to complete and determine if the probe has landed or has crashed.

Again, like the Mars Odyssey, auditoriums all over the University of Arizona campus were filled with scientists, faculty members, donors, space junkies, and friends to witness firsthand this tension-laced period of landing on the surface of Mars.

Peter Smith was in Pasadena at the Jet Propulsion Lab and the campus auditoriums all had a live feed to follow the landing's progress. It is difficult to describe the thrill in writing, but to watch the announcer at JPL mission control call out the landing sequence was something I will never forget.

Here are the final moments (as voiced from mission control):

"Standing by for expected parachute deployment."

"Parachute trigger detected. Heat shield trigger detected." (Applause)

"Land leg deployment trigger detected."

"Altitude 2,000 meters."

"Altitude 1,800 meters."

"Altitude 1,600 meters."

"Standing by for landing separation, 1,100 meters." (Applause)

"Separation detected."

"We are verifying the signal. Gravity turn detected."

"600 meters."

"400 meters."

"250 meters."

"150 meters."

"100 meters."

"40 meters."

"30 meters."

"15 meters. Standing by for touchdown."

"Touchdown signal detected." (Cheers and Applause)

"Landing sequence initiated."

"Phoenix has landed!"

"Phoenix has landed."

"Welcome to the North Plains of Mars!" (Pandemonium!)

Phoenix Mars Mission landing-2007 (artist rendering)

I urge you to take a few minutes and watch this riveting video where Dr. Peter Smith describes the mission and the entire landing sequence with scientists exploding in cheers when word came we had successfully landed on Mars. It is guaranteed to be a goose bump moment for you.

Phoenix Mars Mission (5:44 mins)
https://BobLogan.net/PhxMission7MinutesOfTerror

Bottom line, as exciting as a 4th and goal play to win a football game is, or needing to sink two free throws to win a championship, nothing, and I mean nothing, compares to these moments in science exploration. Thinking back to my coaching days, our football staff would prepare for a week or maybe ten days for an upcoming opponent. Did we work hard? Absolutely. We put in twelve-to-fifteen-hour days breaking down film, chronicling tendencies, preparing our schemes and game plans. It was grueling work and preparation to get ready for a single game. And we did this week after week through an entire season.

But does this work compare in any way to what these scientists do preparing for their mission? Science teams prepare for ten to fifteen years for their key moment! And there are hundreds of people on these science teams. All of them preparing for this one, short, critical moment. Many of these science team members are responsible for one small, tiny piece of the total mission. If they fail, the mission fails. Hundreds of these critical details all need to work in harmony to be successful.

To be in the room with these scientists, engineers, faculty members, and their families in the final seconds of the key moment to their missions is a heart-pumping experience. It is the culmination of years of hard work and validates their time was well spent. The pressure in the room is palpable, and the explosion of cheers and excitement when they are successful brought me to tears every time.

To all those who ask (and they will never totally understand), I will take a science moment like those listed above before any football, basketball, or athletic moment. It is not even close. To me, the change from athletics to science was one I will take every time.

Lessons on Change:

1. Big or small, it's how you deal with, accept, and even embrace change that counts.

2. Reach out to others for perspective when you aren't sure what the next steps are to take.

3. It's okay to be upset, angry, and hurt. But to a point. You have to find a way to deal with the change happening to you. (My strong recommendation is that you never share your feelings in the social media space. When you are upset, angry, and hurt, trust me, those feelings don't translate very well on social media. Even worse, if your feelings involve others, making them public will only make it worse.)

4. Your *reaction* to change is what causes problems—not the change itself.

5. Accept the past (make peace with it) and fight for the future. Sometimes we have a clue that change is coming. Prepare as best you can so it doesn't send you into a tailspin—turn into the skid when you can. Get out in front of the problem. Don't wait.

6. Change can be a massive opportunity for something better when you choose to see it that way.

7. Don't get caught up in your emotions. Sometimes it's better to relax and move on.

8. Know what you can control and what you can't. You can't change the change. Remember the Serenity Prayer.

9. Purpose and passion are the best distraction. Viktor Frankl also said: "Those who have a 'why' to live can bear with almost any 'how.'"[32]

10. Never give up. Persistence rather than resistance. Lou Holtz said it best, "Never tell people about your problems. Ninety percent don't care, and the other 10 percent are happy you have them." Live life. Live well.

CHAPTER 9

THE SEVEN MOST IMPORTANT WORDS

"Did I offer peace today? Did I bring a smile to someone's face? Did I say words of healing? Did I let go of my anger and resentment? Did I forgive? Did I love? These are the real questions. I must trust that the little bit of love that I sow now will bear many fruits, here in this world and the life to come."

— HENRI NOUWEN

Below are Seven Words from the English language that can change your entire life. Literally. We have all heard them and used them but take a moment to think back to certain situations in your life. Look deep down inside of you. Have you used these words enough in your life? Could you have changed a situation if you had swallowed your pride and said, "I'm sorry"? Do you take your family for granted and not say "I love you" enough? Finally, do you show your gratitude to all the people in your life who do things for you?

- I'm Sorry
- Thank You
- I Love You

Pretty simple stuff, but these seven little words, used often, used when necessary, and said with sincerity, authenticity, and grace, will have a considerable impact on your life's path. These seven short words can repair almost any misstep, heal practically any wound, and often will literally make someone's day. All of us long to hear them, and all of us need to use them as often as possible. If you say them regularly, you will find out how amazingly rewarding it is to incorporate them into your daily life.

I'M SORRY

Many of us have a hard time with this one. I don't know if it's because we think it makes us weak by admitting our mistakes or because we have a difficult time taking responsibility for our actions. I have had a lot of practice in this area because I grew up in a military family where there wasn't much gray area when it came to issues of right and wrong. My dad, an Air Force officer and family disciplinarian, taught me the correct way to live. Everything was black and white; if you did something wrong, not only would you apologize, but you needed to fix it.

That was why it had been so difficult for me to quit the Air Force Academy a few years earlier. I knew what a huge disappointment it would be to him—the most significant "I'm sorry" I could ever deliver. I'm sure I apologized a lot, but I'm not sure he ever really understood or accepted it. It was such a crushing blow.

A few years ago, I was cleaning out boxes in one of the unused bedrooms in my childhood home. I came across a box filled with papers and letters. Inside the box were old Air Force Academy documents, as well as a large envelope stuffed with old letters. I turned the large manilla envelope upside down and out fell a trove of personal letters. My dad, God rest his soul, after I had told him I was going to leave the Academy, wrote me an encouraging hand-written letter every single day for the entire time I was in outplacement at the Academy! There were easily thirty letters or more. It was a labor of love. Each letter was a different version of him begging me to change my mind about quitting the Academy. Remember, this was in the days before email, text messaging, and instant communication. It was so humbling to think of the time he spent on these letters, every single day, and I could literally feel his pain and desperation in each one.

In addition, Dad asked local sports heroes and former coaches to write me; he had my brother in Pittsburgh (because of our age difference, I was not that close to him) write a letter. Looking back, I cannot imagine the heartache my decision caused my dad.

Despite the many times I said "I'm sorry" to him, it took many years for him to accept that I had taken full responsibility for my decision, and I was now moving on. I was confident I would still be successful, but in a much different way and likely on a much different path than he expected. It is sad that he passed away before he could see most of the successes I achieved in my life.

That first endeavor was to become a high school teacher and football coach at Salpointe Catholic High School. I do know Dad was very proud of my becoming a teacher and coach. I was coaching with one of Arizona's all-time legendary football coaches, Ed Doherty, and he revered Ed Doherty and became a personal friend of Ed, his wife Irene, and the entire Doherty clan. Dad was incredibly proud of that achievement. He also saw I had become a man, I was living my own life, and even though I didn't follow specifically in his Air Force footsteps, I was doing something positive with my life. He recognized that late in his life.

Learning that critical lesson early on has served me well in my work and my life. While I still have some regrets about leaving the Air Force Academy, I can proudly say I left with my head held high and I owned that decision. People often make decisions based on what *others* think is the best thing to do, and then spend many years on the wrong path. If there is one takeaway here, it is: Live your own life by your convictions—own your life, and you will be a much happier person for it in the end.

A great example is when I began my job at the UA College of Science as a fundraiser. Once I stepped into the position, I discovered there was no donor filing system. We had nearly 90,000 alumni, but I had very few records of those who supported the college. This lack of information made it difficult for me to be effective in my new position. I found out most of the records resided in the seventeen individual departments across the college. The College of Science was highly decentralized, and it took many years to develop strong relationships with the various department heads and units to work with my College of Science central development operation.

All I could do was work with what I had. As I began combing through the files, I came across a donor file with a significant $50,000 donation from nearly twenty-five years ago. The initial gift from this couple was a large collection of seashells collected from around the world. These shells would be part of a research program in our Department of Ecology and Evolutionary Biology (EEB), and the rest were put on display for the public to see in the building. The shells were beautiful.

With the shell collection came a $50,000 gift to create a graduate fellowship endowment. This endowment would fund a graduate student who would curate the collection each year. The initial gift was quite generous considering the year (late 1970s), and by the time I stumbled upon it, the endowment fund had grown to more than $200,000.

I was totally confused, however. If the EEB Department was awarding annual endowment gifts to fund this graduate student, how could the endowment have grown to such a significant amount? A typical endowment pays out 4 percent per year to protect the corpus of the fund. With a typical endowment, this account would continue to grow over time, but very, very slowly.

After much investigation, I tried to find a list of the graduate students who had received the fellowship. My worst fears were soon realized. The reason the endowment fund had grown so large was that not a single graduate fellowship had ever been awarded by the department! This initial gift of $50,000 had continued to grow, earning compound interest every year, but none of the designated funds had ever been used as specified in the endowment agreement. I was stunned. In the development world, this was a grievous mistake and needed to be rectified immediately. I could not believe how mismanaged this gift was, and I wondered if the donors knew any of this information. I dreaded it, but I knew my next step was to reach out to the donors, explain the situation, apologize profusely for the mistake, and hope for the best.

I knew this would be one of the most difficult phone calls I would have in my career. I called the elderly donors and introduced myself as the new development director for the College of Science. I apologized on behalf of the University of Arizona and the College of Science for the incredible oversight. To my relief, the donor was actually thrilled to hear from me! They had been trying to connect with someone at the UA for many years, to no avail. They knew something was wrong but had never been able to find a UA official to get the facts. So, after the small talk, they were just so happy to find someone who cared and could provide the information. What a turn of events.

Here is the power of a well-placed, "I'm sorry." In the fifteen years since I reluctantly made that call to apologize for this major university screwup, this elderly couple has made several more substantial gifts to the College of Science. They continue to be huge supporters and fans of our work. When I left the university, I recall they were considering a substantial estate gift to support the college. They even traveled with us on a memorable donor trip to the launch of the UA Osiris-REx mission launch at Cape Canaveral. And this couple were both in their nineties at the time! After all of this, they became great friends. All because of a well-placed, "I'm sorry."

THANK YOU

Gratitude is one of the most beneficial acts a human can experience. This fact has been confirmed by hundreds of peer-reviewed research studies. Gratitude not only helps us appreciate all the good things in our lives, but it attracts more of them to us. It is so easy to focus solely on what is wrong in our lives, and at times, it may take something to appreciate to make everything right in our world. When we do, it immediately changes the way we see the world and ourselves in it. Showing gratitude is a powerful practice for our well-being and sharing it with others can have many of the same positive impacts on the giver, but the bonus is someone else also gets to feel good.

Do you know what employees will often cite as the most essential thing they desire to stay engaged and be happy at work? Surprisingly, it is not more salary compensation. It is appreciation, acknowledgment, and being recognized for their contributions to the organization. Here are some recent startling statistics to emphasize this point: 55 percent of employees are unsatisfied with their current job situation; 48 percent would take another job offer if presented; and 76 percent of employees are actively looking for another job. No matter how much money you make, it is hard to maintain enthusiasm for your work without some indication from leadership about the value you provide to their organization. Life is too short.

When I am giving one of my happiness keynote talks, I often ask the audience about their experience in bringing in the mail each day. When you bring in a pile of mail from a long weekend and throw it on the counter, which items do you open first? Certainly, it is not the bills or advertising inserts. Now, if you happen to spy a handwritten personal note, a card, postcard, or letter, that is what we all reach for to open before anything else.

We all love to receive personal notes, but few of us take the time to write them when emails or a text are so much easier to send. I'm guilty of this just like you are. I text all the time to people in all aspects of my life. In fact, I look for opportunities to thank people as much as I possibly can.

John Kralik, author of *A Simple Act of Gratitude*, discovered this simple act, and it changed his entire life.[33] His book is about how his life was at an extreme low point, so he decided to identify things in his life that he could be thankful for. He made a New Year's Day resolution to write a thank you note each day for the entire year. As he wrote more and more notes, his relationships improved, his business was on the upswing, and eventually, he achieved one of his biggest life goals. The simple act of looking for things to be grateful for forces you to look at life in a new way.

In many ways, I had a difficult childhood. I lost my entire immediate family at a young age, and I am not incredibly close to any of my cousins or extended family. While I wish I had a big family, I have accepted this is the reality of my life. It is what it is. I have had great opportunities. We are blessed with two awesome sons. I have had great bosses and mentors over the years, I have a supportive spouse, and we have lived a good life. I don't sweat the small stuff, and I genuinely believe it is better to give than to receive. When I write my thank you notes, I feel fulfilled through the entire process, from buying the note cards to thinking of someone to send them to and writing the notes and putting them in the mail.

I have written notes to people I met a single time at an event and to people I see every day in my work or personal life. I have written notes to my dry cleaner and the deli counter guy at my grocery store. If I don't have a physical address or even a last name, I will sometimes hand-deliver them.

Sometimes, I'll buy $5-10 Starbucks gift cards and pop them into the notes to places I frequent as a customer to thank them for their excellent service to me. In a world where most people don't notice the people who serve them, much less take the time to acknowledge or thank them verbally, receiving a handwritten note is a big deal. It blows people away, and one can never replicate the feelings these notes generate. I have had people tell me it's one of the coolest things that ever happened to them at work. Occasionally, I'll even get a call or a thank you note back for my thank you!

ROTARY RANDOM ACTS OF KINDNESS

In 2019, I was named president of my Rotary Club of Tucson. It was a great honor, and I have been a proud Rotarian for many years. During my term, like most presidents do, I wanted to come up with a few ideas that could engage our entire club. We are one of the largest clubs in the world (250-plus members), so this was a difficult task. I came across the idea of having our entire club participate in a kindness exercise, one-by-one. I asked a number of Rotarians to help me by donating $100 to support the exercise. Then at one meeting, I passed out envelopes, each of which contained a $20 bill with brief instructions. The instructions were simply to do something with the $20 in the form of a random act of kindness. You could buy the Coke and popcorn for the person in front of you at the movie theater; you could give it to a homeless person; you could buy some candy and distribute it to a school or a nursing home, etc. Every Rotarian could come up with their own idea. What came back were some incredibly touching stories, and nearly every single one concluded with the Rotarian saying that *they* were the ones who actually benefited from the kindness they shared. The feelings were so strong that some decided to do this exercise on their own on a regular basis in the community. Now that is the power of kindness and gratitude.

During my happiness talks, we discuss the value of gratitude, and to emphasize this point, I show a video that asks 4-5 individual research participants to identify the most influential person in their life. It can be seen below.

A Lesson in Gratitude (7:13 mins)
https://BobLogan.net/ALessonInGratitude

After that significant person is identified, the participants are asked to write a personal note to that individual and explain in detail their feelings for them. At the end of the exercise, the participants assume they are done. However, next they are handed a telephone and told to call the person on the spot and read the note they just wrote about them word-for-word. You can imagine the reactions with these phone calls—lots of heartfelt tears and lots of "I love you."

While I don't ask my audience members to make the phone calls, I do bring a stack of thank you notes, and I hand them out as an exercise during the talk.

All the notes are pre-stamped, and I ask my audience members to write a note to their identified significant person, right then and there. When finished, they are instructed to hand them back to me, and I announce to them I will be mailing all of the notes on the way home after the talk. I always ask for volunteers who might be willing to read theirs aloud to the group, and, invariably, they are incredibly touching and heartwarming.

I LOVE YOU

This one can be tricky. Sometimes we say it so often or automatically that it becomes rote—when we're hanging up the phone or saying goodbye. And just like the phrase "I'm sorry," "I love you" can occasionally be used to provide cover when we've screwed up in some significant way. Many of us will never say it to anyone outside of our immediate family, and that's a shame. When authentically and sincerely shared, it can be the most powerful phrase in any language.

COACH DICK TOMEY—A STORY OF LOVE

UA football coach Dick Tomey, after the 1997 upset of #12 ranked ASU

Early in my career as an athletic director, we hosted an annual luncheon for major boosters and alumni from the Phoenix area. This event occurred after the season, and these rabid Phoenix fans loved to interact with Coach Tomey. Dick would always end the luncheon by answering questions from the audience, and he would stay until there were no more hands raised; he was incredibly gracious, no matter how long it took, he would be there to the end. He also told those who needed to go back to work not to be shy, just get up and leave—no offense taken; he knew these fans had taken time away from work to come to this luncheon.

At this specific event in January 1997, our Arizona team had just concluded a rather average season (7-5 record). Still, unexpectedly, they upset a highly favored #12 ranked 9-3 Arizona State in the season's final game. Most UA fans were surprised since this ASU team was a vastly superior team to ours, and they went on to play in the Sun Bowl game against Iowa that year. That is why this victory was so unexpected.

At the conclusion of Coach Tomey's comments, someone at the back of the room raised his hand and asked, "Coach Tomey, how on earth did we win that ASU game? I think I can speak for many in this room and say very few of us actually expected us to beat ASU this year. How did you do it?" Dick paused for a long moment. He could have answered with a typical media-type clichéd answer, but he chose to tell the entire story and, looking back, what an incredible story he told.

Coach Tomey admitted that ASU had better players and a better team, so he had to search for some way to gain an edge. He decided to appeal to his entire team—one player at a time. Over three days, he brought every single player into his office for a 10-15-minute conversation. It didn't matter if the player was the starting quarterback or the third-string walk-on who never played. Every conversation started the same way. Tomey would ask each player how things were going for them in school and in their life. The talks were very personal. He listened to the problems as well as the dreams and aspirations of each of his players.

However, every conversation ended the same way, with Coach Tomey asking each player to think about someone important to them—someone in their lives they loved and cared about. Once they identified that person, Coach Tomey instructed the player to do three things in the next few days leading up to the game:

Call that person before the game and tell them how important they are in your life and what they mean to you. Tell them "I love you."

Next, explain to that special person when they watch the game on Saturday, that you are playing the game *for them.*

Finally, tell them this ASU game is to honor them for what they have done for you in your life. The message is, "My success is because of you."

You can imagine, with 100 players all playing on behalf of these very special people in their lives, emotions ran high, and the team played far above its capabilities to win in a huge 28-16 upset. Never forget that the best team and the best players do not always win the games or the battles. There is still room for the overachiever. I will never forget that luncheon. There was not a dry eye in the room, and Coach Tomey won many fans that day.

Lessons about the Seven Most Important Words:

1. Saying these three phrases can go a long way toward healing or affirming essential relationships in your life.
2. Don't fret or be uncomfortable. Just speaking in a heartfelt way is often enough.
3. Looking for people to acknowledge or make amends to is so powerful. There is a reason the latter is part of the Twelve-Step process. It's not just for them. It is also for you.
4. Come up with your own version of Random Acts of Kindness.
5. Pick up the phone and call someone you have not spoken to in many years. Trust me; they will be surprised and it will feel like you just talked yesterday!
6. "I am so sorry" can change everything in a situation. It immediately disarms the person you are apologizing to.
7. Every now and then, have a "Stop the Train" moment with your kids or with a coworker. Tell them to stop and listen to what you have to say. Then tell them from the heart how much you love, appreciate, and notice them. It will be amazing.
8. I used to love the old Budweiser commercials when one guy would say to the other, "I love you, man!" Even though the commercial is old, I never tire of saying it to important people in my life. They appreciate it and get a laugh at the same time.
9. Be conscious with your Thank Yous. When at a restaurant, when a server or a bus boy clears the table, I stop, look at them, and say thank you. It is so easy to ignore the people who do everyday tasks in our everyday life. Let them know and say thank you.
10. One of my favorite things to do on the holidays is to thank service workers in our community. They work on our behalf on every holiday. When I see them, I say, "I know it was a sacrifice for you to work on this holiday. I want you to know we appreciate you." It always results in a smile, and often a hug or a tear. Try it.

CHAPTER 10
LAUGHTER

"[Humanity] has unquestionably one really effective weapon—laughter. Power, money, persuasion, supplication, persecution—these can lift a colossal humbug—push it a little—weaken it a little, century by century, but only laughter can blow it to rags and atoms at a blast. Against the assault of laughter, nothing can stand."

— MARK TWAIN

If you've ever been to Tucson, perhaps you've heard of the Bashful Bandit bar. It is the prototypical "biker bar hangout." The tagline on its website is: Bikers Wanted, Everyone Welcome. Over the years, the Bashful Bandit has been home to many brawls, experienced a few murders in the parking lot, and held a prominent place in the news from time to time. With motorcycles lined up out front and no windows, it can seem foreboding from the outside. In my fifty years of living in Tucson, I had driven past the infamous bar a thousand times but never once set foot inside. It was a bit intimidating to me. It's clearly not the kind of place you'd expect a bunch of college academics to hang out and have a drink.

The UA College of Science, on the other hand, is a place of prestige, filled with scientists at the top of their field. Going to a bar, any bar in fact, is not high on the list of things to do for scientists. Let's just say stepping outside the box and having some fun is not the norm for the typical science personality. One year, we decided to spice up the College of Science administration office and arrange for a monthly "staff happy hour" at local pubs around town. When discussing this with some of our staff, we kicked around several popular places in Tucson.

I recalled I had recently seen a social media post of the "top dive bars in Tucson, Arizona." There you go! We had our pool of happy hour locales for the College of Science administration! We even took it to the extreme by creating a "College of Science Dive Bar Tour" punch card!

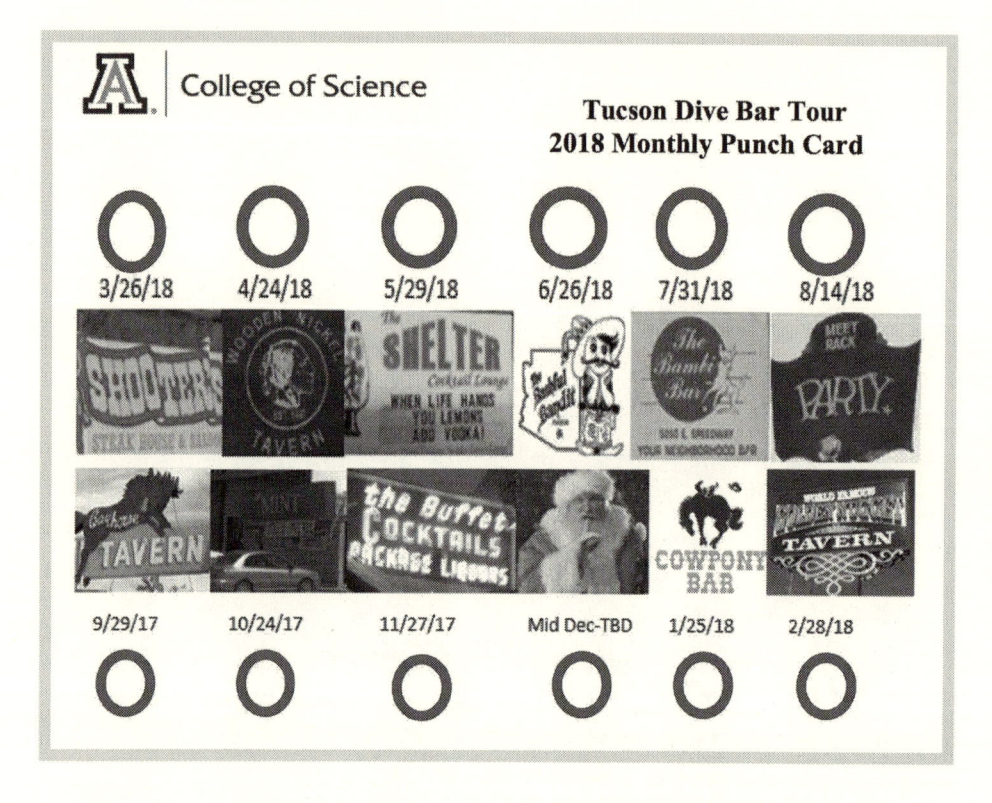

[College of Science Tucson Dive Bar Tour 2018 Monthly Punch Card with dates: 3/26/18, 4/24/18, 5/29/18, 6/26/18, 7/31/18, 8/14/18, 9/29/17, 10/24/17, 11/27/17, Mid Dec-TBD, 1/25/18, 2/28/18]

You can imagine the College of Science academics hanging out with bikers at the Bashful Bandit. It was hysterical. Talk about opposites. Not only did we bond as a group, but we also had a ton of fun visiting these dive bars that few of us would have otherwise entered. These places were from the dregs of Tucson's past, from the John F. Kennedy memorabilia covering walls of The Shelter, to the plethora of scary food choices at The Buffet (open at 6 a.m. and famous for its pickled eggs). From the Bay Horse Tavern with its "big chair" photo op to places with catchy names like The Mint and The Bambi, we had some unique experiences, and we laughed a lot! The local neighborhood folks typically frequent most of these establishments, so when 8-10 strange people walk in as a group, people pay attention. The entire crowd at the bar would invariably turn around and gape at us like we were aliens invading their space. Going as a group to a place that was outside our comfort zone was so much fun.

Here is the point—life can feel so severe and challenging day-to-day that it can be easy to overlook what really makes life great—having fun, playing around, and having a good laugh. I always include some fun and silly activities in my motivational talks to break the ice and help audience members venture outside of their comfort zones. All too often, we sit back for a speaker and expect to be talked to and educated. However, I like to engage with my audiences and include them as much as possible. Connecting with them and having them communicate with one another makes any lecture that much more fun. It can transform what might otherwise be an informative, but perhaps a bit dry and dull, experience into a fun-filled time with some insights and knowledge takeaways to boot.

Laughter not only helps us through some tough times, but many research studies are proving its benefits. We have all heard the phrase "Laughter is the best medicine." That statement has been proven true through much peer-reviewed scientific research. Laughter has a positive impact on our physical health and mental well-being, as well as enhancing our relationships. Additionally, humor has been shown to improve job performance, and laughter has been proven to reduce pain. Stress is the number-one issue affecting the US population, both personally and professionally. Laughter can cut tension like a knife. Introducing more lightheartedness into the workplace will lead to more creativity and even increased productivity. Look at the workplaces of Apple Computer, Google, and other high-tech companies over the past twenty years. These innovative companies include open workspaces with pool and ping-pong tables and more creative, fun spaces. This simple policy encourages employees to gather and interface with one another during non-work times. These companies have found that employees often find solutions to workplace problems and issues by virtue of them spending time with each other socially.

Laughter and Humor from a Medical Perspective

Maybe you are second-guessing me regarding the importance of laughter and humor in your life. Maybe you don't have much of a sense of humor, are an introvert, or just tend to take life more seriously than others. Let's take a brief look at what the scientific research says about how laughter can positively affect the human body. It is quite startling. Consider the following impacts laughter and humor can physically have on you.[34] It may make you look at laughing in a different light!

- **Increases the amount of HDL cholesterol** (the good kind).
- **Reduces catecholamines and inflammatory cytokines**—These are known to have a harmful effect on the cardiovascular system and are especially dangerous to diabetes patients.
- **Improves the inner lining of the arteries**—Multiple studies have shown that stress and negative emotions cause the interior of the arteries to constrict. Humor and laughter expand the arteries and improves blood flow.
- **Reduces pain**—Multiple studies have shown laughter and humor causes a direct reduction of pain. While it has not been determined exactly why this happens, many researchers attribute it to the release of endorphins into the body when one laughs.
- **Laughter improves your pulmonary health**—The act of laughing triggers coughing and clears mucus from the lungs. Laughter also removes carbon dioxide and replaces it with oxygen-rich air to your lungs.
- **Laughter and humor strengthen your immune system**—One study focused on immunoglobulin A (IgA). IgA resides in the mucosal areas of the body and protects you against upper respiratory infections like the flu. Studies have shown that watching comedies and engaging in laughter increases the level of IgA in the body.
- **Reduces stress**—George Vaillant, in his book *Adaptation to Life*, reported that humor was an effective coping mechanism used by many professionals under stress.
- **Improves your heart health**—Many studies have shown that tension, anger, and anxiety have a negative impact on the heart long-term. Laughter and humor reduce the risk of coronary heart disease and hypertension.

Let's review here so we are all on the same page. Laughter and humor improve your heart, lowers your blood pressure, reduces stress, increases HDL cholesterol and reduces pain. And all of these facts are confirmed in peer reviewed scientific studies. Convinced yet? Now, it may be time to take a break from the book and watch some cat videos on YouTube? I think so, you will be better off if you do.

LAUGHTER AT WORK

Surveys conducted as far back as the 1980s have shown the importance of having a sense of humor in the hiring process. One specific study discovered more than 80 percent of vice presidents in major corporations believed employees with a sense of humor were more productive. The surveys summarized that these employees were more creative, less rigid, and more open to new ideas and approaches. Another survey of 700 plus CEOs found that 98 percent would be more likely to hire someone with a good sense of humor than a similarly talented candidate lacking in that area.[35] Even some famous Greek philosophers had an opinion about the importance of humor. Aristotle went so far as to categorize a sense of humor as a moral virtue.

Former Southwest Airlines CEO Herb Kelleher famously demonstrated this when he said, "What we are looking for first and foremost is a sense of humor. We don't care much about education and expertise because we can train people. We hire for attitudes." If you've ever flown Southwest, you've probably experienced their unique brand of humor yourself. Their pre-flight safety talks are famous among passengers. Many can be found on YouTube for your entertainment, even if you don't fly.

Here are a couple of great examples:

Funny Southwest Airlines Flight Attendent #1 (1:57 mins)
https://BobLogan.net/FlightAttendant1

Funny Southwest Airlines Flight Attentent #2 (5:03 mins)
https://BobLogan.net/FlightAttendant2

WORK VS. PRISON

IN PRISON, you spend the majority of your time in an 8x10 cell.
AT WORK, you spend the majority of your time in a 6x8 cubicle.

IN PRISON, you get three meals a day.
AT WORK, you only get a break for one meal, and you pay for it.

IN PRISON, you get time off for good behavior.
AT WORK, you get more work for good behavior.

IN PRISON, the guard locks and unlocks all the doors for you.
AT WORK, you must carry around a security card and open all the doors for yourself.

IN PRISON, you can watch TV and play games.
AT WORK, you get fired for watching TV and playing games.

Dr. Robert Provine, described as the world's leading scientific expert on laughter, drew upon ten years of research for his book *Laughter*. Some of his findings showed that laughter is thirty times more likely in social settings than individual situations. Further, most laughter doesn't come from jokes or comments designed to be funny, but from casual observations or statements from those around us.[36] Understanding that, hanging out with friends or colleagues in any setting, from the copy room to a dive bar, can lead to many good laughs and make life and work more fun.

Laughter is also contagious, which is why we are more likely to laugh when we are with others. Something that might not ordinarily be funny can release guffaws under certain circumstances and in the right crowd. When was the last time you hung out with a group over a shared experience like watching the game, a book club, game night, dinner party, or happy hour? When we have so much technology in our homes, from cable television and streaming movies to iPads and high-speed internet, this constant digital existence may impact our desire to venture outside and meet with other people. Call some friends and go out to dinner or for a drink—the research shows you will be a better person for it!

THE IMPACT OF MEDIA—SOCIAL AND OTHERWISE

Today, many of our "connections" come not from face-to-face interactions but from various social media platforms. Social media has the benefit of quickly finding and staying in touch with people we may not have communicated with for many years. However, studies have continuously shown increased levels of depression because of the lack of human interaction. Social media also has significant downsides; it has led to decreased employee productivity[37] and increased political polarization.[38] While Facebook and other social media channels might be a good escape in small doses, they can also be addictive.

We all know people who can scarcely go a few minutes without going back to get some screen time. The next time you are at a restaurant for dinner, or hanging out at a bar with a friend, take a conscious moment to look around you. Take note of how many people are buried in their iPhones, checking out social media, email, etc. It is amazing how we cannot break away from our phones. The allure of the audible text "ding" for the connected social media user is as powerful as the "next drink" for the alcoholic at the bar. Both individuals are addicted to their specific vices, social media, and alcohol, and both cannot control their respective urges, no matter how hard they try.

In the enlightening Netflix documentary *Social Dilemma*, key high-level executives from social media platforms like Facebook, Google, Instagram, etc. all outline how these platforms design algorithms to "addict" their users. They then use that addiction to sell your information to marketers so they can pinpoint their advertising directly at you. Jeff Seibert, former Twitter executive, said it best in the movie:

"What I want people to know is everything they are doing online is being watched, is being tracked, is being measured. Every single action you take is carefully monitored and recorded. Exactly what image you stop and look at, and for how long you look at it. They know when people are lonely, when people are depressed, whether you are an introvert or an extrovert. They have more information about us than has ever been imagined in human history. It is unprecedented." [39]

Countless studies show the downside of social media, including the loss of our authentic selves.[40] We tend to share only what makes us look good. The flip side is the belief that our lives are far more interesting than they are in reality. We find ourselves checking to see how many "likes" or "comments" our social media posts create. We look for validation not from face-to-face encounters but from more engagement through our digital profiles. The envy that ensues from looking at other peoples' fabulous vacations, new cars, or gala events online can impact our mental state. It is far too easy to fall into the trap of feeling as if our own lives don't measure up to our friends'. As we all know, most people only post the "best" aspects of their lives, not the various issues and problems we all deal with today. Social media creates an image of people that does not present the full picture. Take all of this with a grain of salt and take a hard look at your own social media world and how you interact with it. You may want to consider some changes yourself.

The addictive nature of social media rose to the national stage in 2021 when Facebook data scientist Frances Haugen became a whistleblower and shined the light directly on Mark Zuckerberg and Facebook. When her allegations were released, along with tens of thousands of pages of internal Facebook documents, many initially questioned her legitimacy to take this stance. However, Haugen has a degree in computer science and a Harvard business degree. In addition to Facebook, she spent fifteen years working at Google and Pinterest. There is no doubt about her credibility.

What she said was shocking. The misinformation coming from Facebook and other platforms is palpable. In one interview, Haugen said:

"When we live in an information environment that is full of angry, hateful, polarizing content, it erodes our civic trust, it erodes our faith in each other, it erodes our ability to want to care for each other, the version

of Facebook that exists today (2021) is tearing our societies apart and causing ethnic violence around the world." [41]

I encourage you to spend some time to read her allegations and testimony in front of Congress. It will give you pause and cause you to take a hard look at how you might interact with social media going forward.

Frances Haugen's 60 Minutes Interview (13:36 mins)
https://boblogan.net/Haugen60MinsInterview

The twenty-four-hour news cycle doesn't lend itself to peace of mind either. This steady onslaught of constant news is troubling, and it can make us feel as though everything in our world or our local community is a crisis. This news cycle ends up leaving us unsettled about our sense of place and where we live. Studies have shown that people who watch more television today think the world is a much more dangerous place than it truly is.[42] Conversely, other studies have shown that today is the safest time to be alive in all of human history. There is less violence, longer lifespans, less disease (and more cures for what we do get), and better food access than ever before. What is happening here?

The difference is, today we have more access to news from around the world than ever before. And this news is coming at us from multiple directions constantly, so we immediately hear about every bad thing that happens anywhere in the world on any given day. To compound this situation, we now must deal with politics when watching the news. For some fun, watch Fox News and CNN on the same night and see how they report on the same topic/issue. It is eye-opening to see the obvious right and left slant these "news" organizations apply to their reporting. It is almost comical to watch how extreme each of these channels is each night. It is more a form of political entertainment than learning about the hard news of the day. This 24-7 information pipeline can cause us to feel depressed, overwhelmed, and scared.

With so many news sources to choose from, very few people read a daily printed newspaper anymore. Even my son, Sean, who worked several years for the *Arizona Republic* newspaper in Phoenix, one of the largest dailies in the United States, didn't read his own newspaper in its printed version. Young people have been criticized for only ingesting humorous online news sources such as *The Daily Show*, *The Onion*, or Steven Colbert and other news/comedian programs. I'm in favor of anything that makes us laugh, so perhaps laughing while being informed is okay. Too many of us have fallen into only agreeing with our own specific, homogenized way of thinking, and that can be detrimental. All the polarizing political arguments impact our ability to relate to each other and be persuaded by another viewpoint.

Here in the United States, we also have a limited understanding of the rest of the world. While many countries consume our media and know quite a bit about us, we often know very little about the rest of the world. My older son, Tommy, studied abroad twice, once in New Zealand and later in Italy. On both occasions, upon returning to the United States, he lamented how little Americans know about United States history and/or world history. He was often surprised by foreigners' high level of knowledge, interests, and insights about his own country's history and political system. They sometimes taught him things about his home country!

Why in this chapter about laughter have I diverted to such a degree into the media space? Because it is the primary influencer of how we see our world, our place in it, and our relationships with others. Everything in the press is hyped to the nth degree, and it can cause us to take ourselves too seriously. What is the antidote to that? Read on.

PLAY AND FUN

When I worked in the athletic department in the 1990s, one of my tasks was to oversee the annual intercollegiate athletics United Way campaign for the University of Arizona. Since athletics was one of the largest units on campus, this campaign leadership role came with a responsibility and high expectations for success. Our athletics' United Way effort would be compared to units all over the UA campus, so I wanted the campaign to be successful. Since athletics is a competitive enterprise in its own right, I did everything in my power to have an active campaign and gain campus-wide recognition.

My job as campaign chair was to motivate our 150-person athletics staff members to each make a United Way contribution. In years past, this typically came with quite a bit of arm-twisting, begging, and cajoling. Most employees groaned each year when the topic of the annual United Way campaign came up. Nobody likes to talk about fundraising. In previous years, organizers just passed out the donation forms at a staff meeting. That was it. You waited and hoped for the best. This methodology usually resulted in very low participation numbers and below-average fundraising results.

I decided to take a different approach. I enlisted some of our prominent (and top-rated) coaches to help me, and I convinced them to all dress up as a ridiculous Elvis impersonator band. We all had wigs complete with outrageous costumes and inflatable guitar and saxophone instruments. We performed a short karaoke "air guitar" concert and taped it to show later at one of our monthly all-staff meetings.

At the next all-staff meeting, the room was filled with nearly 150 athletics employees. The room included basketball coach Lute Olson, baseball coach Jerry Kindall, and every one of our men's and women's coaches. We introduced this year's United Way campaign. We passed out the requisite forms, and throughout the room, you could hear the typical groans. Next, we brought down the lights and cued up the Elvis video. People were wondering what was happening. This short, funny skit and video would be the extent of our plea for participation in the fundraising drive for that year's campaign.

The video starred some of our prominent coaches and senior staff leadership, including Rocky LaRose, swimming coach Frank Busch, and other visible and popular administrative staff members. The athletic department staff had never seen anything like it before! Although the video and air band performance made little mention of United Way or about donating, the entire athletic department roared with laughter. As you can imagine, because our United Way ask was fun, and some highly respected coaches and administrators weren't afraid to make fools of ourselves for a good cause, it received rave reviews. The response rate for donations went through the roof, and our athletics department won Best United Way Campaign for the entire UA campus. Again, don't be scared to step out of your comfort zone and have some fun. No one gets hurt in the process (apart from a bruised ego), and the upside is often huge.

Taking this concept a step further, when was the last time you joked around with the bank teller or the cashier at the grocery store? We have these daily interactions with people all the time, and we do the same thing all the time. How about having some fun every now and then with these typically boring daily interactions?

What can you do to make meetings more fun in the workplace? They don't have to be dry and dull. Lighten it up a bit, even if it's just for a moment. Laughter Scientist Paul McGhee suggested twenty-five ideas for building fun into your work setting. Here are a few of them:

1. Establish a fun committee.
2. Encourage spontaneity.
3. Create a humor bulletin board, breakroom, or tension release room.
4. Have a dress-up day.
5. Share photos of employees as children.

You get the idea. Come up with some fun things of your own and be creative. I know of one office that purchased a margarita machine for the end of the day happy hour or when employees met a sales goal. Cotton candy or a popcorn machine would be fun too.

I know someone who received small wind-up toys and spinners for her office when she got her first full-time job. Her mentor, who gifted the items, told her that working in higher education, students would frequently stop by to play with them. They didn't always have a pressing need and were sometimes just killing time between classes. Having toys on hand to distract them would allow her to get some work done while hanging out. She loved having students drop by and having a toy box kept them entertained!

This person reminded me of the Steve Hartman "On the Road" segment I introduced back in Chapter 5 on Grief.[43] If you recall, this little boy, Jaden, who had just lost both his parents now only had one goal in life to bring smiles to people's faces.

This video is always the first story I share in all my happiness talks. This straightforward but incredibly moving story puts life into perspective. While we think we have serious problems, here comes a six-year-old boy trying to make *other* people smile after losing both of his parents. Truly humbling.

So many ways exist to bring lightheartedness to even the worst of circumstances. One of my favorite actors and comedians of all time is Robin Williams. In 1998, he played Patch Adams, the real-life doctor who often wore giant clown shoes and a huge red clown nose during rounds on the hospital's pediatric floor. Nothing is more depressing than a sick child. But no matter how sick a child might be, Dr. Patch Adams could always bring a smile to their and their parents' faces. Patch Adams not only had an excellent bed-side manner; his methods brought about healing as well.[44]

A CAMINO STORY—THE CAMINO DE SANTIAGO AND LAUGHTER

You laugh every day on the Camino. However, laughter is not too frequent at the beginning of the day, waking up in a crowded albergue. And a pilgrim is not usually laughing very much during the intense and challenging 15-20-mile daily walks in all kinds of weather conditions. But at the end of the day, everything changes. Once the pain of the day has subsided, blisters have been tended to, and your clothes are all washed and hung out to dry, it is time to compare notes with your fellow pilgrims. Belly-busting laughter about the daily encounters and experiences on the Camino with friends, often over a glass of wine or dinner, were regular occurrences nearly every night.

Laughing at the end of the day with fellow pilgrims is the motivation to get up and do it all over again the following day. It goes back to the initial concept of the value of being uncomfortable that I mentioned before. After a strenuous day—physically, emotionally, and mentally—people's simple pleasure in being with one another is appreciated even more. Wine, good company, and a bed (even one that may not be that comfortable) are the best.

One night, we were staying in Ponferrada, a medium-sized Spanish city. It was famous for the massive Knights Templar castle from the 1200s right in the center of downtown. That evening, we asked the hotel front desk clerk for a restaurant and dinner recommendation. The clerk replied by asking if we planned to watch the soccer game. I was totally clueless, and I think he could tell by the look on my face. I had no idea what soccer game he was talking about, and since I am not a soccer fan anyway, I said no.

We had no idea we happened to be in town the evening of the European Championship, basically the "Super Bowl" of soccer. Real Madrid was playing Liverpool, which was a huge deal for the locals—and to the entire country of Spain. It began to dawn on us how big a deal this was as we heard cheers and shouts emanating from pubs and restaurants all over town. Once we arrived at our restaurant, it was clear our waiter was also pre-occupied with the soccer match. The funniest moment was when he was taking our order. He was reciting all the dinner specials when, suddenly, a huge cheer went up; someone had scored. Boom, he was gone! Our waiter heard the roar and ran away mid-sentence to check on what had happened. That specific goal was an incredible bicycle kick that was on the front page of the morning papers the next day.

It was a memorable dinner, and to experience first-hand Spain's passion and love for soccer was a real treat. Real Madrid ultimately won the European championship, making every Spaniard we met for the next few days extremely happy. The next morning, we saw the result of the many celebrations (pizza boxes, empty beer and liquor bottles, etc.) littering the streets all over town. When we walked to the train station the next day, we spotted two guys passed out at their small table on the train platform. The table and immediate area were littered with empty beer bottles and remnants of food. Obviously, they'd had a great time celebrating the Real Madrid victory the previous night.

After a long day of walking on the Camino, I would often have a funny experience when I arrived at a nearly full albergue for the night. Whenever a pilgrim arrives late in the afternoon, most of the desirable bottom bunks are already taken and only top bunks are available. The clerk would look me up and down, assessing my hefty 260-pound frame, and take stock of the risk of having me sleep in one of the top bunks that remained in the albergue. He would slowly walk me around, and then politely find and ask someone in Spanish who had already secured a bottom bunk if they wouldn't mind taking the top one instead. I never said a word, but by the looks on their faces, I could tell they did not want to fear me climbing up and possibly crashing down upon them during the night. Of course, they didn't say so in front of me, but I could tell what they were thinking and found it amusing. Who knew there were advantages to being a big guy? It meant I consistently scored a bottom bunk.

I also had many encounters with interesting people, some of whom had humorous personalities or amusing stories to tell. I'll never forget the afternoon Judy and I met three guys in a nearly empty restaurant in the quaint little town of Molinaseca. The bar/restaurant was void of diners except for us and these three guys up at the bar. They were laughing and it was evident they had been there for quite a while. When I went up to order another beer, I could tell they were from England or Scotland since they were all speaking English.

These guys were unbelievable, and their backgrounds were unconventional, to say the least. They were refreshingly open about their interesting lifestyle choices. The first man was a seventy-year-old admitted alcoholic. The second one told me with no hesitation that he sold drugs to make ends meet. The third man was a street musician who played guitar for donations.

These guys couldn't have been more different from Judy and me with our classic American life, kids, 401Ks, full-time jobs, health insurance, and all. But we spent hours hanging out with them and hearing their crazy stories. It was a fantastic and hysterical evening. You never know whom you will meet on the Camino, and their lives may be completely different from yours.

These motley characters live their lives to the fullest and don't care about being judged by others. They just happen to live their lives much differently than we do. They have no responsibilities; they live life day to day and are happier for it.

Who are we to say whether our way of life or theirs is the correct way? They are every bit as happy as we are. The takeaway is not to judge others. We are all humans living on this earth—how you live is up to you. Whatever you choose, I recommend following Ralph Waldo Emerson's definition of success:

> *"To laugh often and much; to win the respect of the intelligent people and the affection of children; to earn the appreciation of honest critics and endure the betrayal of false friends; to appreciate beauty; to find the beauty in others; to leave the world a bit better whether by a healthy child, a garden patch, or a redeemed social condition; to know that one life has breathed easier because you lived here. This is to have succeeded."*

Reminders About Laughter

1. A sense of humor can serve you well in almost all areas of life.
2. Don't take yourself too seriously.
3. Life shouldn't always feel like a grind. It's okay—in fact, mandatory—to have fun and laugh as often as you can.
4. Life is less fulfilling in general without some joking around and laughter.
5. Smile more.
6. Laugh more.
7. Don't worry about the judgment of others. Do what you feel is best for you.
8. Find opportunities throughout your day to laugh with someone.
9. If you find something funny on the internet or on YouTube, be sure to share it with someone you know. Try to get other people to laugh. Try not to go into hysterics watching the video below on helium-infused beer from Germany (it is impossible to not laugh, trust me.)
10. Look forward to April Fool's Day. Promise yourself to come up with a fantastic and fun way to spoof someone! (BTW, the video below about the helium beer was an April Fool's joke, believe it or not!)

Hellium Beer (4:05 mins)
https://boblogan.net/HeliumBeerHysterical

PART III
REDISCOVERY

CHAPTER 11
HAPPINESS

"Happiness does not depend upon accumulating more things, but the mindset we have concerning the things we already do possess."
— FULTON SHEEN, FINDING TRUE HAPPINESS

What does the typical human crave? More than anything, being happy. Being happy in our relationships, happy at our workplace, and happy with our general outlook on life. Happiness is what we all strive to achieve and hold onto for as long as possible. When I speak with clients about speaking opportunities, my keynote on happiness is by far the most requested topic. Working in the College of Science, I have spent many years researching myriad aspects of happiness and how it affects our lives. You would think the research on acquiring happiness would be straightforward, but I have discovered that happiness is an inside job.

Most people think happiness results from external circumstances (a new job promotion), material possessions (a new car or home), or even good health. While these things definitely influence our comfort level for the short term, surprisingly, they do not determine our level of happiness in the long term.

If happiness is not dependent upon your winning the lottery, having the perfect partner, driving a fancy luxury car, or even working in an attractive and well-paying job, what are the formal requirements to become a happier person? It is not nearly as complicated as we try to make it. Happiness is entirely about how you relate to the life you are already living. That's it, really. It is quite simple.

Jealousy, frustration, fear, doubt, comparison, greed, revenge-seeking, judgment, and a host of other emotions will obviously detract from our level of happiness. Conversely, other behaviors, beliefs, and practices also contribute to our happiness. Lessening the former and increasing the latter is all that is required to be happy.

It sounds simple, and it is, but that doesn't mean it's easy to achieve in any way, shape, or form. Over many years of living, we naturally develop particular ways of thinking about our world and the people in it. The longer you are alive, the more firmly ingrained these patterns may be. They won't even appear as patterns. It is just the way the world is. Stephen Covey said, "We see the world not the way it is, but the way we are."

We tend to look at the effect of our thoughts on the world around us, but what about the effect of our own thoughts on ourselves? As we have already learned, latest science shows that we can literally change our brains' neural pathways purely by changing the way we think. Believe it or not, our minds are not hardwired, and we are not predetermined to remain on a fixed track. If ever a phrase was true, it is: We control our own destiny.

This ability to change our brains' neural pathways is called brain plasticity or elasticity. It allows people, with considerable training and rehabilitation, to "remap" their brains. For example, in the UA College of Science, I was able to sit in on some of the amazing research being done with aphasia patients in the Department of Speech, Language, and Hearing. Aphasia is the by-product of stroke or brain injury when a patient or victim loses the ability to communicate. Depending on the severity of the brain damage from a stroke or brain injury, one can transition the speaking portion of the brain to the opposite side. The brain will simply rewire itself to make this happen. To see this in action is truly humbling. If stroke patients dealing with significant communication loss can make their brain learn how to speak again, then it should be easy for each of us to remap our brains to bring happiness into our lives. We just need to be proactive and change *how* we think about our lives and our personal circumstances.

WHAT EXACTLY IS HAPPINESS?

Before we go any further, what exactly is happiness? How is it defined? According to economist Richard Layard, what brings enjoyment or peace of mind may mean different things to different people; happiness in its simplest terms means feeling good, enjoying life, and wanting that feeling to be maintained.[45] Various philosophers have made many other observations over time on the study of happiness. Montaigne and Spinoza define happiness as optimism. Epicurus links it to pleasure. Pascal ascribes it to faith, and Nietzsche to power. From a scientific viewpoint and shown through medical imaging, happiness is a specific, measurable state of activity in different areas of the brain. What makes your brain light up, and how can you get it to occur more often? That is your quest, for you and you alone to discover.

HAPPINESS IS A HABIT

Earlier in Chapter 8 on Change, we discussed the Northwestern study and Dan Gilbert's Harvard research showing the leveling effect on people who won the lottery versus those who became quadriplegics through some type of tragic accident. How is it possible that a paraplegic and a lottery winner could have the same level of happiness? The truth is the impact of something extraordinary happening in our lives (winning the lottery) or experiencing a terrible accident (becoming a paraplegic) doesn't stay with us for very long. Over time, the happy moments and depressing times tend to even out and we ultimately return to the baseline of our personalities. These countless small, seemingly insignificant thoughts and actions have a far more significant impact on our everyday happiness. The little things matter in the long term.[46]

THE DISASTER OF AIR NEW ZEALAND FLIGHT 901— NOVEMBER 1979

The story of Air New Zealand Flight 901 illustrates this perfectly. Because of New Zealand's proximity to the Antarctic, in 1979 Air New Zealand airline created widely popular and innovative sightseeing tours to Antarctica. The flights departed from Auckland and flew for more than eleven hours on a 5,500-mile round trip to Antarctica. Once they arrived in Antarctica, they descended very low (1,500 feet) over Antarctica's continent so passengers could see the ice-bound landscape from the plane's warmth and comfort.[47]

The plane was filled with scientists, naturalists, and other experts to interpret the landscape below them. Passengers took stunning photos and could experience the rugged landscape without so much as donning a light jacket! All in the span of one day. As you can imagine, these tourist flights were very popular, and the first two November flights sold out.

On the third tour, on November 28, 1979, Flight 901 departed as usual, but without knowing it, and without any malice, someone in the organization had accidentally changed the flight coordinates in the computer autopilot program by three degrees. Like all extremely long-haul flights, once the plane reaches cruising altitude, the pilot puts the plane into autopilot and the computer takes over flying the plane for the flight's duration. Although the autopilot was flying the correct flight plan from the computer, the entire route was flying off course by three degrees. To the innocent observer, three degrees doesn't sound like much, does it? But in this case, over the course of 5,500 miles, this small three-degree mistake put the aircraft nearly thirty-five miles off-course by the time they arrived at Antarctica.

On this day, being thirty-five miles off course put Flight 901 on a direct path toward the largest geographical feature on all of Antarctica—a 13,000-foot-tall active volcano called Mt. Erebus. The pilots were flying on autopilot like they usually do on this flight. As they descended lower and lower, they experienced an optical illusion called "sector whiteout."

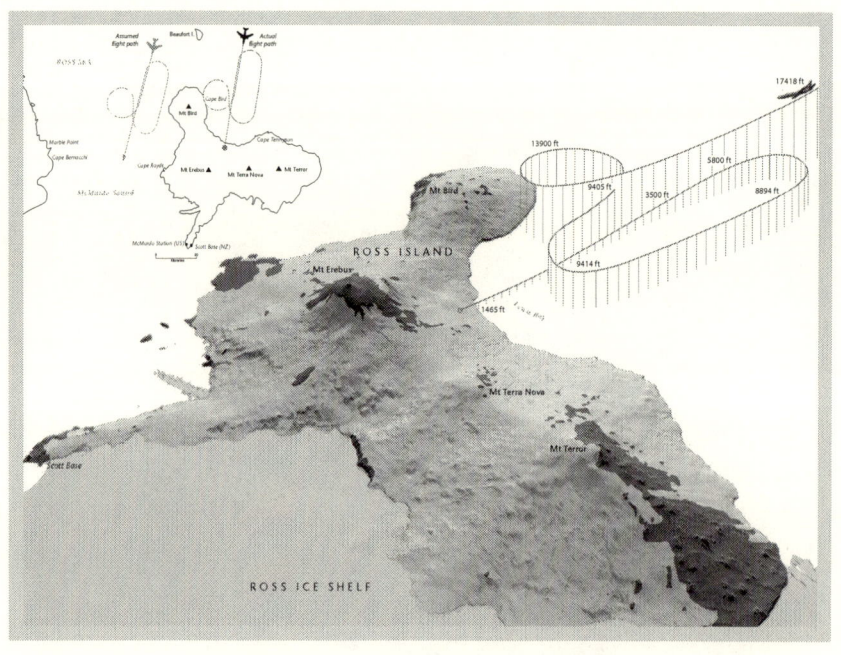

GRAPHIC COURTESY OF NEW ZEALAND GEOGRAPHIC

Sector whiteout is when the snow-covered Mt. Erebus, combined with the white, wispy clouds around them and the white of the icy landmass below, essentially make Mt. Erebus "disappear" from the pilots' view from the cockpit. The pilots had expected to fly thirty-five miles to the east, which would have been a flat landmass below them. When the sector whiteout condition occurred, that was the exact image provided to the pilots. They thought everything was normal. However, when the alarms began to sound in the cockpit, they erroneously assumed there must be a malfunction with the alarm system. In what is still the worst air tragedy in New Zealand aviation history, the low-flying plane in whiteout conditions smashed into the base of Mount Erebus, killing all 257 people on board.

This might not be the kind of story you would expect in a chapter on happiness, but it illustrates an important point. Is your life on autopilot? What is your destination, and how do you plan to get there? Are you off-course for happiness? What would it take to steer you back in the direction you really want to go? Believe it or not, the little things matter. In this case, a three-degree mistake resulted in a tragic accident killing 257 people. But if you truly desire change, you must learn to pay attention to the little things in your life. And when you hear the alarms go off in your head, you must step back and think about what you need to do to turn off those alarms.

Many of us fantasize about quitting our jobs, moving to a different city, leaving a relationship, or starting a new one. We automatically think these drastic changes will bring us happiness and satisfaction. As in the case of Flight 901, small things, if left uncorrected, almost always become big problems. If there is one takeaway from the story of Flight 901, it is that the little things matter. They always matter.

In reality, the small, simple, and secure course corrections in our lives will likely have a longer-lasting impact on our sense of well-being. Drastic changes like winning the lottery or becoming a paraplegic will ultimately level out.

During my extensive research on happiness, I discovered more than 17,000 peer-reviewed articles had been published on this topic. I could not believe it! Coming from a university college of science, with programs like astronomy, geosciences, and chemistry, I was quite familiar with high-level peer-reviewed research. There is even a *Journal of Happiness Studies* bearing the subtitle: An Interdisciplinary Forum on Subjective Well-Being. The University of California-Berkeley has The Greater Good Science Center, which focuses on happiness and living a more meaningful life. If the scientific community has dedicated this amount of effort on happiness, there must be something to it.

Certain traits and techniques came up repeatedly during this happiness research. What was most surprising was how simple the techniques were that would bring happiness. We all know them, and they are all "little things." Like I said before, the little things matter.

Let me emphasize—the following techniques below are all scientifically proven to improve your happiness level if practiced regularly. Don't feel like you have to do them all or even do them every day, but when you regularly include some of these in your life, you will feel happier. Guaranteed!

HAPPINESS TECHNIQUE #1—SMILE MORE

Research has shown it is physiologically impossible to think negative thoughts while smiling or laughing (try it now and see), and laughter is contagious. In fact, laughter yoga is a popular new form of yoga. It involves clapping, yogic breathing, and then just laughing. There are no jokes or funny stories told; someone just starts laughing, and it becomes contagious. Even watching videos of this practice can make you smile. This practice has been shown to reduce stress while creating fun for participants.

Perhaps you've heard that it takes more muscles anatomically to frown than to smile? This is true. Smiling is more natural and our typical default. I play a little game with myself by smiling at people on the street to see if I can get them to smile back. Perhaps you have experienced the opposite. You're walking along in a bad mood when you see a child do something silly or someone you pass smiles at you, and suddenly, your spirits lift and your mouth breaks into a grin. Smiling is a good thing—try it more often.

HAPPINESS TECHNIQUE #2—VOLUNTEER, SERVE, HELP— GIVE YOUR TIME, TALENT, AND TREASURE

The state of the world can get us down from time to time. Studies have shown that people who watch significant hours of television each week think the world is a lot scarier than it actually is.[48] When immersed in the 24-7 news cycle, it can help our individual state of mind to step back from this onslaught of negativity and reach out to be helpful to others. People often talk about genuinely "selfless acts" being performed by others. In reality, it is impossible to do something genuinely "selfless" because it always makes you feel good when you serve others. The donor of the act also receives a benefit. Our brains contain oxytocin, commonly called the "feel good" chemical. When someone helps others or is the recipient of good deeds, both parties get a jolt of oxytocin. Sharing our time, talent, and treasures are what life is all about. John Southard put it this way, "The only people you should ever get even with are those who have helped you."

HAPPINESS TECHNIQUE #3 — NATURE IS GOOD FOR YOU

Several studies show the multitude of benefits from being outside in nature.[49] Just living in an area with green grass and trees contributes to the safety and well-being of residents. Walking barefoot in the grass helps you feel more grounded. Ever look through a telescope at the stars or find shapes in clouds? Numerous organizations are encouraging us to look at the sky, including former astronaut Mae Jemison who recently launched *Look Up*, and Jack Borden who founded the non-profit *For Spacious Skies* to get us to notice our surroundings, including those above us. One fantastic website I stumbled across is Nature-Rx.org. It has a number of spoof commercials about the importance of nature in one's life, and it took a while before I realized they were pulling my leg. Take a look:

Nature-Rx Spoof #1 (1:32mins)
https://BobLogan.net/NatureRXSpoof1

Nature-Rx Spoof #2 (1:37 mins)
https://BobLogan.net/NatureRXSpoof2

One Stanford study showed that simply walking in nature reduces your risk of depression.[50] Others have demonstrated the multiple benefits of exercise, from lowered anxiety and depression to decreased appetite. It's so easy to go take a walk. Anyone can do it, anytime, from anywhere. We are often so stuck in our routines and chained to our desks that forming a habit with this one is crucial. It helps to have a goal. Consider signing up for a race, joining a Meetup, creating your own group to walk with, or train for the Camino. Having a reason provides a great deal of motivation and exercising with others makes it more comfortable.

HAPPINESS TECHNIQUE #4—TRAVEL AND VACATION EXPERIENTIALLY

There is a difference between spending a week somewhere, laying out on the beach basking in the sun, and making your trips meaningful and memorable. Not that there is anything wrong with laying in the sun with a book all day, but travel can be much more rewarding when it gets us out of our comfort zone, makes us think more, and includes contact with local people, projects, and history.

I'm obviously biased toward the Camino de Santiago, but there are many ways to create unique travel experiences. You may not have the budget to fly to another continent or sign up for an expensive cycling tour, but even a weekend road or train trip can offer up something fresh. Have you ever considered the RV life? RVs can cost hundreds of thousands of dollars, but websites like rvshare.com and outdoorsy.com are dedicated to owners of RVs who will rent them at a daily rate.

Ever thought about visiting the setting of your favorite book or movie? My wife and I spent a week this past summer in Scotland. She is a *huge* fan of the television series *Outlander*. While in Scotland, she was always on the lookout for Jamie Fraser!

(You need to watch the show to understand—he is a hunk, and all the women swoon over him.) Seriously, she really enjoyed seeing the Scottish countryside where the *Outlander* books are set, and the television show is filmed.

You can participate in a work or trade experience from as short as a month to many months, working on farms or other projects worldwide. Use your vacation to volunteer in your hometown or anywhere—several organizations can connect you with "volunteer vacation" opportunities around the world and check out one of the many books about volunteer vacations.[51] Visit discovercorps.com or volunteerworld.com to better understand the possibilities. Whether planned for months or years, or totally spontaneous, in your own state or halfway around the world, these travel experiences can provide spiritual, emotional, and physical benefits for you and those you encounter along the way. They will be trips you will never forget.

HAPPINESS TECHNIQUE #5—PLAY AND BE CREATIVE

Being more creative is an essential habit for happiness. Stanford professor Bob McKim has done considerable research on happiness, play, and creativity. He uses several fun activities that were described by sociologist Tim Brown in his TED Talk, which I have used extensively to great effect with my speaking audiences.[52]

I hand out pieces of standard notepaper where the outside border looks like an expensive picture frame. I then ask audience members to pair up with someone they don't know and identify a "Partner A" and a "Partner B." I then announce which partner is going first and give them forty-five seconds to draw the very best portrait they can of their partner. After Partner A is finished, Partner B gets another forty-five seconds to draw their partner's portrait. They are told *not* to allow their partner to see their work in process.

Everyone has incredible angst when asked to do something they are not good at, and most people are not artists by nature. When the exercise is finished, I ask all participants to sit facing each other and on the count of three do the "big reveal." Simultaneously, they expose their artwork to their partner, and the room explodes into laughter, people howling with embarrassment and apologies at their poor drawing skills. It is hysterical.

However, Part II of this exercise explains that Dr. Bob McKim also does this exact same activity with kindergarten children. The responses from these kids doing the exact same task as the adults produce entirely different results. Of course, there is the same laughter and fun, but when it comes to the kindergartners "big reveal," they are incredibly proud of their artwork rather than embarrassed because they know theirs is actually a "masterpiece."

So, I ask you, what happens to us from kindergarten to adulthood? Why are kids at this age so willing to have fun and share their artistic skills with no self-consciousness about their artwork or the outcome in a way adults aren't?

The main point of this exercise is to show in vivid detail the following: as we age, we worry more about the judgment of others, and we are afraid of what other people think. These feelings clearly stifle creativity. If you have ever been involved in brainstorming sessions, especially in a computer environment, you will recall that all thoughts and ideas are given anonymously. If it were not done that way, the comment would have more or less weight given based on the power and prestige of the individual providing it. The point is to get as many ideas on the table as possible in a short amount of time and only to evaluate them afterward as a group.

In the Air Force, there is a common management technique called the "debrief." In essence, after every flight mission *everyone* in the organization, from the pilots to the maintenance crew, all sit in a room and debrief what occurred. Rank does not matter. The voice of the pilot and the lowest enlisted person are treated equally. The point is to find out what went right and what went wrong, and everyone's opinion is equally valued. Trust me; this does not happen very often in corporate boardrooms.

In the media world, an entire entertainment genre is built around pranks and practical jokes. In years past, you may recall shows like *Candid Camera*, *TV's Bloopers & Practical Jokes*, and MTV's *Punk'd*. They were top-rated in their day. Prank phone callers like the Jerky Boys spawned more recent online copy-cats, and Bart's antics on *The Simpsons* were an inspiration to many young boys. *America's Funniest Home Videos* has been on television for nearly twenty years and is still as popular as ever. People who are willing to be creative and who know how to laugh at themselves are very entertaining for the rest of us.

Happiness Technique #5—Taking Play and Creativity to the Extreme (a real-life example)

The year was 1979, and I was in my senior year of college. My friends and I were all terribly excited when we heard the Arizona Wildcats were selected to play in Tempe's Fiesta Bowl against Dan Marino and the Pittsburgh Panthers. The game was to be played on Christmas Day at 1:00 p.m. (This is a critical piece of information for this story).

Christmas Day, 1979 -- Fiesta Bowl Game Day program

My friends and I decided we would take a road trip to Tempe for the game. Before they picked me up, I made an incredulous statement to my buddies: Not only would I get into the game for free without a ticket, but I would be on the field for the halftime show. They had no idea what I was talking about! My brother lived in Pittsburgh at the time, and I had told him to be sure to watch the *entire* game. When he asked why, I told him I would be on television during the game and to absolutely not leave at halftime to make a snack. I did not give him any other details or explain how or why this would happen.

Now for a little background. After his retirement from the Air Force, my father became a real estate salesperson. He was always trying to do nice things for his clients and his Air Force friends. A few years earlier, my dad had purchased a very nice Santa Claus outfit for me. Each year he would identify 10-15 of his best clients and friends who also had small children who still believed in Santa Claus. My dad would work with the parents to get specific Christmas gifts for each of these kids. On Christmas Eve I would show up and surprise the families. These children were in total shock when Santa showed up in their living rooms! The look in their eyes when I slowly reached into my bag and pulled out a toy they had asked for on their

"Santa List" was unbelievable. Their eyes were like saucers and I am sure they all would remember their "Santa Visit" for many years to come. It was a blast to do this, and this Santa suit got a lot for many Christmases. Memories forever to be sure.

Now back to the Fiesta Bowl. That morning, when my friends picked me up for the game, I was dressed in my dad's Santa Claus outfit. Remember, this Fiesta Bowl game was played on Christmas Day. When we arrived at the stadium, my friends got in line to buy their tickets. I just walked right past them and through the turnstile like I owned the place.

The ticket agent came up, grabbed my arm, and asked what I was doing. I turned around and very casually told him, "Well, it is pretty obvious. I'm Santa Claus, it's Christmas Day, and I'm part of the halftime show." The agent stood there with his mouth agape, not knowing what to do or who to call. He then shrugged his shoulders, said "Okay," and let me go. I was in the Fiesta Bowl for free just like I said I would!

I joined my friends in the stands and watched the game until ten minutes before halftime. Then I said, "See you later; I'm going on the field for the halftime show." My buddies were roaring, and they all trained their binoculars on me to see how this would go. I worked my way down the stands, shaking hands with all the kids along the way. Finally, I found my way down to the end zone gate where the mascot and cheerleaders were gathered.

Again, I walked through the field-level gate, and again, a security guard grabbed my arm and asked me what I was doing. I casually said I was Santa Claus, it was Christmas Day, and I was part of the halftime show. He looked up and down at his clipboard. There was no Santa on the list. He said, "I'm going to have to ask you to leave." I responded very calmly, "Here is the way I look at it. You and I both agree that it is Christmas Day, and you agree that I am Santa Claus. Why my name is not on the list, I have no idea. However, what if I am right and someone else made a mistake and forgot to add me to the list? Then, when Santa doesn't show up on the field like he's supposed to, it seems to me like you will be the one in trouble, not me. So, in my mind, you have a very hard choice to make. I wouldn't want to be in your shoes right now. Do you want to be the one responsible for the disappointment of thousands of fans who are waiting to see Santa Claus on Christmas Day with their children? Your call."

The guard thought about it for a second and said, "Okay, go ahead." Now, I was just seconds from being on the field for the halftime show at the Fiesta Bowl!

The halftime show began with the Pittsburgh band. I raced up the sideline to the 50-yard line and waited for the perfect moment to run onto midfield. Near the end of the Pittsburgh band's performance, they rolled a humongous square box onto the middle of the field. I stood there and said to myself, "If there is another Santa Claus inside that box, I'm in big trouble." I waited patiently until they opened the box, sweat pouring down my brow. When they opened the box, there was no Santa Claus! Instead, thousands of balloons came pouring out and went up into the sky. This was my moment! I sprinted onto the field and waved wildly to the fans. Everyone in the stands was so happy that Santa had found time to come to the Fiesta Bowl!

Bob Logan (Santa) on field with Wilbur the Wildcat at 1979 Fiesta Bowl

I then rejoined my friends in the stands, who were howling with laughter for the rest of the game. They could not believe what they had just witnessed. The next day, I called my brother in Pittsburgh to make sure he had watched the entire game. When I asked if he had seen me on television, he said no. I asked if he had watched the halftime show. He said he did. I asked if he had seen Santa on the field waving to the fans. He had, and then I told him that the Santa he saw on the field was me! We both got a great laugh out of this.

Luckily, legendary photographer Jack Shaffer from the *Arizona Daily Star* covered the game, and he took some great photos with me— "Santa"—and the UA mascot, Wilbur the Wildcat. I figured I would need these someday because nobody would ever believe this story. I needed the proof.

To read this incredible story in its entirety, check out the *Arizona Daily Star*'s link on the forty-year anniversary of this event.

Arizona Daily Star Story (December 25, 2019)
https://boblogan.net/LoganCrashesFiestaBowlAsSanta

I tell this story for a specific reason: Acting with purpose and being bold is the key to putting yourself in situations that someone with less confidence might never experience. While I may have snuck into the Fiesta Bowl, there are many similar stories, some on a large scale like people crashing White House state dinners, or on a smaller scale of crashing weddings, conventions, receptions, etc. We all know that since 9-11, security is much tighter than it was thirty years ago, and I'm not advocating you get yourself into trouble by doing something stupid. But there is something to be said about acting with confidence to save time and stress in even more favorable circumstances. I am reminded of the story of a man walking down the middle of a crowded downtown New York Manhattan street. He took huge strides and swung his arms from side-to-side. Very soon, the crowds on the sidewalk began to part, and he was walking freely without obstructions. That, my friends, is walking with purpose. Sometimes, if you just act confidently, like you know what you're doing, you can accomplish things some thought would never be possible.

I also regularly have fun with restaurant servers. Remember, I am a big guy and a former football player at about 260 pounds. At the end of a meal, when the waiter typically asks if we would like any dessert, I look the server in the eye and casually reply with a straight face, "You know, I noticed you were looking right at me when you were describing the desserts to everyone. I think it is so inappropriate that you identify the one fat guy sitting at the table. You should know I'm really self-conscious about my weight." The waiter is usually totally flummoxed and stands there not knowing what to say. I typically wait a few long seconds, and then beam with a huge smile. I tell them I was joking and let out a huge laugh. The relief on their faces is incredible, and believe it or not, every now and then, they will bring us a free dessert anyway!

The new handheld credit card payment devices include a choice to enter the tip amount at the end of the transaction. The options usually include 15 percent, 20 percent, 25 percent, etc. After handing the device to me to enter the tip, the server is often standing next to the table watching and waiting. I take the device and study the screen for a few moments. I then look up and ask why there is not a 5 or 10 percent tip option. I then ask the server to help me input the 5 percent tip and ask them if that is okay. The waiters are uneasy and don't know what to say. I know they cannot look like they are disappointed or disgusted. After a few long, and very awkward seconds, I let them in on the joke. It breaks the tension, and we have a huge laugh together before I select my final "real" tip, usually 20 percent to 25 percent.

The point is: Find opportunities to get out of the "norms" of daily life and do something unexpected from time to time. Saying something totally unexpected when in a normal situation is often a great way to get everyone laughing and having some fun. Don't be afraid to have some fun at your own expense, even in tense circumstances when the mood needs to be lightened up.

HAPPINESS TECHNIQUE #6—PRACTICE GRATITUDE

Proactively looking for things to be thankful for will help you realize how good you have it. The ability to be grateful is a strong predictor of happiness. Take stock daily of what you have to be thankful for and develop a daily practice around it. In her book *Project Happiness*, Gretchen Rubin wrote about her daily practice when leaving or entering her NYC apartment of being thankful for the vibrant city she was stepping out into or for her cozy living space when she came back home. She focused on specific details that made going out or coming home not just another daily act but a ritual of sorts that made her appreciate where she lived on both a micro and macro scale.[53] Sarah Ban Breathnach made a big splash in Oprah circles when she wrote in *Simple Abundance* about her gratitude journaling at the end of each day. Writing down what she was grateful for each day helped her keep recognizing all the blessings she had and spurred countless others to do the same.[54]

This practice can be powerful for you personally, but it can take on even more meaning when you involve others by thanking them for their contributions to your or others' lives. Say it. Write it. There are many wonderful samples of Gratitude Journals on Amazon. Some of them are specifically geared to certain people, like for children or men. Find one you like and express your gratitude daily!

HAPPINESS TECHNIQUE #7—FIND A WORK-LIFE BALANCE

We hear so much about the importance of work-life balance that we sometimes become numb to how to incorporate it into our daily lives. Popular with movie buffs, perhaps the most famous line in *The Shining* is when Jack Nicholson says, "All work and no play makes Jack a dull boy." It merely means we must find a way to balance the various parts of our lives if we genuinely want to be fulfilled.

The pandemic has exacerbated the need for work-life balance. Working from home with our kids with us 24-7 has shown how important our family lives are to us today. Most organizational management experts agree that once the pandemic is over, many companies will retain a certain level of remote work.

During my happiness talks, I ask people to rank the key priorities in their lives (faith, family, friends, work). Without fail, the order usually goes something like this: work, family, friends, faith. Being totally honest and transparent, most of us do put work—where we spend most of our time—ahead of all the other things in our lives. But for others (those who have figured it out), there is a genuine reordering of priorities, and they truly value what is called the "three Fs" (faith, family, and friends).

Balance can come to us in various ways, and we must find the way that works best for us. Some people work hard for a long period (for example, authors writing a book or musicians writing a new album) and then take extended time off. They will cycle from work to relaxation year after year, which is a good thing. Others manage to balance day-to-day by working out, spending time with family and friends, practicing their faith through meditation or prayer, or taking time off from work. Whichever one works best for you; it is crucial to find balance. If you don't, the universe has a way of making things even for you in the end. Maybe you'll have an accident or an illness that lands you flat on your back, forcing you to rest and recover. Better for you to choose the method yourself.

I encourage you to think instead of the most important people and mentors in your own life. Who are the people you can call on anytime, day or night? Teachers or coaches who impacted you? Think of all those who have had a major influence on your own life. Conversely, who are the people you have made a difference for? What about someone you haven't connected with in many years? Which group brings you more joy and connection—the famous people or the people who helped you become who you are today? Sure, our lives may not seem as consequential or glamorous as some of these celebrities, but we are significant and important to those closest to us.

HAPPINESS TECHNIQUE #8—MEDITATION/VISUALIZATION

Countless studies document the benefits of meditation and visualization, not just on our own well-being but on the world around us.[55] Try a simple visualization exercise you can do right now. Close your eyes, and imagine holding various objects in your hand, smelling them, and feeling what they feel like against your skin. Then imagine using them. First, think about Crayola Crayons. Then how about Play-Doh. Finally, Silly Putty. Did that experience take you back to a simpler time? Could you smell those smells and recall the fun times playing with those items? What memories flooded forward from visualizing those objects from childhood?

A CAMINO STORY—HAPPINESS ON THE CAMINO DE SANTIAGO

Happiness can be difficult to quantify on the Camino. Generally, most pilgrims aren't very happy at the thought of walking all day, particularly if the terrain or conditions that specific day will be challenging. There is often a considerable measure of satisfaction in completing a steep section with a lot of climbing, or a day with severe weather conditions like rain, cold, or extreme heat. Even the end of a typical day on the Camino feels good when you can kick back with new friends over a glass of wine or a nice meal. And sleeping on a bed, no matter how uncomfortable the mattress is, can feel luxurious after a long, tiring day of walking.

In 2015, I remember the ecstatic feeling of seeing the first albergue on day one of the Camino. It is only five miles from the traditional starting point, St. Jean

Pied de Port, in the tiny hamlet of Orisson, and many pilgrims feel this ridiculously short walk wastes an entire day on the Camino. However, the alternative is to cross the entire Pyrenees Mountains in one day, a day that takes you straight up and then straight down for twenty-plus miles to the next town of Roncesvalles. It is by far the most challenging day on the entire Camino, and I have heard of many people who hurt their knees, took a fall, or developed blisters so bad they could not go any farther.

However, I did a considerable amount of research before arriving in Spain, and I learned about this terrible first day of hiking over the top of the Pyrenees. So, I did the smart thing and stayed in Orisson, just five miles from the start in St. Jean Pied de Port in France. Even walking only five miles on this first day is a significant undertaking when your muscles aren't used to hiking. These first five miles are literally straight up the mountain. It took me nearly three-and-a-half hours to walk those grueling five miles. By comparison, at home in Tucson on flat ground, I could cover this mileage easily in ninety minutes. It is that hard.

There are many "false summits" on the Camino climbs, but perhaps none are more prominent than that first day when it feels like the lodge is always just around the next corner. When it finally does come into view, almost nothing can cause more happiness. You are totally exhausted, and you feel you cannot walk much farther, and then there it is! An oasis on the side of the mountain!

Many miles later on the Camino, after about three weeks on the trail, is another grinder of an uphill climb that concludes in the fascinating town of O Cebreiro. This mountain climb is the steepest on the entire Camino de Santiago. It is so steep that locals at the base of the mountain have begun offering pilgrims horseback rides to the top for a small fee.

The euphoria one experiences when reaching the summit of these steep climbs almost makes the climb worth it. First, you cannot believe it is over, and the feeling of accomplishment of completing an incredibly difficult task is intoxicating. I feel it is this way with all the challenges in our lives. Overcoming challenges helps us appreciate the quieter, more normal times in our lives and provides a sense of joy on the other side of the challenge.

Many unexpected pleasures happen along the Camino, including beautiful scenery, quaint towns, spiritual experiences, opportunities to be helpful, and many random and memorable conversations. Every day you walk with hundreds of people, all walking in the same direction as you are walking. Wherever and whenever you stop on the Camino, you meet people with a common quest and goal. A conversation about what we're doing and why we're doing it comes easily and makes the walk go faster. Meeting people and having conversations is incredibly smooth on the Camino.

One beautiful morning on the Camino, I met a young man on the trail. As we began talking, I complimented him on his excellent command of the English language. He told me he was from South America—Argentina, I think. He went to college in the US at Columbia University, and he received his law degree from Georgetown University. "Wow, that is an impressive group of schools," I told him. I asked what he was doing for a living with that fancy American education, and I expected him to say he was a doctor or a lawyer. I nearly fainted when he told me he was a potato farmer. What? He explained that when he returned home from his schooling, he realized what was truly needed most by the people of his small community was food, not legal advice. He decided that growing potatoes was one of the best contributions he could make to his family and to his community. It blew me away to hear his story. It is one of the most amazing Camino stories I ever heard. Talk about commitment to the greater good!

Another evening, I was having a glass of wine with a group of people who were a lot like me—from the same socioeconomic background, professionals, etc. A scruffy-looking guy at a table nearby was drinking quite a bit and smoking, and at one point, he invited himself to join us. At first, we were all a bit taken aback by his unkempt appearance and obvious inebriation, but where else could I meet a fascinating Scandinavian tug-boat captain and hear about his varied and exciting background?

That is the magic of the Camino. Unlikely people sometimes become fast friends. It can often take you by surprise, and it makes me think of Forrest Gump's oft-repeated phrase from his momma, "Life is like a box of chocolates. You never know what you're gonna get."[56]

The Habits/Techniques of Happiness

1. **Happiness comes from within.** Recognize that happiness is an inside job and not linked to what you do, what you have, where you live, or who you are.
2. **Happiness is a habit.** Understand that happiness is simply a habit that can be cultivated and maintained by anyone at any time.
3. **Smile and laugh** as often as you can. Even if it's forced, it won't be forced for very long.
4. **Volunteer, serve, and help others.** You can't do that without helping yourself as well.
5. **Get outside and get moving.** Nature and exercise are two of the best mood enhancers there are.
6. **Travel experientially.** Even if you love fancy resorts or beach vacations, consider there might be more rewarding opportunities in using your time off. Create a compelling and memorable experience instead of just a relaxing one.
7. **Play and be creative.** Whether it's playing board games with friends, painting while sipping wine, or numerous other creative and fun endeavors, there are apparent benefits while doing this with others.
8. **Practice gratitude.** Often.
9. **Find balance.** No one ever said on their deathbed, "I wish I had spent more time at the office," as the old adage goes. It is helpful to remember that when planning how you spend your time.
10. **Meditate, visualize, be still.** To whatever extent you wish to delve into meditation and visualization, there are countless benefits to our state of mind. It may be simply to sit still and stare at a stream or into a fire. And there are even more benefits from focusing your mind on a meditative practice or visualization.

CHAPTER 12
VISION AND VISUALIZATION

"Imagination is more important than knowledge. For while knowledge defines all we currently know and understand, imagination points to all we might yet discover and create."

— ALBERT EINSTEIN

SCIENCE AND THE BRAIN

I spent more than twenty years working at the University of Arizona College of Science as an assistant dean. During this time, I was exposed to and fortunate to work with many incredible faculty experts from the areas of psychology, neuroscience, and cognitive science. As we begin this chapter on vision and visualization, it is best to start with the basics, which I learned from these scientific leaders—the science of the brain. While some out there may still not be too sure about the use of visualization and psycho-cybernetics, the truth is this area of visualization is firmly rooted in science, with numerous studies now proving its effectiveness.[57]

One of the leading centers in the UA College of Science was the Evelyn McKnight Brain Institute. My work also put me into contact with the work of the college's top-ranked Department of Speech, Language, and Hearing Sciences program. I have seen firsthand the miraculous work they do, particularly with stroke victims and brain injury patients. They also work with hearing impaired individuals being fitted for cochlear implants so they can hear sound for the first time. Humbling stuff, to say the least.

Anyone who has experienced a loved one suffering a stroke knows one of the major side-effects of strokes is the devastating impact on the brain's communication parts, causing aphasia—the loss of ability to understand or express speech. I touched on this aphasia research and the amazing brain plasticity earlier in Chapter 11 on happiness. Due to recent advances in science and treatment methodology, aphasia is now treated quite differently and quite effectively.

It was impressive to watch aphasia rehabilitation and healing in action, and I was amazed by the story of the CEO of a multi-billion-dollar company who suffered a massive stroke and lost his ability to communicate. Here he was, one day running a multi-billion-dollar company, and the next, he could not speak or communicate. Watching the early rehabilitation videos of this Harvard-educated man trying to form small words and simple sentences was truly painful.

The tragedy with aphasia is all the patient's knowledge and intelligence still reside inside the brain. Stroke and brain injury do not affect intelligence. Unfortunately, those with aphasia have no way to communicate to their full capabilities, either in verbal or in written form. The improvement the CEO experienced over two years working with this UA speech and language program was incredible. He started out reading third-grade-style *Dick and Jane* type books, and over multiple years of intense therapy, he was able to reacquire nearly all his lost communication skills. In essence, his brain rewired itself away from his permanent brain damage and placing that communication ability in a different part of the brain. Amazing.

Depending on where the brain damage occurs and how severe it is, remapping of skills and abilities to different parts of the brain is possible. This remapping is called neuroplasticity, which was only discovered a few decades ago.[58] Scientists now understand in great detail the specific, physical location in the brain where all our skills originate. There is the "reptilian" brain—the part of the brain that worries only about our survival instincts, breathing, eating, fight or flight, etc. Then there is the limbic brain, which is responsible for our emotions. And finally, there is the pre-frontal cortex or neocortex, which controls facts and communication.

These new scientific discoveries of plasticity have also proven the psychological power we all have to turn vision into reality. The brain is actually very similar to a muscle. If adequately trained on a regular and consistent basis, it can demonstrate the power of belief to heal, create, and succeed at levels previously unimagined. In this chapter, I will not only share stories of people who have used this ability to significant effect in their own lives, but we will also dig into how you can do this for yourself.[59]

On a personal note, my mom had multiple strokes while I was growing up, and it's a shame that none of these incredible advances in treatment were available at that time. I am confident many of her essential communication skills and abilities might have been restored with today's treatment methods.

A CAMINO STORY—VISUALIZE SUCCESS ON THE CAMINO

Visualization plays a significant role in both the day-to-day aspects of the Camino and long-term completion. Obviously, most pilgrims start out with a goal to complete either some portion or the entire 500-mile journey, but challenges along the journey can get in the way, including personal issues, financial issues, blisters, weather, or many other unforeseen circumstances. Having a daily goal for how far you want to walk and which town you want to reach that day is imperative for your sanity. In the beginning, walking 500 miles seems impossible, and you cannot imagine ever reaching Santiago.

However, every day you must step back and visualize the original goal. The pilgrim must see in their mind's eye the feeling of arriving on the square in front of the massive cathedral in central Santiago de Compostela. This goal and this very specific image will help keep you going when the going gets tough. There are always highs and lows along the way. I think I was most surprised by the moments of awe and total gratitude that washed over me at intervals, often for no reason whatsoever.

When walking for hours on the Camino, often with only your internal dialogue to keep you company, it is easy to stumble upon thoughts of how fortunate you are. Those thoughts might be for having this Camino experience at all, or taking stock of what you've experienced already, or marveling at everything around you.

The Camino is often said to be divided into three distinct aspects—physical, emotional, and spiritual. The aspect lasts about 7-10 days and is largely physical and it occurs at the beginning of the Camino. Your initial exposure to the Pyrenees Mountains is shocking to your system. As your body gets accustomed to walking many miles each day and learns how to deal with the big climbs, the blisters and sore muscles can overtake your every thought. But our bodies eventually adjust, and the recovery at the end of the day from the long walks becomes shorter and more manageable.

The second aspect of the journey is the mental or emotional part. It hits in weeks two and three on the trail. In the middle of the Camino is a section called the Meseta, when the path is flat and dull, kind of like walking through Kansas or Nebraska day after day. The view is the same day in and day out, and sometimes the main highway is near the trail, making the entire experience unattractive. This is when overcoming the mental chatter and putting one foot in front of the other is critical. One must get over the thoughts of "Will this never end?" or "What am I doing here?" that dominate your mind.

Finally, the last third of the Camino is spiritual. Your body and mind have overcome the initial physical challenges and you can deal with the blisters and uncomfortable nature of daily life on the Camino. You have been on the trail for 3-4 weeks and become emotionally stable with the experience. Now, in the final weeks, you are more open to appreciating the journey and seeing the wonder the Camino has to offer. On this final third of the Camino, you really get closer to God, see the beauty around you, enjoy your pilgrim friends' personalities, and appreciate the small towns and intimate churches you see every day. Humbling feelings of gratitude and appreciation begin to flow all over you.

> *"You can't depend on your eyes when your imagination is out of focus."*
>
> — MARK TWAIN

"WHAT YOU FOCUS ON EXPANDS"

This quote from Oprah Winfrey encourages us to focus on what we want rather than what we don't want. That's exactly what Jim Carrey famously did in 1985 when he wrote himself a personal check for $10,000,000, postdating it ten years into the future. The memo line on the bottom of the check read: "for acting services rendered." Early in his career, Carrey had failed time and time again to get selected for any significant acting roles, but he carried this check around in his wallet and looked at it constantly. He dreamed, and he was sure his time would someday arrive. Carrey just believed it would happen someday. A few weeks before Thanksgiving in 1995, almost to the day when he wrote that check ten years earlier, he landed a starring role in the movie, *Dumb and Dumber*. And what was the payout for this comedy? You guessed it—$10 million! Carrey initially told this story to Oprah Winfrey, who has shared many similar tales in her storied career, and she believes strongly in the power of visualization herself.[60]

In 2018, Oprah Winfrey interviewed Anthony Ray Hinton, someone with a very different life story than Jim Carrey's.[61] Hinton was falsely accused and convicted of murder in Alabama and served thirty years on death row. His book *The Sun Does Shine: How I Found Life and Freedom on Death Row* details how he used visualization daily to get through some of his most challenging periods in prison.[62]

Hinton told Oprah about the many memorable experiences he had visualized while in prison. One time, he had tea with the Queen of England, and then he visited exotic places all over the world, all in his mind. Instead of dwelling on the unfairness and difficulty of his current hopeless situation in prison, he found ways to allow his mind to take him places and envision a better existence someday. Hinton focused on faith and forgiveness to weather the worst of his horrifying experience, and he ultimately left prison a better man.

You may be more familiar with John McCain who used a similar technique to survive an impossible situation. Forced to eject from his plane over hostile enemy territory during the Vietnam War, McCain had two broken arms and one broken leg after the Viet Cong shot down his Navy jet. Ironically, he was captured in the middle of the very town he had just tried to bomb earlier that day. As you can imagine, the Vietnamese were not too kind to him.

Though McCain was offered early release because of his father's position as head of naval forces in the Pacific, he refused freedom, remaining in the infamous Hanoi Hilton prisoner of war camp for five-and-a-half years, mostly in solitary confinement. He was severely beaten multiple times and sustained injuries that still affected him decades later while he served as a US Senator for my home state of Arizona. During his harrowing time as a prisoner of war, he said he was sustained by praying for moral and physical courage. He also used visualization techniques during his time in the Hanoi Hilton. He visualized holidays at home with his family and thought about historical events from books he had read in the past. His constant prayer for relief from pain often yielded results, as he reported in a piece published in *U.S. News and World Report* in 2008.[63]

Another fascinating tale of visualization during prison survival comes from Natan Sharansky, a Ukrainian Jew accused of spying for the Americans when Ukraine was still part of the Soviet Union. Sharansky spent nine years in a Soviet prison, and at one point, his health deteriorated to the point that he was not expected to survive. He kept himself sane, he said, by visualizing playing games of chess during solitary confinement. Many years later, in a 1996 Israeli Chess Exhibition (Sharansky emigrated to Israel after being released from prison), he beat Russian chess champion, Garry Kasparov.[64]

> *"Formulate and stamp indelibly on your mind a mental picture of yourself as succeeding. Hold this picture tenaciously and never permit it to fade. Your mind will seek to develop this picture."*
>
> — NORMAN VINCENT PEALE

As a football kicking coach, I often incorporated visualization techniques when teaching kicking and long snapping techniques with my players. We would practice "extreme" field goals with the kickers, kicking from the sideline through the goalposts. From these extreme sideline angles, the split between the two uprights becomes smaller and smaller as we moved closer to the goal line.

The kickers initially hated this drill because the margin for error was miniscule and the chances for making the kicks go through the goal posts seemed impossible. However, I explained that this drill was more of a mental exercise than a physical one. I would ask my kickers to pick an aiming point well beyond the uprights and concentrate on that single point instead of thinking about making a nearly impossible field goal from this extreme angle. Prior to each field goal attempt, I asked them to close their eyes and visualize kicking the ball so it would land softly on the top of the palm trees far beyond the uprights. Amazingly, they began to embrace these visualization techniques and began to consistently make these extreme field goals.

While visualization worked for the kickers, it was also extremely helpful for the punters. Without boring you with football minutia, as a punter, the absolute worst situation you can be in is punting from the back of your own end zone. When a punt happens mid-field, the punter stands fifteen yards from the long snapper. Now imagine the ball being on your own one-yard line. You are now only ten yards from the center, and the ten defensive players are chomping at the bit to rush this shorter distance to block the punt. It is terrifying. If you are not in total control, both physically and emotionally, the nerves can get the best of you, frequently with tragic results like a blocked or shanked punt, both of which put the opponents in easy reach for a touchdown.

The act of thinking it through ahead of time and experiencing the pressure of standing in the back of the end zone visualizing everything connected to the play helped calm my punting specialists' nerves. They would hear the crowd; they would see the rushers lined up, the perfect snap, the pace of the steps, the football drop, and the punt with a high follow-through, resulting in a high arching spiral, landing fifty-plus yards down the field. All of this off-field slow-motion visualization practice provided the mental acuity to take the necessary actions while on the field. In a more nuanced way, performance improved even with the distractions of a hostile crowd and the game's intense pressure.

Tennis great Andre Agassi used to talk about how he would visualize the tennis ball as traveling slower and being much bigger than in reality. Agassi has described how his vision changes when hitting each tennis ball that comes his way. The balls appear big and slow in his mind's eye, so they are quickly returned. Perhaps this is why Agassi is known as tennis's greatest service returner ever to play the game. I would have my punters incorporate the very same technique as Agassi. I would make them relax, visualize the game slowing down, and block out the on-rushing lineman, all in order to get the punt off quickly.

In 1996, a famous University of Chicago study was done on the use of visualization. Conducted by Dr. Blasotto, the experiment used free throw shooting skills in basketball.[65,66] First, he took a group of students and divided them into three groups. Group 1 practiced shooting basketball free throws for an hour daily for thirty days. Group 2 didn't touch a ball but visualized shooting free throws for an hour each day for thirty days. Group 3 did absolutely nothing—they didn't visualize, and they didn't practice shooting free throws.

What were the results? When free-throw ability was remeasured in each of the groups a month later, not surprisingly, Group 3 showed no improvement. Very surprising, though, was that the first two groups showed nearly the same amount of improvement, with Group 1 showing a 24 percent improvement and Group 2, the visualization group, showing an almost identical 23 percent improvement. The message here is our brains are just like any other muscle in our bodies. The mind cannot detect the difference between actual physical activity *or* the visualization of that same activity. Therefore, intentionally and intensely thinking positive thoughts can have a positive effect on the results we see in our daily lives.

Numerous studies on transcendental meditation's impact demonstrate that even a small group of practitioners can impact the world around them. If meditation and visualization can have these kinds of impacts, what might you gain by taking up this regular practice?

The positive effects of meditation include:
- Decreased stress and anxiety
- Greater emotional well-being and self-awareness
- Increased attention span and better memory
- Improved sleep and higher levels of kindness
- Decreases in blood pressure and pain
- Positive impacts on addiction, illness, and depression.

Follow this link for more:

12 Scientific-Based Benefits of Meditation
https://BobLogan.net/Meditation

You can meditate anywhere, anytime. Even if you don't know how, it isn't challenging to learn. It is as simple as sitting still and focusing on your breath, a candle flame, a mantra, or nothing. When your mind wanders, gently bring it back to the center. If you've never meditated before, start with a short period, like 5-10 minutes, and gradually build up to longer intervals. Numerous apps and online resources can guide you through meditation if that is easier, or you could use them until you feel confident enough to do it on your own.

SPORTS CHAMPIONS

Several athletes attribute their success to visualization techniques. However, the most famous of them all went a little beyond mental practice by loudly proclaiming his status to everyone who would listen by stating he was "the greatest of all time." Muhammed Ali is one of the most celebrated sports figures of the twentieth century and one of the greatest boxers of all-time, possibly because he, himself, began saying so to everyone who would listen at every opportunity possible. Ali was not alone, however, in using visualization practices to achieve unprecedented success. Other athletes include golfer Jack Nicklaus, Olympic skier Lindsay Vonn, and tennis great Andre Agassi.

Nicklaus is regarded by many as the greatest golfer of all-time, having won eighteen major championships in twenty-five years. He was the first to win back-to-back Masters championships, the youngest to win The British Open Championship, and the oldest to win the Masters Tournament, at age forty-six. How did he achieve this success? Were his physical abilities purely far advanced beyond his peers on the PGA tour? I think not. Jack Nicklaus once said he never hit a single shot in a tournament that he had not seen beforehand through visualization.

Let's delve into this a little further. Once interviewed by a golf journalist, Nicklaus said:

> "I never hit a shot, not even in practice, without having a very sharp, in-focus picture of it in my head. First, I see the ball where I want it to finish, nice and white, sitting up high on the bright green grass. Then, the scene quickly changes, and I see the ball flight going there: its path, trajectory, and shape, even its behavior when landing on the fairway or the green. Then, there is a sort of fade-out, and the next scene shows me making the kind of swing that will turn those previous images into the reality of my golf shot."

The night before every competitive round, Nicklaus would play an entire eighteen-hole round—in his mind. He would visualize every hole, landing his drives in the perfect locations, hitting approach shots to the correct parts of the green, and putting with precision through all the rolling and intricate breaks on the greens.

Additionally, Nicklaus's visualization techniques would cross over to the actual round of golf during the tournament. He was famous for his extensive pre-shot routine. He would stand directly behind the ball for what seemed like an eternity, just staring down the fairway. Finally, he would stride up to the ball, take his stance, and take his swing. Nicklaus was visualizing the entire stroke in his mind, including the fade or draw he needed on the shot, where the ball would land on the green, and how far it would roll toward the pin. Feel it, see it, then do it; that is the formula for winning.

Jack Nicklaus, Payne Stewart, and many other top golfers made specific reference to the "mental side of golf" for their success. The founder of the field was Dr. Maxwell Martz and one of his disciples was Dr. Richard Coop, a professor of educational psychology at the University of North Carolina and the author of *Mind over Golf*. Both Martz and Coop embraced the technique of "The Theater of the Mind," where athletes visualize "scenes" of their athletic prowess and play these scenes in their mind's eye like a movie. Amazing stuff.

When Andre Agassi won Wimbledon for the first time and was asked what it was like, he said, "I have already won Wimbledon at least 10,000 times." At first, people thought he was joking until they realized Agassi was touting the power of visualization.

Lindsey Vonn is an Olympic gold medalist who has won four World Cup championships—only one of two women to achieve this feat. She has won twenty World Cup crystal globe titles, a record among men and women skiers, making her the most successful American ski racer and one of the greatest ever. Vonn attributes her success to visualizing each ski run 100 times in her mind, for many hours beforehand.[67] Much like Jack Nicklaus, she goes as far as to physically shift her weight to mimic the run before she ever hits the snow. It's like she is watching a movie of herself skiing these challenging runs.

> "Go confidently in the direction of your dreams. Live the life you've imagined."
>
> — HENRY DAVID THOREAU

HEALING

Besides visualizing success in sports and career to using the mind's power to survive difficult circumstances, visioning has contributed to survival. The Institute of Noetic Sciences has been documenting spontaneous remissions of diseases, primarily cancer, for many decades. Its work has been called the largest database of medically reported cases of spontaneous remission globally, with more than 3,500 references from more than 800 journals in twenty different languages. It put forth a Consciousness Transformation Model that describes the process by which "significant changes in how people perceive and shape their reality" are brought about. This model was developed through surveys of more than 2,000 people who had experienced their own transformations, sixty in-depth interviews with representatives of both ancient and modern wisdom traditions, and a series of studies and focus groups.[68]

> *"If you want to reach a goal, you must 'see the reaching' in your own mind before you actually arrive at your goal."*
>
> — ZIG ZIGLAR

AGING AND STAYING HEALTHY

Can our thoughts slow the ravages of time? Some studies suggest they can. It is inevitable as we get older that people will comment about what we are losing. Even if we aren't experiencing the aging process negatively, being surrounded by so much negativity can contribute to our perceptions. It turns out it may also work in reverse. The December 2018 issue of *The Rotarian* included an article titled "Decline to decline" that describes various studies on aging.[69]

A study by Yale School of Public Health psychologist Becca Levy found that fear of aging may negatively impact how we feel. Her research showed that those with negative views of aging died seven-and-a-half years earlier than those with a positive outlook. Another study determined that women who believed they were at risk of heart disease were 3.6 times more likely to die of heart attacks than women with the same risk factors but a less worrisome attitude. Levy says that cultures with more positive aging views tend to have healthier citizens for a more extended period.[70]

Given all this evidence, there should be no excuse not to seriously incorporate visualization into your daily life. Trust me, it works, and once you experience it for yourself, you will be hooked.

> *"All that we are is the result of what we have thought."*
>
> — BUDDHA

VISUALIZATION IN ACTION

I use visualization techniques regularly, and I have used them throughout my entire career. Visualization is very helpful, especially when preparing for a major presentation or a speaking engagement to a large audience. These high-pressure situations can make anyone nervous. I started using visualization techniques many years ago when I worked for AT&T and delivered high-level corporate presentations. Today, I use visualization techniques for public speaking and other related activities.

First, I must prepare the actual content of the presentation or PowerPoint. Once that is finished, I incorporate my own version of what is called "The Theater of the Mind." I like to imagine myself sitting in a movie theater, watching myself delivering the talk on the big screen in front of me. I see what I'm wearing, what I look like from the audience's perspective, the gestures I use, and the visuals I employ to make my various points.

When I was a young history teacher early in my career, I used visualization in the classroom setting. The first year of teaching a new subject was a challenge because I was not yet comfortable with the material. I didn't know it well enough to accurately ascertain what would and would not work in the classroom, how best to engage students, and what were the most important topics to share during each lecture. After I'd taught a lesson and after consecutive classes, I would start to get into the groove of the material and could visualize what success looked like in the classroom. Not only did I want to ensure students learned the content, but I also wanted them to enjoy it. Extensive planning and visioning were a big part of my teaching practice and my success as a teacher.

VISUALIZATION IN COACHING

An important distinction needs to be made about effectively using visualization techniques as a coach. Despite what has been shared about visualization thus far, thinking that one can just sit around and visualize competitive success without having a semblance of the necessary physical skillset is a fallacy.

Here is where the Law of Attraction folks often miss the mark. Visualization also requires action, as demonstrated in the story of how I became a coach at the University of Arizona. In the early 1980s, I was a high school teacher and coach with a dream of becoming a college football coach. How could I do this? I had no idea. But I'd the fortunate opportunity to work for several years with legendary football coach Ed Doherty.

Coach Doherty was nearing the end of his forty-year coaching career when he became the head coach at Salpointe Catholic High School, my alma mater. I was thrilled to learn from this incredible coaching legend. To give you an idea of this man's impressive coaching career, Ed Doherty is the *only* man to serve as the head coach at both the University of Arizona and Arizona State University. Earlier in his career, he was the head coach at Xavier University and Holy Cross College. He coached in the NFL for the Philadelphia Eagles, and he even coached with Vince Lombardi at one time. I had a chance to learn from one of the masters of the game.

Because of his reputation and impressive coaching resume, Coach Doherty was also well known in the college football coaching circles. He was long-time friends with the current University of Arizona head coach Larry Smith. After getting to know Coach Doherty on a more social level, I learned he and Coach Smith met a few times a year over breakfast or lunch. They would tell stories, compare football notes, and just do what coaches do.

After about a year of working with Coach Doherty, I got up the nerve to tell him I wanted to stop coaching at the high school level and move to the college coaching level. We discussed this at great length, and he provided tons of advice. I ultimately asked if he would mention my name to Coach Smith the next time they had lunch. Taking the initiative to ask for help eventually paid off. Several months later, Coach Smith called me at my home and offered me a job on his coaching staff. I was ecstatic! I had arrived!

> *"If you can dream it, you can do it."*
>
> — WALT DISNEY

A CAMINO STORY—VISUALIZATION HELPS ME MAKE A DECISION

Perhaps the best example of visualization helping me attain a goal was when I decided to do the Camino for the first time in 2012. When I first thought about the Camino, I had little understanding about it and little support from anyone about attempting this trek. If circumstances at work had been different, I might not have felt such a pull to go. This is an example of how significant challenges in our lives can lead to incredible opportunities.

After I saw the movie *The Way*,[71] starring Martin Sheen, I knew I needed to take this journey by myself. The story blew me away and put many of my personal issues into a greater focused perspective. I'm not giving away too much of the plot when I say the film deals primarily with grief, something I'm quite familiar with.

Despite the initial lack of support and not knowing anyone else who had experienced the Camino, it became a self-fulfilling prophecy for me. I knew I was going to do it, and I didn't care what anyone else thought. You must commit 100 percent if you hope to achieve your goals. Ray Bradbury described this idea in a radical way, "Jump off the cliff and build your wings on the way down." Jumping off the cliff commits you. And the Camino was my cliff.

Once I decided to take on the Camino, the rest was in the details. As it turned out, our College of Science has a high-end donor society called The Galileo Circle. Every couple of years, we would develop a special science-based trip to some popular world location. It might be the Large Hadron Collider in France, a trip to Chile to see Giant Magellan Telescope, or something similar. In this specific year, we had built a fantastic two-week trip for the Galileo Circle donors to tour the Vatican Observatory and the Galilean cities of Italy.

As the College of Science's principal development officer, I would be required to help facilitate and plan this donor trip, so it provided the perfect opportunity for me to take on the Camino. Since I would already be in Europe, it would be easy to add a few extra weeks prior to the Galileo Circle trip, fly to Spain first and walk the Camino. I spoke to the Dean of the College of Science, Joaquin Ruiz, about my desire. Luckily, being Hispanic, he was quite familiar with the Camino de Santiago. In fact, he had friends that lived just a few kilometers from the Camino in the town of Lugo. I had his blessing to take the adequate vacation time to walk the Camino and then meet our Galileo Circle donor group in Italy.

You've heard people say that planning a vacation is a big part of the experience. It is true. Why? Because it involves visualizing yourself doing all the things you are planning. It builds anticipation. That's why we seem to be happier in the days leading up to a vacation. On the last day, we are sadly anticipating going home again.

When I returned from my Camino adventure, everything changed in my life and career. The biggest challenge I faced led me to begin the Camino journey, and it, in turn, became my most significant opportunity. Perhaps you've heard luck described as the intersection of preparedness and opportunity. However, upon my return from the Camino, I fell into a fantastic opportunity within a few weeks, and it opened all kinds of new possibilities. Everything about my career changed because I was a changed person.

HOW TO VISUALIZE

1. **Know what you want.** This can be the most challenging part for many people. Consider that we often think we know what will make us happy, but we aren't always right. Material possessions will rarely lead to a life of contentment. It might be fun to imagine yourself driving a new red Ferrari, but it is more likely the freedom and excitement of the experience you desire. Getting clear about the feelings you desire to experience may be more helpful in the long run. Starting with feelings can make this process more comfortable and fulfilling than focusing on a single object of desire.
2. **Be Specific.** The details are essential. Just as we were taught long ago about goal setting, writing down what you desire can be a powerful experience. It provides clarity and cements the details in your mind to commit them to paper. It makes it easier to go back and review them when they are in

writing. Going through the process of writing down goals can make the end of the year exciting. There is no greater satisfaction than seeing how many of your written goals you have achieved during the past year.

3. **Imagine and Visualize.** Here is where the rubber meets the road. It is the actual practice of visioning yourself doing, having, or being. It is important to use as many of your senses as possible when doing the actual practice—see, feel, taste, touch, and hear what is happening around you.

4. **Find Quiet time.** For visualization practice to be successful, you must find the "perfect place" without distractions and other people. It may be in bed just before you fall asleep, or it may be a quiet place in the yard without anyone interrupting you. Surprisingly, just closing your eyes for 3-5 minutes during the day can be enough.

5. **Practice Daily.** This practice must be regular to be effective. It doesn't have to take a long time each day, but it usually takes time to bring about your desires.

6. **Persevere.** With practice, we can manifest more clearly and faster, but this doesn't often happen overnight. Being patient and persistent will serve you well.

Develop a practice that works for you. Choose the time of day, place, and format that will contribute to your committing to this daily task. It may be during your lunch break, before you go to bed at night, or first thing in the morning. Because I get up earlier than my wife on most days, my practice is to pour a cup of coffee and get comfortable in my easy chair for 10-15 minutes of visualization every morning. It is essential to turn off your phone and ensure that you will not be interrupted.

Just as this practice can help you manifest things—I know someone who got a new car this way, and I got a new career after clearing my head on the Camino—it can also help in your relationships. I have never been a fan of the worst-case scenario handbook idea because it has us imagine the worst possible things that could happen to us with the assumption that we will be better prepared for bad situations when they occur. A great quote refutes this idea: "If you want bad things to happen to you, think about bad things."

I prefer to imagine the best-case scenario and visualize a win-win outcome for tough conversations, whether they take place in personal or work relationships. When you've known someone for a while, you can usually imagine the way an upcoming conversation might progress. But bad things happen if we approach a situation from a perspective of wanting to one-up or "win" the conversation.

If we approach the conversation from a win-win mindset, and a willingness to be vulnerable instead, it changes the entire dynamic. Instead of wanting to be right, we want to be loved or admired, and we want to provide the same thing to the person to whom we are talking. Visualizing the best possible outcome for everyone involved, through a willingness to share your feelings and be vulnerable rather than dominate, can radically change your conversations and, as a result, your relationships.

Ten Health Benefits of Visualization

1. **It improves your performance:** Professional athletes, from Jack Nicklaus to Tiger Woods to Arnold Schwarzenegger, have all incorporated visualization techniques into their daily lives.

2. **It helps you reach your potential:** Imagining something you want to achieve, be it a physical activity or a personal situation, can help you reach your highest level of potential and define your goals.

3. **It reduces stress:** Similar to meditation, visualizing positive experiences has been shown to reduce stress.

4. **It brings joy to your life:** When my friend was angry at work, thinking about the beach made her happy. While she wasn't actually on the beach, imagining herself at that moment—the ocean breeze blowing through her hair, the hot sand under her toes, a cold beer in her hand—brought her joy.

5. **It increases focus:** Regular concentration and visualization will help you improve your focus during stressful times.

6. **It can spark inspiration:** Thinking about doing something amazing can create amazing experiences.

7. **It boosts confidence:** People generally can be negative. Doing (and accomplishing) something that nobody else thinks is a good idea can only serve to expand how you feel about yourself.

8. **If you're sick, it can help you get better faster:** Numerous studies have shown how positive thoughts and visualizing yourself being healthy can change the physical nature of your ailment.

9. **It makes you more creative:** The more vivid the image, the stronger the results will be.

10. **It can help you overcome nervousness:** Visualization is a safe and secure way to put yourself in uncomfortable situations at no risk. If you can visualize doing something you are not looking forward to, the chances of having a good experience are higher.

CHAPTER 13
LEADERSHIP

*"Before you are a leader, success is all about growing yourself.
When you become a leader, success is all about growing others."*
— JACK WELCH

I firmly believe that leaders are made and not born. Anyone can be a leader. Leadership is not about holding a position or a "title," but about inspiring others to create a shared vision. Leadership is an acquired skill that comes from years of watching and learning from others you admire. Who you become is based upon many years of relationships, leaders who may have influenced you, and, most importantly, what you have learned along your own path of life.

We all have different personalities, and what works for me may not work for you. Motivation comes from being appreciated and knowing your contributions to the organization or to the team are valuable. When leaders express that clearly and concisely, they are sure to get the best from those around them. When things go wrong, leaders take responsibility, and when things go right, they share the credit.

Everyone has some innate leadership skills, either internally, or possibly externally with their immediate family, workplace, or their friends. But it is also essential to understand that not everyone needs to lead on a larger scale. Everyone has an essential role in life, some as leaders, and others as followers and team members. Leaders don't get very far (and aren't truly leaders) if they don't inspire others to follow. At the same time, it is okay to be a follower in the game of life.

I find it fascinating to google the term "Leadership" or put "Leadership" in the search box at Amazon. Google comes up with 4.4 million results, and in 2021 Amazon had 57,136 books with leadership in the title. Thousands of books have been written on leadership, but what if you were not cut out to be a leader and have no desire to become one? How many books do you think are written on "following"? Again, performing the same Google search, it is hard to find any true books on becoming a follower, unless you want to read how to "follow" the Lord, or "follow" people on social media, etc. The topic of following others or following leaders is just not in the mainstream literature.

An important distinction exists between leading and following, and one depends on the other for success. Being a follower, believe it or not, is perfectly fine. If you happen to be an introvert and have no aspirations for leadership development, that is perfectly okay, and you do not have to feel you are less of a person by not being a leader. All organizations need different types of employees, all with different skillsets. They need to all work together seamlessly to become successful. If you are a follower, run with it and be the very best follower you can become!

Leadership and management also have a clear distinction. While both are important, leadership is visionary and sets the direction for the organization. Their dedication to the cause and vision is often more substantial because of the visionary ideas great leaders provide for their people. On the other hand, managers might play an essential role in carrying out the vision through project planning, progress tracking, and determining tasks.

Still, those being "managed" are often more concerned with avoiding retribution by doing the bare minimum expected of them. In other words, it is rare to see managers inspiring people to go above and beyond to create some grand vision as leaders do. The manager's focus tends to be more on hitting deadlines, checking off a to-do list, and plugging away at the implementation of specific project tasks. In contrast, leadership at its best can inspire others to "walk through the fire," "take a bullet," and do more than followers themselves may have seen themselves capable of doing.

Throughout history, many such leaders have inspired me. I love researching and learning about great leaders from history and sports. Below is a list profiling a few such individuals. I encourage you to research and learn about leaders from your past as well. There is much to be learned and much to emulate.

JOHN F. KENNEDY

John F. Kennedy was truly inspiring during the Cuban Missile Crisis's tense days in 1962. Russia and its leader Nikita Kruschev had taken us to the brink of nuclear war by placing missiles in Cuba, well within reach of the United States. Knowing that any small slip of communication might result in nuclear annihilation, Kennedy calmly reviewed the information, evaluated the Russian communication messages, and firmly and confidently made hard decisions.

MARTIN LUTHER KING, JR.

I lived during the Civil Rights Movement of the 1950s and 1960s. The racial tensions in this country then were like nothing I had ever experienced. Martin Luther King, Jr. was at the center of this movement, and he chose to lead in a much different way. While many black activists decided to strike, protest, and make their voices heard, they often did so in bloody and violent ways. King was an advocate of non-violent resistance. He led many peaceful marches and is most famous for his "I Have a Dream" speech, given in Washington, DC on August 28, 1963. If you have not heard it, visit the link below:

Martin Luther King, Jr. "I Have a Dream" Speech (5:45 mins)
https://boblogan.net/MLKIHaveADreamSpeech

VINCE LOMBARDI

Vince Lombardi was my hero growing up. Everything about his leadership style was tough. Was he autocratic? Yes. Could he, at times, belittle his players? Sure. Did he engage his players in his decision making? Probably not. However, if you ask anyone who played for or coached with Vince Lombardi, they will unanimously say how they *loved* the man. Leadership comes in all different shapes and styles, and it is essential to recognize this should you want to be successful as a leader yourself. Was Vince Lombardi demanding? Yes. Did he lead with an iron fist? Absolutely. But he also instilled great pride in the mission, and everyone had their role and responsibility for the team to be successful. Great leaders give their people the road map, and then they expect them to do their job. Plain and simple.

MOHANDAS KARAMCHAND GANDHI

Gandhi was an Indian lawyer, anti-colonial nationalist, and political ethicist who employed non-violent resistance to lead the successful campaign for India's independence from British Rule. In turn, he inspired movements for civil rights and freedom across the world. The honorific Mahātmā (meaning "great soul") was first applied to him in 1914 in South Africa and is now used worldwide. With his unique yet powerful political tools of Satyagraha and non-violence, he inspired several political leaders worldwide, including Nelson Mandela, Martin Luther King, Jr., and Aung San Suu Kyi. Apart from helping India triumph in its fight for independence against the English, Gandhi also led a pure and righteous life, for which he is revered, even today.

Gandhi's early life was very ordinary, but he became a great man through his life experiences. One reason Gandhi is followed by millions is he proved one could become a great soul during one's life, should they possess the will to do so.

I was always impressed with how Gandhi lived his life. Coming from a non-prominent family and a very normal upbringing, he could get millions of Indians to follow his cause toward liberation from British rule. The takeaway here is to understand that great leaders can lead in drastically different ways and still be incredibly successful.

GENERAL COLIN L. POWELL

When one thinks of great military leaders from United States history, names like Eisenhower, Patton, Grant and Lee from the Civil War, Nimitz, Marshall and Bradley are all at the top of the list. But one name stands out, in my opinion. That man was General Colin L. Powell and he set himself apart from all the rest because of his statesmanship and service in the political arena.

Powell served as Secretary of State and as the Chairman of the Joint Chiefs of Staff, where he oversaw 28 crises during his term, including leading Operation Desert Storm against Iraq in 1990-1991. He was one of the rare military leaders who had allies on both sides of the aisle, Republican and Democrat. To illustrate, in the 2016 United States Presidential election, he won three electoral votes, despite the fact he was not even a candidate!

Colin Powell served with dignity, with honor and leadership oozed out of his every pore. In a wonderful exchange at a charity event, Powell fielded a question asking him to define the key characteristics of effective leadership. He answered from the heart, "Trust…Good leaders are people who are trusted by followers. Leaders take organizations past the level that the science of management thinks is possible." (watch this short talk below.)

Powell was famous for the rules of leadership he kept under the glass on his desk. Finally, he addressed the 13 Rules of Leadership and these rules have taken on a life all their own. A few of them include: Share credit; Check the small things; Remain calm; Be kind; and Get mad then get over it. All great thoughts and guideposts to live by in leading a team or an organization.

Sadly, Colin Powell died of COVID-19 complications in 2021 at the age of 84.

The Essence of Leadership (2:42 mins)
https://BobLogan.net/ColinPowellTheEssenceofLeadership

In their specific way, each of these leaders inspired legions of followers in extremely challenging and sometimes dangerous missions. Many of these causes changed the lives of millions of people and entire nations. While some leaders fought violently for independence, others used non-violent means to achieve freedom for their people. In every case, all these leaders, despite their wildly divergent styles, faced a tremendous amount of risk. Risk is inherent with leadership, and great leaders absorb as much risk as possible to minimize the risk endured by their followers.

ESSENTIAL QUALITIES OF GREAT LEADERS

While most of us will likely never be in a position of leadership as monumental as John F. Kennedy or Martin Luther King, Jr., the embodiment of leadership qualities in the roles we play are just as important in fulfilling our own individual leadership missions. Following are the essential qualities of great leaders:

Enthusiasm

I define enthusiasm as showing up "with bells on." Not just going through the motions, but genuinely being excited and inspired to action. Some would say if you are lacking enthusiasm for a mission, it's not your mission. People can detect when you are not engaged in the task.

Integrity

Integrity can be defined in two ways: 1) honest and moral uprightness, and 2) wholeness and unity. The first is more in alignment with how I see it: making tough decisions even when it's hard. It also means making the right decisions, even if no one else is watching. Doing the right thing is everything. The second is more about functionality: Think about a bicycle wheel's integrity missing several spokes. Both can be useful ways of looking at issues. Does this way of being work in a broader sense? Does it have integrity?

Empowerment

Even the best leaders can't do it all themselves, and leaders who aren't effective may feel that having followers who are unquestioning or non-threatening is best. I have always felt that surrounding yourself with people smarter than you is the absolute key to success. Hire the very best people and empower them to do their part in the organization. Empowered people perform at high levels. Micro-managing and requiring blind loyalty do not promote the best from people and ultimately will not be what's best for the organization or mission.

Trust/Loyalty

Do your best for those who have trusted and done their best for you. To be satisfied, always be "all in" at all times. This quality relates to advice from *The Four Agreements* (always do your best)[72] by Don Miguel Ruiz and *Leadership Challenge* by authors Kouzes and Posner.[73] From their many years of research, both hail as the first law of leadership: If you don't believe in the messenger, you won't believe the message. They call it credibility and often describe it by the acronym DWYSYWD (Do what you say you will do).

Competence

The Peter Principle describes the organizational fallout when staff members are continuously promoted to their highest level of incompetence. To be successful as a leader and effective in any realm, competence is a foundational requirement. If you are promoted to a level of perceived incompetence, the previous qualities will help—surround yourself with people who are smarter than you; empower them; be enthusiastic; have integrity; and be trustworthy. Also, don't be afraid to ask for help to gain the competence you need to do your job well.

Decisiveness

Leadership requires the ability to be comfortable in making decisions. That doesn't mean you won't make mistakes, but mistakes help us learn, and when we act with integrity, mistakes can be easily fixed or cleaned up. Often, new professionals struggle with this one. Too many have a fear of making mistakes. Worrying about doing the wrong thing can trap you in analysis paralysis or relying too much on advice from others. Both traits are acceptable to some degree, but to be a leader, you must learn how to make the critical decisions you feel are best for the mission and make them in a timely fashion. Decide and live with the results. Own the decision, whether the outcome is good or bad; that's what good leaders do.

Confidence

Developing confidence may require you to "fake it till you make it." It is a quality that can come from two equally valid sources, both of which are important:

Act as if—even if you don't feel it yet, building a sense of confidence from the inside and projecting it will help it become more real. Eventually, the energy makes it so.

Practice makes perfect. Repetition and trial and error help ingrain skills so they are available when needed. This kind of discipline builds confidence over time.

Charisma

This may seem very much like enthusiasm, but it is distinctly different. Enthusiasm is *for* something, and charisma is *from* somewhere. It is possible to find both enthusiasm and charisma generated internally. However, enthusiasm is created for a mission, vision, or goal, while charisma is embodied from within and expressed outwardly. It is not strictly required to be charismatic to be a good leader, but exuding passion for what you do will make it easier to attract others to the cause.

Communication

Especially when they are charismatic, leaders can feel the need to "sell" their viewpoints and talk too much, or they may think they must have all the answers. A good leader is also a good listener, a better leader is a better listener, and a great leader is a great listener. Listening is key. The great leader asks lots of questions and involves others in the process. Communication is vital in both the development and sharing of the vision. It is impossible to be a good leader (or a productive human for that matter) without being a skillful, patient, and open communicator.

A STORY OF INSPIRING LEADERSHIP

How can one have a chapter on leadership and not include the story of President Volodymyr Zelensky and the job he is doing in his country of Ukraine? At this writing, no one knows how the 2022 Russian invasion at the hands of Vladimir Putin will turn out, but it is clear from all sides that Zelensky has handled this crisis in a way that nobody saw coming, considering his background as an actor and comedian. When reviewing the traits necessary to be a successful leader, Zelensky has shown all of them—enthusiasm, confidence, empowerment, charisma, and communication. By his single-minded purpose and fearless attitude, he has brought the entire democratic world together in unity. Even Switzerland, long a bastion of neutrality on the world stage, has pledged its support. Zelensky is my hero, and I wish there were more leaders like him in the world.

A FEMININE APPROACH

As this book was being written, a renaissance for women was taking place. The many women's marches, #MeToo movement, and the #Time'sUp movement, not to mention a wave of diverse women elected to Congress in 2018 dominating the news 24-7. These events brought more attention to issues important to women and shined a light on the unique way women lead. Multiple studies have explained the success of organizations with more women in leadership positions.

In 2014, *Forbes Magazine* published an interview with scientist Janet Crawford, who created a workshop for companies called "The Surprising Neuroscience of Gender Inequality." Crawford said that feminine leadership traits like connectivity, communication, and collaborative sharing are the future of business and shared the following[74]:

1. MIT research suggested that group intelligence is related to the number of women on a team.
2. Gallup found that retail stores with more gender diversity experienced significantly higher revenues.
3. Catalyst research reported that Fortune 500 companies with the highest percentages of women board directors produced an average of 66 percent higher ROI than those with the least.

Crawford went on to say:

> *"Both men and women can exhibit feminine leadership qualities, but the tendency, both biologically and culturally, is for women to embody them more. These include a host of characteristics such as long-term and global perspective-taking, nurturing, empathy, conversational turn-taking, credit distribution, inquiry, networked thinking, etc. Promoting feminine leadership is less an issue of male vs. female, but a question of whether we are overlooking qualities that may be crucial to navigating 21st Century business challenges."*

The Athena Doctrine authors compiled surveys with 64,000 women and men in thirteen countries that classified 125 human traits—half of the sample by gender and the other half by which characteristics are most important to leadership, success, morality, and happiness today. Respondents consistently chose what they considered "feminine traits" or values, such as selflessness, empathy, collaboration, flexibility, and patience as the most important.[75] The majority also rejected masculine notions of control, aggression, and black-and-white thinking that underlie many of our business, political, and social structures. Two-thirds thought the world would be a better place if men thought more like women.

DIVERSITY IN LEADERSHIP AT THE UNIVERSITY OF ARIZONA

I am proud to say the University of Arizona was a leader in hiring diversity of thought, color, and gender well before it became the norm. Before there was ever a John Thompson from Georgetown, a John Chaney from Temple, or a George Raveling from Washington State, there was Fred Snowden. In 1972, the UA hired Fred Snowden, an African American out of Detroit. He became the first black Division I basketball coach in the United States. Snowden coached from 1972 to 1982, and he laid the groundwork for the incredible national success of Wildcat basketball under Lute Olson, Sean Miller, and now Tommy Lloyd. In an irony of ironies, in January 1994, Snowden passed away on MLK Day at the young age of fifty-seven.

Fred Snowden – UA Head Basketball Coach 1972-1982

The year 2022 is the fiftieth anniversary of the passing of Title IX, the landmark legislation that provided equal treatment for women's athletics vs. their male counterparts. The UA led the way in landmark Title IX hiring in the early 1980s. Led by Dr. Cedric Dempsey, our senior athletic administration included two of the most prominent female administrators in the United States, Mary Roby and Kathleen "Rocky" LaRose. During my time in intercollegiate athletics, I experienced firsthand the leadership of these two amazing leaders, and they provided the foresight and support to identify and hire two outstanding women in traditional male-dominated roles. Implementing Title IX was controversial in those days, but the University of Arizona was at the forefront of the movement and necessary change. While significant progress has been made in Title IX, much more work must be done nationally.

Mary Roby

Kathleen "Rocky" LaRose

Sue Hillman was hired in 1983. She became the first head athletic trainer in the United States. She was our head athletic trainer when I was coaching with Larry Smith, and she totally took charge of the entire athletic training operation for all seventeen sports. She was an inspirational and committed leader.[76] Later, in 1997, Hillman became the first female athletic trainer in NFL history, working for the Pittsburgh Steelers.

Sue Hillman Interview (3:26 mins)
https://boblogan.net/SueHillmanInterview

Sue Hillman with Pittsburgh Steelers Head Trainer, John Norwig

Only two years later, we hired Meg Ritchie Stone to become head of our strength training program. Meg competed in the shot put and discus for Scotland in the 1980 Olympics (Moscow) and the 1984 Olympics (Los Angeles). Meg had the strong Scottish accent, and she also had quite the personality. When our big tough football players were grumbling under their breath about having a woman lead them in the weight room, word got back to Head Coach Larry Smith. Coach Smith asked Meg to address the squad in a team meeting. The auditorium was packed, and Coach Smith said to Meg, "Meg, tell me a little about your program and your strength-training goals." Meg, in her Scottish brogue, said, "Coach Smith, I don't want to take up much of your valuable time because I know you have a lot to cover with the team. But regarding our strength goals, I only have one. And that is to get every member of our team to be as strong as me! It may take some time, but if our players can squat, clean, and bench as much as me, we will be one of the strongest teams in the PAC-10!" That answer certainly got everyone's attention! Coach Smith loved her response and having him support her in the way he did went a long way toward helping Meg succeed.

Meg also took this bravado into the weight room. Again, when some of the players were complaining, she addressed it head on with them. She took the biggest, baddest, and strongest players on the team and challenged them to a bench press contest! When Meg threw on about 335 pounds on the barbell, laid down on the bench, and proceeded to rapidly do six to eight reps, she made her point! The players immediately knew whom they were dealing with, and Meg became a fixture and a friend to everyone.

Meg Ritchie-Stone

In 1990, *Sports Illustrated* did a story on Ritchie and former UA former Wildcat linebacker Chris Singleton. Singleton was selected by the New England Patriots in the first round of the NFL draft. Singleton says Ritchie's knowledge of weight training was the biggest point in her favor. "Guys came around in a hurry once they started working with her," says Singleton. "Man or woman, it didn't matter. She knows what she's talking about."[77]

Ritchie never lacked confidence when she walked into the job. And she did not feel any pressure to succeed because she was a woman. In the same *Sports Illustrated* article, Ritchie said, "Quite honestly, and I hope this doesn't sound big-headed, I knew that because of my background, I was as qualified, if not more qualified, than anyone." Well said, Meg. You were the greatest to work with, and you inspired me when I saw how you handled this male-dominated football world.

LEADERSHIP ON THE CAMINO

Self-leadership plays a significant role in first getting someone onto the Camino. The Camino is not something most people just wake up and decide to do one day. It takes months of planning and conditioning, a ton of logistical arrangements, securing and packing the right supplies, and convincing many people to support you in taking on this adventure.

Numerous Camino leaders have paved the way for others to embark on this journey, including those who write books on the Camino, produce outstanding Camino films, and give community talks on the Camino as I do regularly. The pilgrimage has been made immeasurably more accessible by those who have taken a leadership role in helping others attain this goal.

Once you arrive in Spain to begin the pilgrimage, considerable motivation and self-discipline are required to keep going. You must continuously put one foot in front of the other despite blisters, heavy backpacks, bad weather, muddy paths, language barriers, and the myriad other challenges you face along the way. When you are out on the Camino, you see leaders of all types emerge. Some speak different languages and act as translators for pilgrims in need. Some have walked the Camino multiple times and can offer expert advice and guidance from their experiences. And finally, some provide constant encouragement to those who may be struggling.

Leadership comes in many forms, and leaders emerge in various ways at different times to make the path easier to navigate. Sometimes you lead, and sometimes you follow; sometimes you walk alone, and sometimes you are part of a group. At times, you may be frustrated by your travel companions, and other times incredibly grateful for them, but no matter what, I can guarantee that someone is always acting as a leader.

Review of Leadership

1. Leaders are made, not born. Not everyone needs to lead; it is perfectly acceptable to be a follower and a team player to help an organization thrive.

2. Leadership is not based on job titles, and it doesn't require a specific endorsement. At any moment, you can exercise your leadership muscle to inspire others to action.

3. Whom you associate with and what you learn shape whom you become. Take opportunities to grow, and choose wisely who you want as a mentor.

4. Management and leadership are both essential and at the same time distinct from each other. Managers ensure goals are met on time and keep the trains running. Leaders set the vision and inspire followers who wish to make them proud.

5. Good leaders know how important it is to properly recognize their people. It may mean a public display of appreciation at a team meeting or it could be a private moment when the leader pulls the team member aside.

6. Great leaders accept the blame when things go wrong and give others credit when things go well.

7. Leaders encourage risk taking and innovation. They provide support when something new or risky is being attempted. And they support their team when things do not go quite as planned.

8. Leaders are not afraid to act, and act decisively. They know they will never have all the perfect information. This breeds confidence in the team.

9. A leader works to develop the team. A good leader is not afraid to add people who are smarter than themself to the organization.

10. A leader has a desire to serve a purpose greater than themselves.

CHAPTER 14
SIMPLICITY AND BALANCE

"The more often you decline invitations to spend time with friends or family because you are too busy with either work or other activities, the more you should realize that your life is not in balance."

— BYRON PULSIFER

When she said it, I was a bit taken aback, but now I reflect with gratitude on the day my wife told me, "Bob, you have to dial it down. You don't see things the way I do. You are doing way too much, you say yes to everyone, and it is affecting your health and ultimately how long you're going to live. I am serious."

My wife saw before I did the impacts of my hectic lifestyle. I was overweight, pre-diabetic, suffering from sleep apnea, and struggling with painful sciatica. My job stress was in high gear, and I said yes to practically anyone who asked me to serve on a local board, chair a gala, or raise money for an important cause. Everything I was doing felt significant and essential to me, and I justified my crazy schedule because I thought it was necessary to do my job well. No doubt this was all true, but I was doing so at the expense of myself and my family. I felt honored when someone wanted me to be involved with their cause, and because of that, I rarely stopped to think about whether I had the time or capacity to serve. It was clear all this involvement made me feel important and needed, but my wife was correct. Something had to give. My life was way out of balance.

Around this time, I saw the movie *The Way* and recognized the stark contrast between how the father and son lived their lives in the film.[78] Played by real-life father and son Martin Sheen and Emilio Estevez, the film depicted a father so focused on his optometry practice and his "country club" lifestyle, the professional side of life, that he could not connect to his son. He didn't understand his son's wandering ways and desire for "frivolous" travel until a tragedy forced him to see things differently. It took his son dying in the mountains of the Pyrenees for him to step back and take stock of his own life. Seeing that movie, filmed entirely on the Camino, made me look at my life completely differently. I will never forget walking out of that theater, amid my own internal work and personal crises, and saying to myself, "I need to do this." I was hoping walking the Camino de Santiago would put things into perspective for me as well. Looking back today, I can say it did.

A CAMINO STORY—SIMPLICITY AND BALANCE ON THE CAMINO

What was my primary takeaway from walking the Camino? As simple as this sounds, one truly understands the beauty of simplicity. Each Camino day is very much like the hysterical Bill Murray movie *Groundhog Day*. You wake up and do the same thing over and over, day after day. It can feel very much the same as putting one foot in front of the other for hours on end, and each pilgrim is on the same path no matter what their motivations might be. One of the revelations was how humbling it was to meet so many people on the trail and not care what people did for a living. Surprisingly, it rarely came up in conversation since it is often the first question we ask here in the United States when we meet someone new.

And for me, in my role as a university executive and major gift fundraiser, I was always evaluating the people I would meet day to day. What people do for a living, the roles they play in the community, the titles they have, the cars they drive, or where they live are critical for me to do my job successfully. These are all characteristics that, when put together, help me develop a "profile" for whether I should continue to cultivate this person as a potential donor. Understand that I have evaluated people like this for my job for nearly thirty years!

However, you learn very quickly on the Camino that *none* of these characteristics matter on the Camino. No one cares what you do, where you live, how much money you make, or how big or fancy your car or house is. Needless to say, it was an incredible relief to meet people for who they are, not what they represent. I began to understand how we are all just humans on this Earth, living a life and trying to do good things. Conversely, the Camino helped me see I could let go of my identification with those things.

Balance took some more intention, though, and I recognized this most clearly when I walked with my wife Judy in 2018 to celebrate our thirty-fifth wedding anniversary. I had walked the Camino twice before, in 2012 and 2015, and I was looking forward to her seeing the Camino in the same way I did.

However, when we arrived in Spain, I realized this journey would be more difficult than I initially imagined. Judy generally walks slower than me; at our individual paces, over the course of one hour, I would be over a mile ahead of her on the trail. She walks about two-and-a-half miles per hour, and I walk three-and-a-half. Clearly, I would have to adjust my gait if we were going to enjoy this experience together. While walking slower was unnatural for me, I realized this walk was totally new for Judy. Unfortunately, she had more physical issues with her feet and developed several painful blisters that impacted her speed. I asked myself, "What can I do to make her experience great?" In my previous Caminos, I would stay in traditional albergues with bunk beds and a communal lifestyle, sacrificing privacy in the process. It meant group meals and fighting to get a hot shower or access to the clothes dryers. After all, this is the Camino that "pure" pilgrims experience.

But I could not subject my wife to that type of Camino lifestyle. I would have to adjust so she could have an enjoyable experience. That often meant staying in a hotel with a private room rather than an albergue with bunk beds, like I would have preferred. Also, we might decide to stay an extra night instead of walking every single day. We might only walk six to nine miles instead of the more traditional twelve to twenty miles. After all, it was not a race, and it was an experience you must allow to grow on you gradually.

One example of how I adjusted was to avoid the Meseta, the long, flat, and boring part of the Camino that takes 6-8 days. I decided to just skip this section and cut off about 100 miles. We took a train, and honestly, it was beautiful. Before, I was so strict about everything related to the Camino, but with Judy, it was invigorating to not worry about all of it anymore. It sent a message to me; one I will never forget—accommodating others can help us have an experience we may have missed out on otherwise.

I recognize not everyone can fly to Spain and spend a month on the Camino, but there are many other things you can do to rebalance and simplify your own life. Slow down, step back, and take stock. Are you spending your time the way you want? Do you have friends who are there for you? Are you doing work (paid or unpaid) that makes a difference and feels fulfilling to you? Are you doing too much and not being discerning enough before saying yes? Sometimes just saying no is the right answer. What are you willing to change? What will it take—outside of your comfort zone—to have what you truly want?

I think every inquiry should begin by looking at the four essential areas of life—faith, family, friends, and work—as we discussed earlier. Many of us have these out of balance. Poor life choices take a toll on our sense of well-being, our emotional state, and very possibly our physical health. Balance rarely is attained perfectly, but with enough focus and attention to its importance, it is achievable over many weeks, months, and years. When you encounter a hectic period, as we all do from time to time, you must step back and make time for a corresponding period of rest.

One easy barometer of balance is looking at how Americans use their vacation time. Are you using all the vacation time allocated to you each year? Americans typically get less paid vacation time than people in other parts of the world, and more than half don't use all the vacation time due to them. In 2018, 768 million vacation days went unused in the US, and 236 million days were totally forfeited—the equivalent of more than $65.5 billion in lost benefits.[79]

U.S. Travel Association Report
https://BobLogan.net/USVacationUse

Why is this? Research has shown that the typical American worker feels they cannot leave their job for that amount of time, when, in fact, most managers *want* their employees to take their earned vacation time. There is a disconnect in the American worker's mindset. We have a long way to go on the work-life balance front.

If you recall, back in Chapter 4 on Adversity, we spent some time talking about UA softball coach Mike Candrea. In addition to the adversity he faced in his career, he had a family experience that put his entire work-life balance into perspective. Mike will readily admit today his work lifestyle and career success in softball came at the expense of his family. Work was always first for him. The pressure to maintain his success was constant. If it wasn't with the UA, it was with the Olympic softball program.

When Mike was a candidate to become the USA Softball coach in the mid-1990s, his son Mikel came to him and said the dreaded, "Dad, can we have a talk? I have something important I need to go over with you." Mike's worst thoughts immediately came to mind. Did Mikel get his girlfriend pregnant, or was he failing some of his high school classes? What could it be?

Mike and Mikel sat down in the living room and Mikel said, "Dad, would you consider withdrawing from consideration to become the US Olympic softball coach?" Mike was totally shocked and taken aback by his son's request. He replied, "Why would you ask me to do this?" Mikel explained he was entering his senior year at Casa Grande HS, and after all these years of playing junior high and high school baseball, his dad had never seen him play in a baseball game. Mikel said, "Dad, I really want you to come watch me play my senior year of baseball. I would love to have you sitting in the stands each game."

What a stunning blow to Mike. It was like a sledgehammer to his forehead. He could not believe what he had become. He was crushed and suddenly realized how he had allowed his life to spin out of control regarding work. He recognized immediately how totally out of balance his life was, and he set out to change it for the better. Mike did pull out of Olympic consideration, and he dedicated the next year to supporting his son. It was the best year of his life.

This experience of work-life balance allowed him to recalibrate his entire life. Today, Mike speaks to audiences about "live where your feet are" or "living in the moment." Every couple of years, I invite Mike to speak at my Rotary Club since he is such an engaging and entertaining speaker. Most in the audience are surprised when he doesn't make a single reference to NCAA championships, wins,

All-Americans, or anything connected to "on the field softball success." He *never* talks about softball. His entire talk focuses on having balance in our lives.

Mike Candrea speaking at my Rotary Club of Tucson, 2019

Mike references the importance of key relationships in our lives and making sure to understand that work should never surpass the importance of family, friends, or faith. Too many people live in a world where they were wronged by someone many years ago. Mike says, "You cannot change the past, and you cannot let past events control your life today. Those days are long gone and should be forgotten. Conversely, you cannot predict the future, so manage only the things you can control in your life." He talks about living in the moment and living in the here and now. I loved one of his frequent quotes: "Live where your feet are…" Mike believes it should be the motto for all of us to live our lives by. Good advice for everyone.

During an interview with the Arizona Wildcat student newspaper, Mike said, "The experience with my son Mikel hit me like a ton of bricks and really made me realize I was losing that balance in life. If there's one thing I preach to young coaches and players, it's that we all must have some balance, and balance to me is the balance between your family, your religion, and your profession. Also, I think we all need some spiritual help in our life, and you can't wait until something happens to get it; it's got to be a part of your life now. When I found balance in my life, I discovered I was a happier person, a more productive dad, and a more productive coach." Well said, Mike Candrea, well said.

One public speaking seminar I lead is called True Colors. It's a program very similar to the well-known Myers-Briggs Type Indicator (MBTI), which is a way to understand personalities better and how they operate. At the beginning of my program, I ask the audience to introduce themselves by sharing three simple things about themselves:

1. Name
2. Two adjectives that would describe them
3. Something we wouldn't know from looking at them

While these ice breaker questions are elementary, I've been floored many times by the responses. Some of the things people share are amazing. For example, one time, we had a former Olympic skating team member! It was interesting to see the reaction of her coworkers at this session. They all turned to her in shock because they were not aware of this information about her background. It came as a total surprise to everyone in the room. There is a message here—if you desire to take a relationship beyond the superficial, you must be willing to ask different questions and converse at a much deeper level.

From my experience, it doesn't take much because, believe it or not, most people enjoy talking about themselves if given the opportunity. Just as important as the questions you ask is how you listen to the answers. Active listening is the key to communication. We all know people who are only thinking about what they want to say next when they are in a conversation with you. It is maddening to talk to those people. They only care about themselves and rarely ask you about your own life. Listen more if you're going to grow your relationships with your circle of friends, family, and coworkers. Everyday life can mirror the intense Camino interactions if we are willing to be more intentional about how we relate with one another.

Bronnie Ware, an Australian palliative care nurse who spent her life attending to people on their deathbeds, shared this valuable information in her book, *The Top Five Regrets of the Dying—A Life Transformed by the Dearly Departing*.[80]

The dying wished they had:
1. Pursued their own dreams and aspirations instead of living the life others expected of them.
2. Worked less (all of the men and many of the women shared this one).
3. Had the courage to express their feelings and speak their minds.
4. Stayed in touch with friends better.
5. Let themselves be happier.

Think about this list for a second. Where you are today, right now, at your current state of life, would you agree with one or more of these five regrets? I believe many people would say yes. Do we work too hard and to the exclusion of our friends and family? Yes. Do we stay in touch with our old friends as much as we used to? Probably not. That is clear just from Christmas cards. We used to receive three to four times as many cards as we do today. What is going on? How many of us live a life that is unfulfilling instead of pursuing our passions and our dreams? Many of us, it seems. If you have gotten yourself this far into this book, then you have time. You have time to change and make a difference. Take the initiative. Do it now, and you will be happier for it.

Tips for Creating Balance and Simplicity in Your Life

1. Quit accumulating so much stuff and pare down what you already have.
2. Settle for "good enough." Brené Brown talks at length on how we spend a lot of time striving for perfection in our projects and even personal development. You are good enough now, and what you produce is too. Strive to be "good enough."
3. Put down your device and interact with someone face-to-face; turn off the TV and talk!
4. Do work that you love as much as possible (paid or unpaid) and work to live rather than living to work.
5. Take stock of your life to determine if you are living the way you want to. If not, do whatever you can to change that. Start now and be patient if it takes a while to create a life you love.
6. If you are turning down invitations to spend time with family and friends for work, find a way to change that. Pick up the phone and call someone you haven't spoken to in a while.
7. Ask yourself repeatedly if you genuinely *want* to do what people ask you to do (or even those things you initiate). Make it a goal to only do those things that elicit a "hell yes." The more you do this, the easier it will become.
8. When in doubt, do *something*.
9. We are often afraid to die. Don't be afraid to live!
10. Read Bronnie Ware's book so you don't have the same regrets at the end of your life.

CHAPTER 15

A RANDOM WALK THROUGH LIFE

Commit to Your Path And Have Some Stories to Tell at the End....

"The quality of a person's life is in direct proportion to their commitment to excellence, regardless of their chosen field of endeavor."

— VINCE LOMBARDI

Throughout these pages, I have shared several stories about finding my path in life. I hope they might have helped you find your path. Whether consciously or unconsciously, many of us find ourselves following a path predetermined or encouraged by someone else in our lives. This is so unfortunate on many fronts. Maybe we are in a situation where we are trying to please our spouse or earn our parents' respect. Many famous comedians, artists, and musicians have told the familiar story of disappointing their parents' dreams of them becoming a doctor or lawyer by following their passion. Often, we aren't even aware of consciously choosing our direction, so we end up following the winds of change wherever they lead us.

As it turns out, landing on a path we would never have considered can at times be a blessing, and at other times, a curse. My wife often tells me I have been able to convince her to do things she never would have considered otherwise—like packing up our lives and moving to Italy. My career choices often led to more work and sacrifice for her. This scenario has occurred many times and I appreciate the sacrifices she made to accommodate me and the pursuit of my next great job. However, when looking in the rearview mirror, Judy almost always tells me she is glad she went through the excitement of all this change.

As this book draws to a close, I would like to leave you with some straightforward advice I hope will inspire you to find and follow your own authentic path no matter what or where it may take you. We will finish with a random list of stories and messages for you to digest.

One difficult message you will face during your life is the judgment of others. Do not be deterred. Do not fall victim to their negative opinions. They do not see the world the way you do, and you will have to stay firm on your convictions. Your goals may seem crazy to others in your life, and you may only find discouragement when striving to reach them. Do it anyway. Failure can be a good thing, and it is often necessary to find the successes. It's never too early or too late to follow your dreams. Though sometimes you may feel like you have to put your nose to the grindstone when you're young and save your passions for your free time or retirement, I encourage you not to wait. Right now, you may think you are too young and inexperienced to follow your dreams, but consider the following:

DID YOU KNOW:

1. Tiger Woods was just three when he shot 48 for nine holes.
2. Julie Andrews was eight when she mastered an astounding four-octave singing range.
3. Mozart wrote his first symphony, also at the age of eight.
4. Paul McCartney was fifteen when John Lennon invited him to join a band.
5. Bill Gates co-founded Microsoft at nineteen and became a billionaire at thirty-one.
6. Joe DiMaggio was twenty-six when he hit safely in fifty-six consecutive games.
7. Henry David Thoreau was twenty-seven when he moved to Walden Pond, built a house, planted a garden, and began a two-year experiment in simplicity and self-reliance.
8. Ralph Lauren was twenty-nine when he created Polo.

9. William Shakespeare was thirty-one when he wrote *Romeo and Juliet*.
10. Thomas Jefferson was thirty-three when he wrote the Declaration of Independence.

Are you too young to share your talents, follow your dreams, and choose your own path? Not if any of the fine folks above are any indication! Matthew Kelly calls this journey 'the rhythm of life' and I think that is an appropriate way to look at things.[81]

Conversely, maybe you are on the other end of the life journey and now worried you might be too old. The responsible person at this age means staying put and not trying new things. Again, consider the following:

DID YOU KNOW:

1. Mother Teresa was forty when she founded the Missionaries of Charity.
2. Jack Nicklaus was forty-six when he shot 65 in the final round, and 30 on the back nine, to win the Masters.
3. Henry Ford was fifty when he started his first manufacturing assembly line.
4. Ray Kroc was a fifty-two-year-old milkshake machine salesman when he bought out Mac and Dick McDonald and officially started McDonald's.
5. Pablo Picasso was fifty-five when he painted *Guernica*.
6. Winston Churchill was sixty-five when he became Britain's Prime Minister.
7. Nelson Mandela was seventy-one when he was released from prison after twenty-seven years, and four years later, he was elected President of South Africa.
8. Michelangelo was seventy-two when he designed the dome of St. Peter's Basilica in Rome.
9. Benjamin Franklin was seventy-nine when he invented bifocal eyeglasses.
10. Frank Lloyd Wright was ninety-one when he completed his work on the Guggenheim Museum.

Adding more to these impressive accomplishments from older people is that many of these feats occurred when lifespans were far shorter than they are today. Also, the challenges were far more significant technically (without modern conveniences). Given all that, with a better quality of life today, ease of travel, and many innovative tools at our disposal, there is no excuse for us not to at least take a stab at fulfilling our unique purpose, no matter how old you are.

OSIRIS-REX—THE TRIP OF A LIFETIME

One of the memorable experiences I had during my twenty years in the College of Science was being exposed to the work of our astronomy department and our lunar and planetary laboratory (LPL). LPL has been involved in every single mission since NASA was formed in the 1960s, and it even mapped the entire lunar surface of the moon for the Apollo landings. People are amazed when I tell them this fact.

In September 2016, I experienced a launch at Cape Canaveral and the Kennedy Space Center for the OSIRIS-REx mission. OSIRIS-REx was a seven-year mission to the near-earth asteroid Bennu. Once it reached the asteroid, it would gently touch the surface and scoop up a sample of the soil for return to Earth. The engineering behind this mission is something to behold. OSIRIS-REx had to travel for two years and 509 million miles to catch up to Bennu. For scale, Bennu is about the size of the Empire State Building. Then, while traveling at 61,300 mph, OSIRIS-REx had to precisely time its entry into orbit around Bennu, a feat in and of itself. After mapping the surface of Bennu for 500 days, OSIRIS-REx slowly approached the asteroid and grabbed some soil from the surface with its TAGSAM (Touch and Go Sample Acquisition Mechanism) device. OSIRIS-REx will return to Earth and deliver the capsule with this precious soil to the Utah desert on September 24, 2023.

Why is this mission so important? The asteroid Bennu is a carbon-rich body, and the scientific community believes it was formed at the beginning of the Big Bang. The soil collected could very well provide the keys to understanding the beginning of our universe!

I was one of the lead administrators from the UA, and we hosted 150 friends, donors, and family members in south Florida for the launch of OSIRIS-REx. Since we were part of the mission, we were able to participate in many behind-the-scenes NASA briefings and had access to the private launch location. Needless to say, it was a sight to behold to watch the dedicated work of hundreds, if not thousands, of scientists launch high into the atmosphere. The joy these scientists and engineers felt rivaled any Final Four or Rose Bowl I may have attended in my athletic past. It provided an indelible memory, to say the least.

A RANDOM WALK THROUGH LIFE | 243

Dr. Dante Lauretta, Principal Investigator, and the author

The OSIRIS-REx launch, as seen from the beach

WHAT OTHER PEOPLE THINK OF YOU IS NONE OF YOUR BUSINESS

Dick Tomey was the winningest coach in the University of Arizona football history, winning ninety-five games, coaching five future first-round NFL draft picks, and twenty All-Americans. After thirteen years in the role, with poor results for the two most recent seasons, Tomey had many loyal fans who supported him, win or lose. He also had a growing number of detractors. Coach Tomey was known as a "players coach," and he always put the team above his personal goals. He had a huge heart and a generosity of spirit rarely seen in major college football.

This spirit played out firsthand when one of his players, Damon Terrell, collapsed from heat exhaustion during a summer pre-season practice in August 1995. The team was devastated, but Coach Tomey felt he had to stay by the family's side during this emotional time. While Terrell was in the hospital for a couple of weeks fighting for his life, the season had already begun. The top-twenty ranked Wildcats already had played games at home against Pacific and in Atlanta vs. Georgia Tech. On the night of the Georgia Tech game, Tomey was notified that Terrell had passed away. Tomey and the entire team were distraught.

The following week Arizona was scheduled to play a huge intersectional game against Big Ten opponent Illinois in Champaign. Tomey felt so strongly about his commitment to support Terrell's family that he chose to miss this crucial game so he could attend Terrell's funeral in California. The entire team did their part and honored Damon Terrell during the pre-game by kneeling on the field in formation, forming the huge letters "DT" for everyone in the stadium and on television to see. It was a touching moment and a heartfelt tribute to Damon Terrell.

For a head coach to miss a significant intersectional top-twenty football game was unheard of in college football, but Tomey garnered the universal support of everyone around him. Tomey understood the value of football vs. the value of life. There is no comparison, and he taught his team, the fans, and everyone connected to Arizona athletics the important lesson of balance.

At the time, many fans were talking about replacing Dick Tomey. The boo-birds had arrived. Coach Tomey knew he was not the most popular person to many Arizona fans and influential alumni at the time, but he still chose to do what he felt was right, even if it contributed to the possibility that he might lose his job. If you make decisions based solely on "polling data," you won't be effective. In the end, you must look yourself in the mirror and feel good about your actions. Your own opinion is the one that matters most. For many, that is a hard lesson to learn.

PRACTICING GRATITUDE PERMANENTLY CHANGES YOUR PERSPECTIVE

It is impossible to feel sorry for yourself when you are grateful. When you begin actively searching for things in your life to be thankful for, you will be amazed by how beautiful your life truly is. The same life that previously had you complaining about everything will suddenly be much better, even though absolutely nothing has changed. It is all about your perspective and how you see the world around you. You choose to be happy, and you choose to show appreciation and gratitude.

When I give my talks, I always start with an eye-opening exercise for the audience. I first ask the audience members to raise their hands if any of the following situations have ever touched them, a family member, or a friend. I assure them I will not call on anyone specifically to speak about their situation. I want them to feel comfortable and have total transparency. Below are a handful of situations I ask them about:

- Suicide
- A cancer diagnosis
- A tragic accident
- Financial issues
- Being fired from a job
- Dealing with end-of-life issues for parents

I ask these questions one by one. After each question, hands go up and then come down. People take side glances to see who else has their hands up. In the end, I ask the entire audience to first put all their hands down. Then, I ask them to raise their hands if they said yes to *any* of these scenarios. As one can imagine, when you look around the room, *every* single hand is in the air.

What exactly does this mean? It means that life is messy, and believe it or not, many people around you have problems much worse than you have. Stop wallowing in self-pity and start to understand and appreciate the many blessings bestowed on you. If it is only a roof over your head, food to eat, and family nearby, you have more than most people in the world. Start showing appreciation and gratitude more often—you will be a better person for it.

How you do this is up to you. It could take the shape of writing personal notes to others, keeping a gratitude journal, saying daily prayers of thanksgiving, or just taking note of the first and last thing every day. Either way, develop a practice of gratitude if you want to have the most empowering perspective on your life that you can. Wayne Dyer famously said, "When you change the way you see things, the things you see change." Gratitude helps you realize the abundance all around you.

IF YOUR WHY IS STRONG ENOUGH, YOU WILL FIGURE OUT THE HOW

Simon Sinek's famous TED Talk encourages us to begin with figuring out our why. At last count, this fantastic TED Talk has been viewed fifty-nine million times![82]

You deserve to see it yourself:

Simon Sinek TED Talk (18:01 mins)
https://BobLogan.net/SinekStartWithWhy

Sinek says most people and most organizations can easily verbalize "what" they do. And many more can also verbalize "how" they do "what" they do. However, Sinek contends many people and organizations struggle with the "why." What is their purpose; what is their "why"? If our motivation for doing anything is powerful enough, we will make it happen.

THE LITTLE THINGS MATTER

William Harry McRaven is a retired Navy Admiral who headed the U.S. Special Operations Command. He jokes that no one remembers much about his distinguished military career. Still, people often remark on the advice he gave during a 2014 commencement address at The University of Texas:[83]

If you make your bed every morning, you will have accomplished the first task of the day. It will give you a small sense of pride, and it will encourage you to do another task and another and another. By the end of the day, that one task completed will have turned into many tasks completed. Making your bed will also reinforce the fact that little things in life matter. If you can't do the little things right, you will never do the big things right.

I would add that life begins at 8 a.m. What I mean by that is if you don't start right, you won't finish right. Whether you start with gratitude, meditation, exercise, or cooking yourself a great breakfast, it will be better than repeated snooze-button hitting, complaining, and worrying.

Admiral McRaven Commencement (19:01 mins)
https://BobLogan.net/McRavenEntireSpeech

Admiral McRaven Commencement (edited) (10:04 mins)
https://BobLogan.net/McRavenSpeechShort

BEING PART OF "WALTON'S WORLD" FOR A DAY AT BIOSPHERE 2

If you looked up the word "eccentric" in the dictionary, you are likely to see a photo of former UCLA All-American Bill Walton. To say Walton brings a special flair to his basketball broadcasts is the understatement of understatements. You either love Bill Walton as a basketball television analyst or you hate him. Watching him is almost like watching NASCAR and waiting for the big crash. You know the moment will eventually come and you just can't take your eyes and ears away from the screen. You don't want to miss it and you want to see what happens next.

Anything is fair game to come out of Bill Walton's mouth. He will always make a reference to the Grateful Dead and Jerry Garcia. (Did you know Walton has seen the Dead in concert more than 850 times!) Or he may talk about the huge Teepee he has in his backyard. Walton has a special love for Tucson and the University of Arizona Wildcats since his son, Luke, played at Arizona for Lute Olson from 1999 to 2003.

Knowing how Walton loves to promote local treasures when he is coming to a PAC-12 city for a broadcast, we thought we could convince him to come out and visit Biosphere 2 and get a big mention during his halftime show, "Walton's World." That day came on January 16, 2015, when he was in Tucson to broadcast the Utah Utes game against the UA. Walton did respond and I was fortunate enough to lead him on a tour of the iconic Biosphere 2 facility. He was amazed to hear about the science at the Biosphere, and yes, we were able to get significant airtime during "Walton's World." What a treat.

Bill Walton loves Biosphere 2

Bill Walton Does Crazy Things (2:26 mins)
https://youtu.be/381OiBkie2U

Walton's World Tribute (1:05 mins)
https://youtu.be/pF4m6T5cy7w

LIVE A LIFE THAT WILL PROVIDE GREAT STORIES TO TELL

I am often very self-conscious when asked to tell stories about my various adventures. However, I feel incredibly blessed to have lived the kind of life that people are intrigued enough to want to hear more details. A good friend of mine always puts it this way: "Go write your obituary first, and then go out and live it."

When I tell the stories, I realize how cool many of my life experiences are, and I think about others whose stories motivated me to take risks and follow my passion. My daring got me into the stadium and onto that Fiesta Bowl field in a Santa suit all those years ago. My desperation to get a coaching job found me leading a team of non-English speaking football players in Bologna, Italy. My desire to find answers had me walk hundreds of miles on the Camino de Santiago even though I was out of shape and didn't speak Spanish. My willingness to accept risk landed me in the College of Science when I thought of myself as only a dumb jock. Now, as I'm retiring from a long university career, I'm starting a new one as a speaker, author, and consultant at age sixty-five. I have always said, "Life's too short." Ferris Bueller said it even better in one of my all-time favorite movies, "Life moves pretty fast. If you don't stop and look around once in a while, you could miss it."

A CHANCE MEETING WITH BASKETBALL LEGEND DEAN SMITH

When I was an associate athletic director at the University of Arizona, one of my duties was to handle all future football and basketball schedules. While the PAC-10 ensured eight conference football games and eighteen conference basketball games, it was my job to schedule all of the non-conference opponents for upcoming seasons. Working with Coach Lute Olson was very interesting in this regard. Typically, we would play six to eight non-conference games, and Lute wanted a handful of easy wins over teams in McKale. These games are called "buy" games. We schedule a lesser opponent to come to McKale, pay them a ton of money, get the easy win, and we don't have to worry about scheduling a return game. It was a win-win for both teams. The lesser team helped with their annual budget, and they gave their players the experience of playing a highly ranked Arizona team in a packed McKale Center.

Dean Smith — North Carolina Head Coach, 1961-1997 (Photo courtesy of UNC Athletics)

But Lute also wanted to play a few significant teams every year. He believed it helped in the March Madness seeding if we played a handful of top-notch, highly ranked opponents. He would not shy away from anyone. We played Duke, Illinois, Georgetown, Michigan, Kansas, Purdue, LSU, and many others over the years. One year, Lute thought we should schedule a home and home arrangement with North Carolina. Wow! What a great series this would be for college basketball.

I pulled out my NCAA directory and contacted North Carolina. You never know who handles football and basketball scheduling at other schools. It could be an assistant coach, an assistant athletics director like me, or a basketball operations person. It was all over the map, so I called the North Carolina athletic director's office to find out who handled North Carolina basketball scheduling.

I was connected to a Mr. Smith. I didn't think anything of it at the time, but after a few minutes of conversation, and when Mr. Smith began asking personal questions about Lute Olson and his wife Bobbi, I realized I was dealing with someone who knew Coach Olson quite well. Then it dawned on me! This was not just Mr. Smith; this was basketball coaching legend Dean Smith! I could not believe it. Dean Smith had retired from coaching a few years earlier in 1997, and his long-time, thirty-plus-year assistant coach Bill Guthridge had taken over the head coaching duties.

Coach Smith, the winningest basketball coach in NCAA history at the time, stayed in the North Carolina athletic department to handle alumni, fundraising, and obviously, basketball scheduling duties! Once I figured it out and stopped stammering from nervousness, Coach Smith and I had a great conversation. And by the way, we did schedule a home and home arrangement with North Carolina in 2006 and 2007.

A GOLFER'S LIFE-TIME MEMORY— ST. ANDREWS GOLF CLUB

I love a challenge. It's like a drug to me to have something that needs fixing and figure out how to do it. Whether it's around the house or with my car, I'm always willing to take on something challenging. You can learn almost anything by watching YouTube. Also, and very importantly, I'm not afraid to pick up the phone and ask for help. Maybe it comes from asking people for money all of these years, but so much of getting what you want in life is just asking someone else to help you. The worst they can say is no, right?

My persistence recently got me onto the oldest and perhaps most revered golf course in the entire world, St. Andrews Golf Club—called the Cathedral of Golf. This is the place where the sport of golf was founded, and golf has been played here since the early fifteenth century.

In the summer of 2019, my wife and I attended the International Rotary Convention with 15,000 Rotarians in Hamburg, Germany. Attending this annual Rotary convention was a requirement in my role as the recently elected president of my local Rotary Club of Tucson. While the convention itself was a fantastic experience, one highlight was it was located in Hamburg. Anni, whom I walked with for eleven days on the Camino in 2012, happened to live in Hamburg, so I knew we would be able to reconnect! What a small world.

In addition to the Rotary Convention, since we were already in Europe, Judy and I decided to extend our stay and see more of Europe. After much discussion, we decided to spend an additional week in Scotland. Scotland is a great place to visit. We began planning where to go and what to see. Because of the ease of travel and the city's history, Edinburgh quickly rose to the top of the list.

Coincidentally, at the time our oldest son Tommy worked for the world-famous Fairmont Hotels and Resorts. I started to research the Fairmont Hotel directory to see if there might be any Fairmont Hotels we could stay at in Scotland. Lo and behold, there was a beautiful Fairmont property in of all places, St. Andrews! St. Andrews is only a couple of hours away by car from Edinburgh, so we decided to stay there next. And one cannot argue with the handsome discount our son was able to negotiate on a gorgeous room.

As a golfer, I immediately wondered if I could play the famous course, though I assumed it would be nearly impossible. I have heard about people needing to book a round at St. Andrews many years in advance. I did not have high hopes. As a single player, my only option was to arrive at 2:30 a.m. and wait until 6:00 a.m. when golfers would start teeing off for the day. If someone didn't show up for their tee time, I could join that foursome. That was not my idea of fun, so I researched various golf operators who broker St. Andrews rounds, but it would cost a ton of money. I couldn't justify that to my wife, so I was resigned to tour the countryside.

Finally, just doing some internet browsing, I pulled up the calendar for St. Andrews Links and discovered a Rotary golf tournament was scheduled for the same week we would be in Scotland. What were the chances? When I called to inquire, I was told there were no spots available, and people were flying in from all over the world to compete in this event. I initially surmised this Rotary tournament was somehow directly connected to the Rotary International Convention in Germany I had attended the previous week. After an email exchange with the tournament director, he told me that was not the case; in fact, this tournament had been going on for sixty-five years!

Eventually, the director took pity on me and allowed me to play in the first two practice rounds of the event. No idea how he got me in but was I ever grateful. To play St. Andrews on a week's notice and at a discounted rate was beyond my wildest dreams. I was placed in threesomes on day one with players from Finland and Ireland

and on day two with players from Sweden and Estonia. I also took advantage of my time on the course to have my caddy take pictures of me on the famous Swilican stone bridge on the eighteenth fairway. This bridge was where Arnold Palmer, Jack Nicklaus, Tom Watson, and Gary Player all stood and waved goodbye to the British Open fans in their final rounds. To pose on the bridge similarly to those famous golfers was an incredible experience all-around.

Bob Logan at famous Swilican Bridge

**Logan with his good friend Tom Watson
(special thanks to Adobe Photoshop)**

THE SPORTING DAY OF A LIFETIME—
THE MASTERS AND THE FINAL FOUR

Staying on this golf theme for a bit, on Monday, April 14, 1994, I can say I experienced arguably the most amazing single day in spectator sports history. On that day, some friends from the UA and I attended the Masters Golf Tournament in Augusta, Georgia, and walked the hallowed grounds of that entire course. Later that same evening, we were sitting in the Charlotte Coliseum watching Arkansas upset Duke for the NCAA Men's Basketball National Championship!

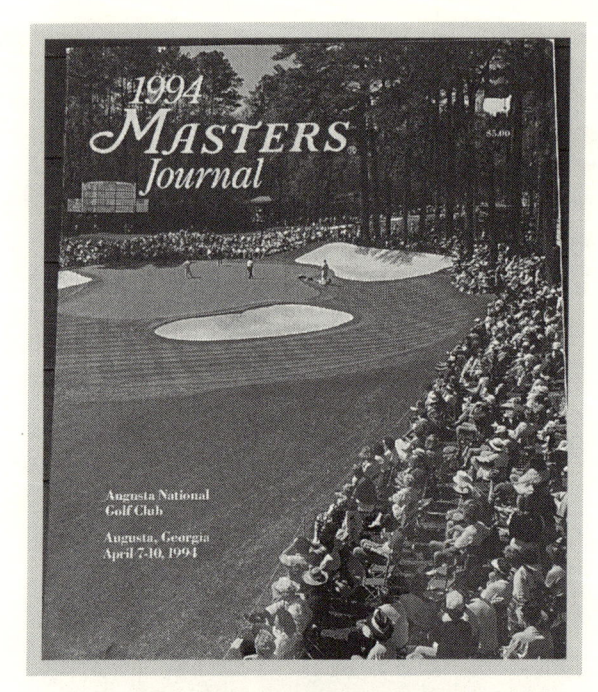

The 1994 Masters program

1994 NCAA Final Four program

Here is the background so you can put all of this in perspective. In 1994, the University of Arizona had another outstanding men's basketball team. We were ranked much of the year in the top ten, had a final record of 26-9, and played in the Final Four in Charlotte, North Carolina.

On Saturday, April 2, we played Coach Nolan Richardson's 31-3 Arkansas Razorbacks in the first round of the Final Four and lost 91-82. They were just too good for us. In the hotel after the game, we were sitting around the lobby bar talking about the game and how anti-climactic it would be to watch the national championship game on Monday night with Duke playing Arkansas.

One of our drinking buddies then piped up with a great idea. He said, "Look, the Masters starts next week; let's jump in a car, drive to Augusta, Georgia, and walk the practice rounds on Monday. I just read it only costs $10 to get a practice round ticket! Then we could drive back to Charlotte in the late afternoon and watch the national championship game that night. Would that be a crazy day or what?" (Since then, The Masters $10 practice round tickets being open to the public has ended. No chance today.)

And that, my friends, is exactly what we did. As it turns out, Augusta is only a two-and-a-half-hour drive from Charlotte and can easily be done in one day. We might be a few minutes late to the game, but who cares?

What a day, I must say. If you are a golfer at any level, you *must* put a visit to The Masters on your bucket list. The grounds, the grass, the people, the Masters store, the food—it was all amazing.

It is still a day I will never forget.

CREATING A LIFE-TIME MEMORY AT THE UNIVERSITY OF NOTRE DAME

My occasional boldness has often paid off for my kids. Most notably, I was able to call on my old football connections to allow my fifth-grade son Sean to experience his lifetime memory. One year, our family decided to take a summer vacation to Chicago to visit the home where my dad grew up. Sean had been telling us for years that his dream was to be part of a future Fighting Irish football team. Sean noticed South Bend, home of the University of Notre Dame, wasn't that far from our Chicago summer vacation spot. He begged us to take a couple of extra days to detour to South Bend and Notre Dame. He wanted to see his dream school (and as a big Notre Dame fan, I did too).

I took charge of the rest by reaching out to a couple of contacts in the Notre Dame athletic department I had worked with many years earlier at the University of Arizona. Mike Low was the Director of Trademarks and Licensing, and Rob Ianello was Notre Dame's football recruiting coordinator and wide receivers coach. These guys made Sean's dreams come true. First, we visited Mike Low's office on campus. Mike Low oversaw all licensed Notre Dame logo apparel for the entire university. He had a closet full of this stuff. The room was *filled* with Notre Dame merchandise and paraphernalia. Sean came home with no fewer than nine branded Notre Dame caps and a handful of ND shirts. He was on cloud nine.

Next, I had asked Rob Ianello if he could surprise Sean at Notre Dame's football stadium. We walked to the stadium at the appointed time when Rob casually walked out and introduced himself. Rob said to Sean, "Coach Logan here tells me you're a pretty good football player. Would you like to take a tour of our locker room and catch some passes on the football field?" Sean's eyes were like saucers.

We slowly entered the locker room and saw all the national championship rings in a trophy case along with the Heisman trophies. Sean even tried on some of the bright gold football helmets hanging in the lockers! Then we went through the tunnel and onto the field. What a thrill!

I need to emphasize how big a fan Sean was for Notre Dame. It is safe to say Sean was pretty bold too. When he was in fifth grade, he was a huge fan of everything Notre Dame, and specifically an online Notre Dame football recruiting website. He was enamored with this website and knew *everything* about the Notre Dame recruits. He was continually posting content on discussion boards talking about the team and the players' qualities. He was always researching and posting his findings. He must have impressed someone at the website because after a few months of non-stop posting activity, the website contacted Sean via email to ask if he was interested in becoming a contributing author. They said his knowledge and talent at expressing himself about Notre Dame football and recruiting was very impressive. Sean immediately said yes.

Sean Logan inside the Notre Dame football locker room (the helmet fits!)

Later, I asked him if they knew he was only twelve. "Nope. They never asked." He wrote for this website for quite a while, and he must have had some good writing skills since he later graduated from the ASU Cronkite School of Journalism. Sean spent the early part of his career as a photo/video journalist for the *Arizona Republic* newspaper in Phoenix. He has subsequently won two Emmy Awards for excellence in journalism. He is an amazing kid.

LOST IN ANOTHER WORLD—BOLOGNA, ITALY

Many years earlier, when I had just arrived in Bologna, Italy to coach my football team, I was struggling with the Italian language. Bologna is not exactly a tourist destination, so very few people there spoke English. I was wearing out an Italian-English translation book because I depended on it to find the correct Italian words. One morning, a woman standing in line behind me in a small coffee shop took pity on me. She stepped up to the front of the line and helped me communicate with the café owner. She spoke perfect English, and I was grateful to her for showing up at my absolutely worst time.

After we enjoyed our espressos together, as a gesture of appreciation, I offered to carry her many bags of groceries back to her flat, and she invited me in to meet her husband. As it turned out, I learned they owned a beautiful ranch with many horses, and that spawned an idea for me. I knew Judy was not so enamored to get on a bus each Saturday for a long bus ride to watch the Bologna Doves play a football game. Most of our games were anywhere from 2-4 hours away. Judy would be a trooper and not complain, but I knew she would dread these road trips each week.

When she was younger, Judy used to own a horse, and she was quite the equestrian back then. When I found out my new English-speaking Italian friends liked to ride their horses at their ranch every weekend, I asked if it were possible for Judy to join them. They enthusiastically said yes, and it was the start of quite a friendship. We had dinner with them many times over that year, and they became one of the lasting memories we had from our time in Italy. All because of a chance encounter in a small, local café. Who would have guessed?

Now go out and live your life and let your own path find you. After all, since we are all on this Earth for a short while, take advantage of every opportunity presented to you. Famed author and mythologist Joseph Campbell was known for his work covering many aspects of the human experience. Campbell's best-known book is _The Hero with a Thousand Faces_ (1949).[84]

One of his famous quotes seems like a fitting end to this book.

> "If you can see your path laid out in front of you step by step,
> you know it's not your path.
> Your own path you make with every step you take.
> That's why it's your path."

ACKNOWLEDGMENTS

While writing this book, which is part memoir and part self-help, I was able to look back at my past and remember all the people who helped me along the path to success. I was fortunate to have had incredible bosses and mentors throughout my career. My early days of football coaching truly established the baseline for my personal and professional development. Legendary coaches Ed Doherty and Dennis Bene at Salpointe Catholic High School; Larry Gray at Flagstaff and Flowing Wells High Schools; Head Coach Larry Smith at the University of Arizona, and UA assistant coaches Moe Ankney, Tom Roggeman, and Bobby April. To work with this stable of outstanding coaches was truly humbling.

As for my professional career, Dr. Cedric Dempsey and Jim Livengood thought enough to hire me out of the corporate world of AT&T. It was a wonderful ten-year ride, and they were amazing mentors during my time in the world of athletic administration. And, of course, Tom Sanders and Kathleen "Rocky" LaRose were there as well. Two of my counterparts, Mark Harlan and Chris del Conte, went on to become directors of athletics at Utah and Texas, respectively. They were amazing to work with and I could see back then they would be uber-successful in the field of athletics administration.

Of course, I need to thank College of Science Dean Joaquin Ruiz for taking a chance on me to lead his development operation, hiring me from the world of intercollegiate athletics. It was a huge risk for him, but it ended up being a crazy ride of 20+ years. Associating with so many world-class scientists, was humbling, to say the least. Working together, I am proud to say we raised the visibility of the College of Science, both locally and nationally.

My family deserves a special place here. My wife and I have two amazing sons, Sean and Tommy, and they are both very successful in the Phoenix area. It is nice to have children who always did well in school, never got in trouble, always did the right thing, and still talk to their parents in adulthood today! It is a parent's greatest gift, and we are extremely proud of both of our sons.

Finally, my wife Judy. To live with me takes a special person, trust me. Judy has been by my side since 1980, and this may be difficult for some to believe, but we rarely have a fight or a disagreement. As you've read in this book, the sacrifices she made on my behalf are truly incredible. Early in our relationship, when my father was dying of lung cancer, Judy dropped everything and moved into our home and provided him extraordinary loving care. She was amazing in every way and still is, and it did not take me long to realize she was the right one at that time. This book has been a labor of love over the past few years, and Judy, it is truly gratifying to be able to say this now for everyone to read—I love you.

Bob Legan

ENDNOTES

1 Roosevelt, Theodore. (1910, April 23). Citizenship in a Republic: The Man in the Arena. Sorbonne, Paris, France.

2 NASA In-Depth: Mars Climate Orbiter https://solarsystem.nasa.gov/missions/mars-climate-orbiter/in-depth/

3 "Metric Mishap Caused Loss of NASA Orbiter." CNN.com. September 30, 1999. http://www.cnn.com/TECH/space/9909/30/mars.metric.02/

4 NASA In-Depth: Mars Climate Orbiter https://solarsystem.nasa.gov/missions/mars-climate-orbiter/in-depth/

5 "NASA Reveals Probable Cause of Mars Polar Lander and Deep Space-2 Mission Failures. SpaceRef.com. Keith Cowing. March 28, 2000. http://www.spaceref.com/news/viewnews.html?id=105

6 Jones, Tom. *Sky Walking: An Astronaut's Memoir.* 2006. Washington, DC: Smithsonian Books and Harper Collins, 2016. p. 3-9, 183-189, 211-212.

7. Nicholas, Stephanie. "So Close Yet So Far: The Jammed Airlock Hatch of STS-80." NASA Kennedy Space Center, 2012. https://www.nasa.gov/pdf/740020main_SCSC-R-0113%20Basic.pdf

8. Gilbert, D. *Stumbling on Happiness*. New York, NY: Alfred A. Knopf, 2006. p. 187-192.

9. Estevez, Emilio Dir. *The Way*. (2010) United States, Spain: Filmax, Elixir Films.

10. Estevez, Emilio Dir. *The Way*. (2010) United States, Spain: Filmax, Elixir Films.

11. Brown, Brené. *Rising Strong: How the Ability to Reset Transforms the Way We Live, Love, Parent, and Lead*. New York, NY: Random House, 2017.

12. Wimbrow, Dale. *The Guy in the Glass*. 1934. Reprinted with permission from Wimbrow family.

13. Merrill, Elizabeth. "He grieved his wife's death, now U.S. softball coach must carry on." ESPN.com June 18, 2008.

14. American Psychological Association. The Road to Resilience. Washington, DC, n.d. Retrieved from: https://www.apa.org/helpcenter/road-resilience.

15. "After losing parents, 6-year-old embarks on smile mission." *On the Road with Steve Hartman, CBS Evening News*. August 7, 2015.

16. Cruz de Ferro [web log]. *Camino Ways Blog*. February 11, 2012. Retrieved from: https://caminoways.com/cruz-de-ferro

17. Scott, B., Russell, B. (1969). *He Ain't Heavy, He's My Brother* [Neil Diamond]. Single. United States: Universal City Records. November 5, 1970.

18 "Teacher Value Evident Here." Arizona Daily Star. A collaboration with Tucson Values Teachers and "My Favorite Teacher" Contest. Sunday, November 30, 2008, Page A10, Tucson, Arizona.

19 Mantovani, Andrea. "Kintsugi and the Art of Repair: Life is What Makes Us." https://medium.com/@andreamantovani/kintsugi-and-the-art-of-repair-life-is-what-makes-us-b4af13a39921

20 "Kintsugi–Art of Repair." Traditional Kyoto article. https://traditionalkyoto.com/culture/kintsugi/

21 Skrzycki, Cindy. "NCR Corp Agrees to AT&T Merger." *Washington Post*. May 7, 1991. https://www.washingtonpost.com/archive/business/1991/05/07/ncr-corp-agrees-to-att-merger/bc710870-7bd9-4904-843e-31571440e2f7/.

22 Keller, John J. "Disconnected Line: Why AT&T Takeover Of NCR Hasn't Been A Real Bell Ringer." *AP News*. September 19, 1995. https://apnews.com/article/c9b97e27a670ce4ff650523b69137a78.

23 Valee, Jean-Marc Dir. *Wild*. United States: *Fox Searchlight*, 2014. With Reese Witherspoon.

24 Poppel, S. "Michael Jordan didn't make varsity at first." *Newsweek, Special Edition*. October 17, 2015. doi: https://www.newsweek.com/missing-cut-382954

25 Gilbert, D. and Wilson, T. "The Impact Bias Is Alive and Well." *Journal of Personality and Social Psychology*. 105.5 (2013): 740-8. https://www.researchgate.net/publication/258501158_The_Impact_Bias_Is_Alive_and_Well

26 Gertner, Jon (2003). "The Futile Pursuit of Happiness." *The New York Times Magazine*. September 7, 2003. https://www.nytimes.com/2003/09/07/magazine/the-futile-pursuit-of-happiness.html

27 Brickman, P., Coates, D., and Janoff-Bulman, R. "Lottery winners and accident victims: Is happiness relative?" *Journal of Personality and Social Psychology.* 36.8 (1978): 917-927. http://dx.doi.org/10.1037/0022-3514.36.8.917

28 Skrzycki, Cindy. "NCR Corp Agrees to AT&T Merger." *Washington Post.* May 7, 1991. https://www.washingtonpost.com/archive/business/1991/05/07/ncr-corp-agrees-to-att-merger/bc710870-7bd9-4904-843e-31571440e2f7/.

29 Nieburh, Reinhold. "Serenity Prayer." 1932.

30 ESPN. March 4, 1993. New York, NY. (Jimmy Valvano was awarded the inaugural Arthur Ashe Courage and Humanitarian Award at the first annual ESPY Awards)

31 National Aeronautics and Space Administration (NASA). 2001 Mars Odyssey Arrival Press Kit, October 2001. https://mars.nasa.gov/system/downloadable_items/44749_odysseyarrival1.pdf

32 Frankl, Viktor E. Man's Search for Meaning. 1946. Boston: Beacon Press, 2006.

33 Kralik, J. *Simple Act of Gratitude: How Learning to Say Thank You Changed My Life.* New York: Hyperion, 2011.

34 McGhee, Paul, PhD. *Humor: The Lighter Path to Resilience and Health.* Author House, 2010.

35 Hodge Cronin & Associates. Humor in Business, A Survey. Rosemont, Illinois: Hodge Cronin & Associates, 1986.

36 Provine, R. R. *Laughter: A Scientific Investigation.* New York: Viking, 2000.

37 Andreassen, C. S. et al. "Use of Social Network Sites for Personal Purposes at Work: Does It Impair Self-Reported Work Performance?" *Comprehensive Psychology.* 2014.

38 Holmes, J. W., and McNeal, R. S. "Social Media, Participation, and Attitudes: Does Social Media Drive Polarization?" (R) Evolutionizing Political Communication through Social Media. (2016): 1-21. doi: 10.4018/978-1-4666-9879-6.ch001

39 Netflix Documentary. *Social Dilemma,* Directed by Jeff Orlowski-Yang. Interview with former Twitter Executive Jeff Seibert, 2015.

40 Shahrinaz, I., and Latif, R. A. "Authenticity Issues of Social Media: Credibility, Quality and Reality" *World Academy of Science, Engineering and Technology.* 74 (2013): 254-261.

41 Pelley, Scott (2021). "Whistleblower: Facebook is misleading the public on progress against hate speech, violence, misinformation." *60 Minutes.* October 4, 2021.

42 Mean world syndrome. (n.d.). Wikipedia. https://en.wikipedia.org/wiki/Mean_world_syndrome. Retrieved November 7, 2019.

43 "After losing parents, 6-year-old embarks on smile mission." *On the Road with Steve Hartman, CBS Evening News.* August 7, 2015.

44 Oedekerk, S. Dir. *Patch Adams.* [Motion Picture] Universal City, CA: Universal Studios, 1999. With Robin Williams.

45 Layard, Richard. *Happiness: Lessons from a New Science.* London: Penguin, 2011.

46 Brickman, P., Coates, D., and Janoff-Bulman, R. "Lottery winners and accident victims: Is happiness relative?" *Journal of Personality and Social Psychology.* 36.8 (1978): 917-927. http://dx.doi.org/10.1037/0022-3514.36.8.917

47 "Air New Zealand Flight 901." (November 19, 2019). https://en.wikipedia.org/wiki/Air_New_Zealand_Flight_901. Retrieved November 24, 2019.

48 Mean world syndrome. (n.d.). Wikipedia. https://en.wikipedia.org/wiki/Mean_world_syndrome. Retrieved November 7, 2019.

49 "11 Scientific Benefits of Being Outdoors." November 2, 2015. https://www.mentalfloss.com/article/70548/11-scientific-benefits-being-outdoors. Retrieved November 24, 2019.

50 Stanford University. "Stanford researchers find mental health prescription: Nature." April 9, 2016. https://news.stanford.edu/2015/06/30/hiking-mental-health-063015/. Retrieved November 24, 2019.

51 McMillon, B. et al., Volunteer Vacations: Short-Term Adventures That Will Benefit You and Others. Chicago: *Chicago Review Press*, 2012.

52 Tim, B. Serious Play 2008. Pasadena. February 2017. Retrieved from https://www.ted.com/talks/tim_brown_on_creativity_and_play?language=en

53 Rubin, Gretchen. (2019). *The Happiness Project: Or Why I Spent a Year Trying to Sing in the Morning, Clean My Closets, Fight Right, Read Aristotle, and Generally Have More Fun.* New York: Harper Luxe, 2019.

54 Breachnach, Sarah Ban. *Simple Abundance.* n.p.: Universe Publishing, 1998.

55 Thorpe, M. "12 Science-Based Benefits of Meditation." July 5, 2017. https://www.healthline.com/nutrition/12-benefits-of-meditation. Retrieved November 24, 2019.

56 Zemeckis, Robert Dir. *Forrest Gump.* Paramount Pictures. 1994. With Tom Hanks.

57 Maltz, Maxwell. *The New Psycho-Cybernetics.* New York, NY: Prentice-Hall Press, 2002. p. 51-54.

58 https://www.forbes.com/sites/taraswart/2018/03/27/the-4-underlying-principles-to-changing-your-brain/#2ca8855a71c3

59 "If You Can See It, You Can Achieve It: Why Visualization is The Key To Hitting Your Goals." https://blog.sanebox.com/2018/08/08/visualization-key-to-hitting-goals. Retrieved August 8, 2018.

60 *The Oprah Winfrey Show*. Harpo Studios. February 17, 1997. CBS. https://www.youtube.com/watch?v=-CbAcNDuEyA. Retrieved January 12, 2020.

61 *Oprah's Super Soul Conversations*. Podcast conversation with Anthony Ray Hinton. Oprah Winfrey. June 11, 2018. https://www.youtube.com/watch?v=2mFAWjn5Ego

62 Hinton, A. R., and Hardin, L. L. *The Sun Does Shine: How I Found Life and Freedom on Death Row*. London, Gr. Brit.: Rider Books, 2019.

63 McCain, J. S. "John McCain, Prisoner of War: A First-Person Account." *U.S. News & World Report*. January 28, 2008. https://www.usnews.com/news/articles/2008/01/28/john-mccain-prisoner-of-war-a-first-person-account.

64 "Natan (Anatoly) Sharansky." https://www.jewishvirtuallibrary.org/natan-anatoly-sharansky. Retrieved January 20, 2020.

65 Cicio, P. "Power of Visualization." August 12, 2016. https://www.philcicio.com/power-of-visualization/. Retrieved November 24, 2019.

66 Haefner, Joseph. "Mental Rehearsal and Visualization: The Secret to Improving Your Game Without Touching a Basketball!" https://www.breakthroughbasketball.com/mental/visualization.html. Retrieved October 20, 2014.

67 Lindsey Vonn. https://en.wikipedia.org/wiki/Lindsey_Vonn. Retrieved January 20, 2020.

68 Institute of Noetic Sciences (IONS). https://noetic.org/. Retrieved January 20, 2020.

69 Bures, F. "Decline to Decline." The Rotarian. December 2018. doi: https://www.rotary.org/en/column-attitude-helps-aging-process.

70 Greenwood, M. (2018, February 7). "Positive attitudes about aging reduce risk of dementia in older adults." https://news.yale.edu/2018/02/07/positive-attitudes-about-aging-reduce-risk-dementia-older-adults. Retrieved January 20, 2020.

71 Estevez, Emilio Dir. *The Way.* 2010. United States, Spain: Filmax, Elixir Films. With Martin Sheen and Emilio Estevez.

72 Ruiz, Don Miguel. *The Four Agreements.* Carlsbad, CA: Hay House, 2008.

73 Kouzes, James M., and Posner, Barry Z. *The Leadership Challenge: How to Keep Getting Extraordinary Things Done in Organizations.* San Francisco: Jossey-Bass, 2007.

74 Hwang, V. W. "Are Feminine Leadership Traits The Future Of Business?" August 30, 2014. https://www.forbes.com/sites/victorhwang/2014/08/30/are-feminine-leadership-traits-the-future-of-business/#19ceb70598e5

75 Gerzema, J., and D'Antonio, M. *The Athena Doctrine: How Women (and Men Who Think Like Them) Will Rule the Future.* San Francisco: Jossey-Bass, 2013.

76 Morales, Javier. Podcast: Interview with legendary Arizona head athletics trainer Sue Hillman in 50th Anniversary of Title IX. *All Sports Tucson.* March 17, 2022. http://allsportstucson.

com/2022/03/17/podcast-interview-with-legendary-arizona-head-athletics-trainer-sue-hillman-in-50th-anniversary-of-title-ix/

77 Banks, Leo. "The Wildcats' Weight Watcher—Meg Ritchie is Division I's Only Female Strength Coach. *Sports Illustrated.* October 15, 1990. https://vault.si.com/vault/1990/10/15/the-wildcats-weight-watcher-meg-ritchie-is-division-is-only-female-strength-coach

78 Estevez, Emilio Dir. *The Way.* 2010. United States, Spain: Filmax, Elixir Films. With Martin Sheen and Emilio Estevez.

79 U.S. Travel Association. "State of American Vacation 2018." May 8, 2018. https://www.ustravel.org/research/state-american-vacation-2018.

80 Ware, Bronnie. *The Top Five Regrets of the Dying: A Life Transformed by the Dearly Departing.* Carlsbad (California): Hay House, 2012.

81 Kelly, Matthew. Rhythm of Life. *Project Gutenberg Literary Archive Foundation,* 2006.

82 Sinek, Simon. *Start With "Why."* TED Talk. October 2017. https://www.youtube.com/watch?v=2Ss78LfY3nE

83 McRaven, W. H. "University of Texas - Austin 2014 Commencement." Austin, TX. https://www.youtube.com/watch?v=pxBQLFLei70

84 Campbell, Joseph. *The Hero With A Thousand Faces.* Original copyright by Bollingen Foundation. Published by Pantheon Books, 1949.

READING LIST

There is an old quote that says our personalities are developed by the people we meet, the relationships we build, and the books we read.

As mentioned earlier, I *love reading* good books. Below is a short sample of books you might enjoy. Note that these books are all over the map, from leadership and biographies to self-help, Camino, and novels. All of them are good; it just depends on what you are looking for. Some are recognizable, and others you may have never heard of before.

GENERAL BOOK RECOMMENDATIONS

1. *The Tipping Point: How Little Things Can Make a Big Difference* by Malcolm Gladwell
2. *Leaders Eat Last* by Simon Sinek
3. *Start With Why: How Great Leaders Inspire Everyone to Take Action* by Simon Sinek
4. *The Last Lecture* by Randy Pausch
5. *Sea Stories: My Life in Special Operations* by Admiral William McRaven
6. *Leaders: Myth and Reality* by General Stanley McChrystal (U.S. Army Retired)
7. *Make Your Bed: Little Things That Can Change Your Life…and Maybe the World* by Admiral William McRaven

8. *The Way of the Shepherd: Seven Secrets to Managing Productive People* by Dr. Kevin Leman and Bill Pentak
9. *Everyday Greatness* by Stephen Covey
10. *Grit* by Angela Duckworth
11. *Jump: Take the Leap of Faith to Achieve Your Life of Abundance* by Steve Harvey
12. *Uncommon: Finding Your Path to Significance* by Tony Dungy
13. *The 21 Indispensable Qualities of a Leader* by John C. Maxwell
14. *Failing Forward: Turning Mistakes into Stepping Stones for Success* by John C. Maxwell
15. *Dig Your Well Before You're Thirsty* by Harvey Mackay
16. *Man's Search for Meaning* by Viktor E. Frankl
17. *What It Takes To Be #1: Vince Lombardi on Leadership* by Vince Lombardi, Jr.
18. *The Kite Runner* by Khaled Hosseini
19. *The New Psycho-Cybernetics* by Maxwell Maltz
20. *Ciao America!—An Italian Discovers the U.S.* by Beppe Severgnini
21. *Playing for Pizza* by John Grisham
22. *Wonder* by R. J. Palacio
23. *Hillbilly Elegy* by J. D. Vance
24. *Lincoln on Leadership* by Donald T. Phillips
25. *All I Really Needed to Know I Learned in Kindergarten: Uncommon Thoughts on Common Things* by Robert Fulghum
26. *Stumbling on Happiness* by Dr. Daniel Gilbert
27. *The Happiness Advantage* by Shawn Achor
28. *The Connector's Way* and *The Trusted Way* by Patrick Galvin
29. *Wins, Losses, and Lessons* by Lou Holtz
30. *Landing on My Feet: A Diary of Dreams* by Kerri Strug

CAMINO DE SANTIAGO BOOK RECOMMENDATIONS

While I know you will enjoy many of the books on the general reading list, some of you might also be intrigued about the possibility of walking the Camino de Santiago in Spain. Is this something you might consider doing? These books will help you find your way to the Camino. I hope you do!

1. *The Camino Way: Lessons in Leadership from a Walk Across Spain* by Victor Prince
2. *A Million Steps* by Kurt Koontz
3. *Pilgrim Strong* by Steve Watkins
4. *I'll Push You: A Journey of 500 Miles, Two Best Friends, and One Wheelchair* by Patrick Gray and Justin Skeesuck
5. *Camino to Santiago: A Spiritual Companion—Stories compiled* by John Rafferty
6. *To Walk Far, Carry Less* by Jean-Christie Ashmore
7. *Walk in a Relaxed Manner: Life Lessons from the Camino* by Joyce Rupp
8. *Spiritual and Walking Guide* by Stacey Wittig
9. *I'm Off Then* by Hape Kerkeling
10. *Off the Road: A Modern Day Walk Down the Pilgrim's Route Into Spain* by Jack Hitt
11. *Seven Tips to Make the Most of the Camino de Santiago* by Cheri Powell

CAMINO DE SANTIAGO GUIDEBOOKS

1. *Camino de Santiago* by John Brierly
2. *A Village-to-Village Guide* by Anna Dintaman and David Landis
3. *The Camino Frances* – A Wise Pilgrim Guide
4. *Camino de Santiago* – Rother Walking Guide

INDEX

A

acceptance
   of change, 124, 144
   Kintsugi tradition, 100–102
   lessons/takeaways on, 106
accountability, 48, 146–148
Adams, Patch, 168
Adaptation to Life (Vaillant), 160
addiction, 163–166, 202
adversity, 2, 55–71
   asking for help, 67–68
   on Camino de Santiago pilgrimage, 55–59
   Candrea, Mike, 65–68
   lessons/takeaways on, 63, 68–70
   UA–ASU football rivalry and, 59–65
   vulnerability and, 67, 68–70
Agassi, Andre, 201, 203, 204
aging, 205–206
Air Force Academy
   author experience at, 9–14, 17–18
   father's response to author leaving, 15, 16, 146–147
   routines at, 12–14
Air New Zealand Flight 901, 177–179
albergues, 4, 29, 46–47, 104, 112, 113
alcoholism, 73–74, 97–98
Ali, Muhammed, 203
Alvernon Bridge story, 136–137
Amazon, 120
ambition, 23–24, 25
America's Funniest Home Videos, 184
Andrews, Julie, 240
Aneto Peak, 32
anger, 144, 160
Ankney, Moe, 60, 62

anxiety, 160, 182, 202
aphasia, 176, 195–197
Apollo missions, 18, 242
apologizing, 145–148, 155
Apple Computer, 159
April, Bobby, 131
April Fool's Day, 172
Arizona Daily Star, 93, 188
Arizona Republic, 165, 259
Arizona State University (ASU)
   UA rivalry with, 59–65, 68–70
   UA victory over, 152–154
Arizona Wildcats, 121, 184–185, 222, 235, 248
Arthur Ashe Award for Courage, 139
Ashikaga, Yoshimasa, 101
asking for help, 67–68, 71, 124
asteroid mission, 242
astronomy, 18. *See also* College of Science; Odyssey mission; Phoenix mission
ASU. *See* Arizona State University
AT&T Computer Systems, 18, 109, 138
Athena Doctrine, The (Gerzema & D'Antonio), 221
athletics, 16, 200–204
Aung San Suu Kyi, 216
author
   backyard football team barbecue, 99–100
   chance meeting with Dean Smith, 250–252
   childhood experiences, 95–100
   family background, 74–79
   loss of immediate family, 73, 150

MBA degree path, 16–18
other jobs held by, 2, 15, 18, 109, 138
photos of, 3, 10, 60, 85, 93, 128, 129, 243
as Santa at 1979 Fiesta Bowl, 184–189
at St. Andrews Golf Club, 252–255
at University of Notre Dame, 257–259
Avon Cosmetics, 15

B
balance, 2, 229–237
  on Camino de Santiago pilgrimage, 230–232
  happiness and, 190–191, 194
  importance of achieving, 232–236
  tips for creating, 237
Bannister, Roger, 118, 119
basketball, 91–93, 201–202, 223
Beckett, Samuel, 119
Bennu (asteroid), 242
best-case scenarios, 28
Bezos, Jeff, 120
Biosphere 2, 247–249
Bishop, Joey, 74
Black Lives Matter movement, 1
Blaslotto, Judd, 201–202
"Blessing Bags," 135, 136
blood pressure, 160, 202
Bologna Doves, 32–37, 260
  author coaching style change, 127–130, 132–133
  author introduction of special teams, 131–133
  author's challenges, 121–123
  team background, 126–127
Borden, Jack, 181
boundaries, 48
Bradbury, Ray, 208
brain plasticity, 176, 195–197

brain stem, 28, 196
BRAVING acronym, 48
Breathnach, Sarah Ban, 189–190
British Open Championship, 203, 254
Brown, Brené, 48, 237
Brown, Tim, 183
Buddha, 206
Burnett, Carol, 124
Busch, Frank, 167

C
Camino de Santiago pilgrimage, 3–5, 20, 114, 135
  adversity and, 55–59
  author's reasons for doing, 44, 108–109, 208, 229–230
  background, 29–30
  balance and simplicity on, 230–232
  challenges on, 107–118
  criticism and, 51–53
  Cruz de Ferro, 81–86
  effect on author's life, 51–53
  fear and, 29–32
  grief and, 81–86
  happiness and, 191–193
  humor/laughter on, 169–171
  leadership on, 227
  logistics, 114–118
  messiness of life and, 103–105
  opposition to author's doing, 44–47
  preparing for, 107–111
  purists' view of, 46–47, 57, 115–116
  reason why people walk, 30–31, 135
  transport service, 47, 115–116
  visualization of doing, 197–198, 208–209
Camino Francés (French Way), 30
Campbell, Joseph, 260
cancer, 69, 75, 77, 97, 139
Candid Camera, 184
Candrea, Mike, 65–68, 233–235
Candrea, Sue, 66–67

cardiovascular system, 160
Carrey, Jim, 198–199
catecholamines, 160
Catholicism, 73, 76, 77, 79, 81
CBS News, 79–80
Cecil, Chuck, 60, 62–64
challenges, 107–124
   benefits of, 118–119, 192
   on Camino de Santiago pilgrimage, 107–118
   coaching in Italy, 121–123
   College of Science, 44–45, 108–109, 120–121
   lessons/takeaways on, 124
Chaney, John, 222
changes, 2, 125–144
   career, 140–143
   coaching experience in Italy, 127–130, 132–133
   embracing, 124, 144
   gradual, 125, 134–137
   lessons/takeaways, 144
   proactive, 125, 137–138
   shifting perspective, 139–140
   sudden, 125, 133–134
charisma, 220
Churchill, Winston, 241
Civil Rights Movement, 215
Clark, Frank A., 48
CNN, 165–166
coaching, 207–208. *See also* Bologna Doves
Coelho, Paulo, 9
cognitive science, 176, 195–197
Colbert, Steven, 165
Cold War, 1
College of Science
   astronomy and space roles, 18, 23–24
   author challenges at, 44–45, 108–109, 120–121
   author leadership position at, 38

   fundraising efforts at, 45, 52–53, 108, 147–148
   LPL, 18–19, 22–23, 141, 242
   OSIRIS-REx mission, 140, 148, 242–243
   Phoenix mission, 22–23, 140–143
comfort zone, 118–119
communication, 220
comparisons, 124, 176
competence, 219
confidants, 68–71
confidence, 25, 39, 219–220
Confucius, 119
connection, 106
Consciousness Transformation Model, 205
constructive criticism, 41–44, 54
   effectively giving, 48–49
   embracing, 42–44
convictions, standing by, 9–14
Coop, Richard, 204
coronavirus pandemic, 1, 190, 217
courage, 27, 39, 106, 139
Covey, Stephen, 176
COVID-19 pandemic, 1, 190, 217
Crawford, Janet, 221
creativity, 183–189, 194
credibility, 219
criticism, 41–54
   author's facing of, 44–47
   discerning when to listen to, 51–54
   effectively giving, 48–49
   handling, 41–44
   ignoring, 49–50
   lessons/takeaways on, 46, 54
Cruz de Ferro, 81–86
Cuban Missile Crisis, 1, 215
curated content/image, 163–164
curiosity, 119
cytokines, 160

D

Daily Show, The, 165
Dante (writer), 73
Davis, Sammy, Jr., 74
death, 2, 73, 80, 150
    Candrea, Sue, 66–67
    Cruz de Ferro and, 83–86
    Gadea, Diego, 81–83
    of Jose's son, "Guapo," 94–95
    Logan, Edward Patrick, 75
    Logan, Jean, 74
    Logan, Jim, 76
    Powell, Colin L., 217
    Reitan, Julie, 66
    Sanders, Tom, 69
    Terrell, Damon, 244
DeBow, James, 63, 65
decisiveness, 219
Declaration of Independence, 241
Dempsey, Cedric, 69, 223
Department of Speech, Language, and Hearing Sciences, 176, 195–197
depression, 163–166, 182, 202
Diamond, Neil, 86
DiMaggio, Joe, 240
discomfort, 107–108, 114
Disney, Walt, 55, 208
Doherty, Ed, 147, 207
doing the right thing, 36, 39, 102, 106, 218
    Alvernon Bridge story, 136–137
Dooley, Mike, 124
door-to-door sales experience, 15
doubt, 176
Dumb and Dumber, 199
Dyer, Wayne, 246

E

economic crash of 2008-2009, 53
Edison, Thomas, 23, 119
EDL (Entry, Descent, and Landing), 141
Einstein, Albert, 195
Eller College, 16, 18
Emerson, Ralph Waldo, 171
Emery, Jim, 36, 127, 131
emotional/social fear, 27
empowerment, 218, 220
endorphins, 160
enthusiasm, 218, 220
Entry, Descent, and Landing (EDL), 141
Epicurus, 177
ESPY Award, 139
"Essence of Leadership," 217
Estevez, Emilio, 31, 44, 230
European National Championship (Eurobowl), 36, 127
Evelyn McKnight Brain Institute, 195–197
Extra-Vehicular Activity (EVA) failure, 22–23

F

Facebook, 163–164
failure, 2, 9–25
    author's Air Force Academy experience, 9–14, 17–18
    fear of, 9, 27–28, 119
    learning from, 18, 25, 120
    light bulb invention, 23–24
    MCO, 19–20
    MPL, 20–22
    Space Shuttle Mission STS-80, 22–23
False Evidence Appearing Real (FEAR), 27–28
Faulkner, William, 49
fear, 2, 27–39, 176. *See also* opinions of others
    of aging, 205–206
    Camino de Santiago pilgrimage and, 29–32
    of failure, 9, 27–28, 119

internal, 27–29, 37–38
of unknown, 32–37
FEAR (False Evidence Appearing Real), 27–28
feedback, 42–44, 48–49, 54
feminine leadership, 222–228
Fiesta Bowl (1979), 184–189
finding one's path, 239–260. *See also* opinions of others
   figuring out one's "why," 246
   gratitude and, 245–246
   importance of little things and, 246–247
   inspirational examples, 240–242
Finding True Happiness (Sheen), 175
Finisterre, Spain, 32
"flight or fight" mechanisms, 28
Floyd, George, 1
football. *See also* Bologna Doves
   role in author's life, 2, 11, 16, 74, 99–100
   special teams, 131–133
   UA–ASU rivalry, 59–65, 68–70
   UA victory over ASU, 152–154
   visualization techniques, 200–201
Forbes Magazine, 221
Ford, Henry, 124, 241
For Spacious Skies non-profit, 181
forward thinking, 106
Four Agreements, The (Ruiz), 219
Fox News, 165–166
France, 29, 32, 46, 106, 192–193
Frankl, Viktor, 144
Franklin, Benjamin, 241
Fraser, Jamie, 182–183
French Way (Camino Francés), 30
frustration, 176
Fuller Brush Company, 15
fun, 158–159, 162, 166–168
fundraising, 38, 44
   at College of Science, 45, 52–53, 108, 147–148
   fun while, 166–167

G

Gadea, Diego, 81–86
Galileo Circle, The, 208–209
Gandhi, Mohandas Karamchand, 216
Garcia, Frank, 99
Garcia, Jerry, 248
Gates, Bill, 240
GCC (Glendale Community College), 33
generosity, 48
German helium-infused beer, 172
Gilbert, Dan, 28–29, 133–134, 177
Glendale Community College (GCC), 33
GMAT (Graduate Management Admissions Test), 17
goal-setting, 23–24, 25
Goldwater, Barry, 14
golf
   Masters Golf Tournament (1994), 203, 255–257
   St. Andrews Golf Club, 252–255
   visualization in, 203–204
Google, 159, 163–164
gradual change, 125, 134–137
   Italy coaching experience, 126–133
Graduate Management Admissions Test (GMAT), 17
Grateful Dead, 248
gratitude, 106, 246, 250
   despite messiness of life, 245–246
   expressing, 145–146, 149–150
   happiness and, 189–190, 194
   simplicity and, 104–105
Greater Good Science Center, The, 180
greed, 176
grief, 73–87
   Camino de Santiago pilgrimage and, 81–86
   Cruz de Ferro and, 83–86

lessons/takeaways on, 87
remembering loved ones, 81–83
Groundhog Day, 230
Guernica (Picasso), 241
Guggenheim Museum, 241

H

Haeger, Fred, 33–36
Hanoi Hilton prison, 199–200
happiness, 2, 175–194
    Camino de Santiago pilgrimage and, 191–193
    challenges and, 192
    defining, 176–177
    failure and, 18
    gratitude and, 189–190, 194
    as a habit, 177–178, 194
    importance of little things to, 177–180
    "Lesson in Gratitude" (Logan), 151
    lessons/takeaways on, 194
    meditation/visualization and, 191, 194
    nature and, 181–182, 194
    play/creativity and, 183–189, 194
    serving/helping/volunteering and, 180–181, 183, 194
    smiling and, 180, 194
    studies on, 134, 177
    travel/vacation and, 182–183, 194, 232–233
    work-life balance and, 190–191, 194
Hartman, Steve, 79–80, 168
Haugen, Frances, 161, 164, 165
HDL cholesterol, 159
"He Ain't Heavy, He's My Brother" (Diamond), 86
health
    author, 32, 45–46, 107–108
    benefits of visualization on, 198–202, 212
    grief and, 81

humor/laughter and, 160
helping others, 180–181, 183, 194
Hero with a Thousand Faces, The (Campbell), 260
Hillman, Sue, 224, 225
Hinton, Anthony Ray, 199
Holtz, Lou, 50, 144
homelessness, 134–137
honesty, 218
Hopkins, Anthony, 37
Hubble Space Telescope, 18
humor, 2, 157–172
    on Camino de Santiago pilgrimage, 169–171
    media/social media and, 163–166
    medical benefits, 159–160
    play/fun and, 166–168
    reminders about, 172
    at work, 159, 160–162

I

Ianello, Rob, 258
IBM, 18
"I Have a Dream" (King), 215
imagination, 195. *See also* visualization
immune system, 160
impact bias, 28–29, 133–134, 177
Inferno (Dante), 73
inflammatory cytokines, 160
Instagram, 163–164
Institute of Noetic Sciences, 205
integrity, 48, 218
internal fears, 27–29, 37–38
International Rotary Convention, 252–253
Israeli Chess Exhibition (1996), 200

J

Jackson, Michael, 50
James, St. (apostle), 29–30
James Webb Space Telescope, 18
Japan, 100–102

jealousy, 176
Jefferson, Thomas, 241
Jemison, Mae, 181
Jerky Boys, 184
Jernigan, Tamara, 23
Jet Propulsion Lab (JPL), 141–143
Jimmy V Foundation, 139
John, Jay, 16, 68–69, 91–92, 94
Jones, Tom, 22–23
Jordan, Michael, 118, 119
"Jose," 91–95
Journal of Happiness Studies, 179–180
JPL (Jet Propulsion Lab), 141–143

K
Kamen, Dean, 91
Kasparov, Garry, 200
Kelleher, Herb, 161
Kelly, Matthew, 241
Kennedy, John F., 215, 218
Kindall, Jerry, 167
kindness, 79–80, 136–137, 150–152, 155
King, Martin Luther, Jr., 107, 215, 216, 218
Kintsugi tradition, 100–102
Knight, John, 133
Korean Conflict, 9
Kralik, John, 149–150
Kroc, Ray, 241
Kruschev, Nikita, 215

L
Labossiere, Stephan, 41
LaRose, Kathleen "Rocky," 167, 223, 224
laughter, 2, 157–172
    on Camino de Santiago pilgrimage, 169–171
    media/social media and, 163–166
    medical benefits, 159–160
    play/fun and, 166–168
    reminders about, 172
    at work, 159, 160–162
Laughter (Provine), 162
laughter yoga, 180
Lauren, Ralph, 240
Lauretta, Dante, 243
Lawford, Peter, 74
Law of Attraction, 207
Layard, Richard, 176–177
leadership, 18, 213–229
    on Camino de Santiago pilgrimage, 227
    diversity at UA, 222–227
    essential qualities, 218–220, 228
    Gandhi, Mohandas Karamchand, 216
    Kennedy, John F., 215
    King, Martin Luther, Jr., 215
    lessons/takeaways on, 228
    Lombardi, Vince, 215–216
    Powell, Colin L., 216–218
    women in, 222–228
    Zelensky, Volodymyr, 220–221
Leadership Challenge (Kouzes & Posner), 219
Lennon, John, 240
Leon, Spain, 31, 32, 46, 112
"Lesson in Gratitude" (Logan), 151
lessons/takeaways
    on adversity, 63, 68–70
    on apologizing, 155
    on balance and simplicity, 237
    on challenges, 124
    on changes, 144
    on criticism, 46, 54
    on doing the right thing, 36, 39
    on failure, 25
    on fear, 39
    on gratitude, 155
    on grief, 87
    on happiness, 194
    on humor/laughter, 172

on kindness, 155
on leadership, 228
on love, 155
on messiness of life, 106
workplace warning signs, 109
letting go, 106
Levy, Becca, 205–206
light bulb, invention of, 23–24
limbic brain, 28, 196
little things, importance of, 59, 117
    finding one's path and, 246–247
    happiness and, 177–180
Lloyd, Tommy, 222
Lockheed Martin, 19–20
Logan, Edward Patrick, 9–10, 69–70
    Air Force medals/ribbons, 76, 77–78
    alcohol use, 73–74, 97–99
    death, 75
    lung cancer, 69, 75, 77, 97
    response to author's decision to quit Air Force Academy, 15, 16, 146–147
    role as father, 99–100
    smoking cessation, 74–75
Logan, Jean, 73–75, 97–99
Logan, Jim, 69, 75–76
Logan, Judy
    caretaker role for author's father, 75
    confidant of author, 69–70
    discomfort over Camino trip, 32, 45–46, 52, 108
    situation with Jose from Mexico, 91–94
Logan, Sean, 84, 165, 257–259
Logan, Tommy, 84, 166, 253
Lombardi, Vince, 124, 128, 207, 215–216, 239
Look Up (Jemison), 181
Lotz, Anne Graham, 124
love
    expressing, 145–146, 150–154
    lessons/takeaways on, 155

Low, Mike, 258
low self-esteem, 14, 15, 37
loyalty, 219
Lugo, Spain, 209
Lunar and Planetary Laboratory (LPL), 18–19, 22–23, 141, 242
lung cancer, 69, 75, 77, 97

M

Madrid, Spain, 68, 112–114
management, 214
Mandela, Nelson, 27, 216, 241
"Man in the Arena, The" (Roosevelt), 6
"Man in the Glass, The" (Wimbrow), 50–51
"Man in the Mirror" (Jackson), 50
Marino, Dan, 184–185
Mars Climate Orbiter (MCO), 19–20
Mars Exploration Rovers, 21
Mars missions, 18–22. *See also* Odyssey mission; Phoenix mission
Mars Polar Lander (MPL), 20–22
Martin, Dean, 74
Martz, Maxwell, 204
master of business degree (MBA), 16–18
Masters Golf Tournament (1994), 203, 255–257
Mayfield, Ollie, 100
MBTI (Myers-Briggs Type Indicator), 235
McCain, John, 199–200
McCartney, Paul, 240
McDonald's, 241
McGhee, Paul, 167–168
McKim, Bob, 183–184
MCO (Mars Climate Orbiter), 19–20
McRaven, William Harry, 246–247
media, 163–166
meditation, 191, 194, 202, 212. *See also* visualization
menial jobs, 15, 25

messiness of life, 91–106
  author childhood experiences, 95–100
  Camino de Santiago and, 103–105
  doing the right thing, 102, 106
  gratitude despite, 245–246
  Kintsugi tradition, 100–102
  lessons/takeaways on, 106
#MeToo movement, 1, 221
Michelangelo, 241
Miller, Sean, 222
mindfulness, 2, 67
Mind over Golf (Coop), 204
mistakes, 25, 48, 146–148, 219
Montaigne, Michel de, 177
moral uprightness, 218
Mother Teresa, 241
motivation, 240–242, 246
Mozart, Wolfgang Amadeus, 240
MPL (Mars Polar Lander), 20–22
Mt. Erebus, 178–179
Murray, Bill, 230
Myers-Briggs Type Indicator (MBTI), 235

N
Napoleon Route, 32
NASA. *See also* Odyssey mission; OSIRIS-REx mission; Phoenix mission
  EVA failure, 22–23
  LPL collaboration, 18–19, 22–23, 141, 242
  MCO failure, 19–20
  MPL failure, 20–22
nature, 181–182, 194
NAU (Northern Arizona University), 15, 16, 23–24
NCAA Final Four program (1994), 255–257
NCR Corporation, 109, 138
negative emotions, 133–134, 176

negative feedback, 42–44, 48–49, 54
neocortex, 196
neuroscience, 176, 195–197
New England Patriots, 226
news media, 165–166
Nicholson, Jack, 190
Nicklaus, Jack, 203–204, 212, 241, 254
Nietzsche, Friedrich, 177
non-violence, 216
Northern Arizona University (NAU), 15, 16, 23–24
Northwestern University, 134, 177
Norwig, John, 225
Nouwen, Henri, 145
nuclear weapons, 1

O
Obama, Barack, 124
O Cebreiro, Spain, 192
Odyssey mission, 140–141
Olson, Lute, 167, 222, 248, 250–252
Onion, The, 165
On the Road with Steve Hartman, 79–80, 168
open workspaces, 159
Operation Desert Storm, 217
opinions of others
  fearing, 39, 50, 54, 119, 184
  ignoring, 184, 239–240, 244–245
Opportunity rover, 21
organizational power structures, 108–109, 137–138
Orisson, France, 103, 192
OSIRIS-REx mission, 140, 148, 242–243
Outlander, 182

P
pain, 107–108, 114, 160, 202
Palmer, Arnold, 254
path. *See* finding one's path

Peale, Norman Vincent, 200
Pearson, Gary, 127
perfectionism, 100–102, 106. *See also* messiness of life
persistence, 17, 25
perspective, 106, 139–140, 144, 245–246
Peter Principle, 219
Phoenix mission, 22–23, 140–143
physical fear, 27
Picasso, Pablo, 241
pilgrims, 29–32, 47
  albergues, 113
  Cruz de Ferro, 84–86
  increasing numbers, 114–116
Pinterest, 164
Pittsburgh Panthers, 184–185
Pittsburgh Steelers, 224, 225
play
  happiness and, 183–189, 194
  humor/laughter and, 166–168
Player, Gary, 254
political divisiveness/polarization, 1, 165–166
Ponferrada, Spain, 169–170
positivity, 71, 106, 124, 133–134
Powell, Colin L., 216–218
pre-frontal cortex, 196
presentations, 206–207
pressure, handling, 63
prison, 162
proactive change, 125, 137–138
Proctor & Gamble, 18
productivity
  humor/laughter and, 160–162
  media/social media and, 163–166
Project Happiness (Rubin), 189
Provine, Robert, 162
psycho-cybernetics, 195
psychology, 176, 195–197
public speaking, 206–207
pulmonary health, 160

Pulsifer, Byron, 229
Punk'd, 184
Putin, Vladimir, 1, 220
Pyrenees Mountains, 29, 32, 44, 103, 192

Q

QR codes/videos, 3
  Air Force Academy cadet training, 12, 13
  author as Santa at 1979 Fiesta Bowl, 188
  benefits of meditation, 202
  Camino de Santiago pilgrimage, 5, 30
  "Essence of Leadership," 217
  Frances Haugen interview, 165
  German helium-infused beer, 172
  "I Have a Dream" (King), 215
  James DeBow Goal Line Stand, 65
  Kintsugi tradition, 101
  "Lesson in Gratitude" (Logan), 151
  Mars Phoenix Mission, 143
  McRaven University of Texas commencement address, 247
  Nature-Rx.org, 181–182
  Simon Sinek TED Talk, 246
  Southwest Airlines pre-flight safety talks, 161
  Steve Hartman CBS News On The Road – "Smiles," 80
  Sue Hillman interview, 224
  unused vacation time, 232
  Valvano Arthur Ashe Award for Courage speech, 139
  Walton, Bill, 249

R

Rabanal del Camino, Spain, 104
Random Acts of Kindness, 150–152, 155
Raveling, George, 222

Real Madrid Football Club, 169–170
Reitan, Julie, 66
reliability, 48
remembrance, 81–83
reptilian brain, 28, 196
resilience, 65–68, 71
resistance to change, 137–138, 144
revenge-seeking, 176
Richardson, Nolan, 257
Rieke, Marcia, 18
Rising Strong (Brown), 48
risk-taking, 25, 120–121, 217–218. *See also* ambition
Ritchie-Stone, Meg, 225–226
Roby, Mary, 223
Roggeman, Tom, 60, 62–64
Romeo and Juliet (Shakespeare), 241
Roncesvalles, Spain, 32, 192
Roosevelt, Theodore, 6, 124
Rose Bowl, 59
Rotarian, The, 205
Rotary Club of Tucson, 150–152, 252–253
Rubin, Gretchen, 189
Ruiz, Don Miguel, 219
Ruiz, Joaquin, 51, 209
Rules of Leadership, 217

S

Salpointe Catholic High School, 16, 147, 207
　basketball team, 91–93
　Gadea, Diego, 81–83
Sanders, Tom, 69
Santiago de Compostela, Spain, 29, 32, 46, 197. *See also* Cruz de Ferro
Satyagraha, 216
saying "sorry." *See* apologizing
saying "thank you." *See* gratitude
Schwarzenegger, Arnold, 212
sector whiteout, 178–179
Seibert, Jeff, 163

self-esteem, 14, 16, 37
self-knowledge, 106
self-leadership, 227
selfless acts, 180–181, 183, 194
self-pity, 245–246
self-reliance, 15–16
Serenity Prayer, 139, 144
serving others, 180–181, 183, 194
"Seven Minutes of Terror," 141–143
Seven Words. *See* apologizing; gratitude; love
sexual abuse, 1, 221
Shaffer, Jack, 188
Shakespeare, William, 241
Sharansky, Natan, 200
Sheen, Fulton, 175
Sheen, Martin, 4, 31, 44, 208, 230
shifting perspective, 139–140
Shining, The, 190
Simple Abundance (Breathnach), 189–190
Simple Act of Gratitude, A (Kralik), 149–150
simplicity, 229–237
　gratitude for, 104–105
　importance of achieving, 232–236
　lessons from Camino de Santiago, 230–232
　tips for creating, 237
Simpsons, The, 184
Sinatra, Frank, 74
Sinek, Simon, 246
Sirleaf, Ellen Johnson, 124
60 Minutes, 161, 165
"Smiles" report, 79–80
smiling, 180, 194
Smith, Dean, 250–252
Smith, Larry, 33, 62–64, 121–122, 141–143, 207–208, 224, 225
smoking, 74–75, 95–97
Snowden, Fred, 222–223
Social Dilemma, 163–166

social/emotional fear, 27
socializing, 158–159, 162
social media, 144, 163–164
Southard, John, 181
Southwest Airlines, 161
Southwestern Books, 43–44
space, 18. *See also* Odyssey mission; Phoenix mission
Space Shuttle Mission STS-80, 22–23
Spain, 3–5, 112–114. *See also* Camino de Santiago pilgrimage; *specific Spanish cities*
special teams (football), 131–133
Spinoza, Baruch, 177
Spirit rover, 21
sports, 200–204
Sports Illustrated, 226
St. Andrews Golf Club, 252–255
St. Christopher medal, 77–78
St. Cyril Catholic School, 81–83
Steves, Rick, 30
Stewart, Payne, 204
St. Jean Pied de Port, France, 29, 32, 46, 192–193
St. Jude Thaddeus medal, 77–78
St. Peter's Basilica, 241
stress, 160, 202, 212
stroke, 74, 176, 195–197
Stumbling on Happiness (Gilbert), 28, 133
success, 171, 213. *See also* visualization
sudden change, 125, 133–134
Sun Does Shine, The (Hinton), 199
"Surprising Neuroscience of Gender Inequality, The" (Crawford), 221
Swilican Bridge, 254–255

T

TAGSAM (Touch and Go Sample Acquisition Mechanism) device, 242
takeaways. *See* lessons/takeaways
Tansik, David, 17
tennis, 201, 203
tension, 160
Terrell, Damon, 244
Tew, Robert, 124
"Theater of the Mind" technique, 204, 206
13 Rules of Leadership, 217
Thompson, John, 222
Thoreau, Henry David, 204, 240
#Time'sUp movement, 221
Title IX, 223
Tolstoy, Leo, 125
Tomey, Dick, 152–154, 244
Top Five Regrets of the Dying, The (Ware), 236
Touch and Go Sample Acquisition Mechanism (TAGSAM) device, 242
toxic work environment, 1–2
transcendental meditation, 202. *See also* visualization
transport services, 47, 115–116
traumatic events, 133–134
travel/vacation, 182–183, 194, 232–233
True Colors seminar, 235
trust, 217, 219
Tucson Conquistadors, 94
Tucson Values Teachers, 93–94
TV's Bloopers & Practical Jokes, 184
Twain, Mark, 124, 157, 198
Twitter, 163

U

UA. *See* University of Arizona
Ukraine, 1, 220–221
United States Air Force Academy. *See* Air Force Academy
United Way organization, 51, 166–167
University of Arizona (UA). *See also* College of Science
    Arizona Wildcats, 121, 184–185, 222, 234, 248

ASU rivalry with, 59–65, 68–70
basketball team, 222
Department of Speech, Language, and Hearing Sciences, 176, 195–197
Eller College, 16, 18
leadership diversity, 222–227
victory over ASU, 152–154
University of California-Berkeley, 180
University of Notre Dame, 257–259
University of Texas, 246
US Air Force Academy. *See* Air Force Academy
U.S. News and World Report, 200
Utley, Mort, 43–44

V

vacation, 182–183, 194, 232–233
Vaillant, George, 160
Valvano, Jimmy, 139
vascular system, 160
Vietnam War, 9
visualization, 118, 124, 195–212
  aging and, 205–206
  in athletics/sports, 200–204
  benefits of, 198–202, 212
  best-case scenarios, 28
  in coaching, 207–208
  of doing Camino de Santiago, 197–198, 208–209
  happiness and, 191, 194
  how-to techniques, 209–211
  neuroscience and, 176, 195–197
  presentation/public speaking and, 206–207
volunteering, 180–181, 183, 194
Vonn, Lindsay, 203, 204
vulnerability, 67, 68–70, 97

W

Walton, Bill, 247–249
Ware, Bronnie, 236, 237
Watson, Tom, 254, 255
Way, The, 4, 31, 44, 208, 230
Welch, Jack, 213
Western culture, 30–31
Wilbur the Wildcat, 187–188
Williams, Channing, 63
Williams, Robin, 168
Wimbledon, 204
Wimbrow, Peter Dale, Sr., 50
Winfrey, Oprah, 198–199
women in leadership, 222–228
Wooden, John, 50
Woods, Tiger, 212, 240
work
  humor/laughter and, 159, 160–162
  performance evaluations, 41, 43
  prison versus, 162
  toxic environment, 1–2
  warning signs, 109
work-life balance, 2, 229–237
  happiness and, 190–191, 194
  importance of achieving, 232–236
  lessons from Camino de Santiago, 230–232
  tips for creating, 237
workplace performance evaluations, 41, 43
World War II, 9, 77–78
World War III, 1
worst-case scenarios, 28
Wright, Frank Lloyd, 241

Y

Yale School of Public Health, 205
yoga, 180

Z

Zelensky, Volodymyr, 220–221
Ziglar, Zig, 205
Zuckerberg, Mark, 164

ABOUT THE AUTHOR

Bob Logan has led an incredibly varied life, rooted in strict military family values. Attending six schools in the first twelve years of his life as the son of an Air Force fighter pilot, Bob learned early on that change can be a good (and sometimes exciting) thing.

Originally, Bob was to follow in his father's footsteps by attending the U.S. Air Force Academy. However, life got in the way, and he ultimately took a different path to complete his undergraduate work at Northern Arizona University and his MBA graduate work at the University of Arizona (UA).

The early formation for his career came as a football coach and teacher, working for some of the best in the business at the time. He coached in three consecutive college bowl games at the University of Arizona and went on to become the head coach of the Bologna Doves in the Italian-American Football League. It was here, he was proud to say, where he was one victory away from coaching in the Super Bowl! However, this was not the Super Bowl we all know so well; it was the Super Bowl (it was actually called this) for the Italian National Championship.

Following earning his MBA, Bob spent time in the corporate world as a sales manager for AT&T Computer Systems when local area networks and connected computing were taking over the business environment. He was one of the most successful AT&T sales managers nationally before NCR corporation merged with AT&T.

For the next twenty-eight years, Bob worked in a senior level capacity at the University of Arizona. The first ten years were as an Associate Director of Athletics. He helped manage the development operation and the Wildcat Club of UA Athletics. He then was recruited to the University of Arizona College of Science where he was an Assistant Dean for Corporate and External Relations. Here, instead of Final Fours and football bowl games, he experienced watching mission lift-offs at Cape Kennedy that landed on Mars with the Mars Phoenix mission and looking far back into our solar system with some of the largest telescopes in the world. He was exposed to some of the most renowned academicians and leading scientists in the world.

While at the UA, Bob was responsible for securing some of the largest gifts in the university's history. This included the $100 million gift of the iconic Biosphere 2, and a $20 million naming gift for the Richard F. Caris Mirror Lab, where the largest telescope mirrors in the world are built. He helped fund hundreds of scholarships and multiple endowed chairs for the UA College of Science.

Bob's successful stints as a coach, a teacher, a salesman, and a fundraiser have given him a unique understanding of people and what motivates them to perform at their best. Bob currently shares what he has learned with others as a highly sought-after motivational speaker, coach, and consultant.

HOW TO CONNECT WITH BOB LOGAN

EVENT PLANNERS, COMPANY RETREATS, ASSOCIATION EVENTS, AND MEETINGS

To book Bob Logan to speak or facilitate at your next conference, company retreat, or meeting, feel free to reach out to him here:

Website: **www.boblogan.net**
Email: **bob@boblogan.net**
Speaking requests: **info@boblogan.net**

ATTENTION BOOK CLUBS!

Bob Logan would be happy to be a featured author for your book club. He can provide discounted copies for your members, and depending on location, visit your book club in person or via Zoom. He loves book clubs and everything they do to support the publishing industry. Feel free to reach out; he would love to help!

Made in the USA
Middletown, DE
12 February 2023